# The Ninth Circle

FRONTISPIECE. U.S. Navy R4D crashed at Hallett Station
with Adelie penguins (photo October, 1960).

THE

# NINTH
# CIRCLE

A Memoir of Life and Death in Antarctica, 1960–1962

# John C. Behrendt

*To Art,*

*From one old Antarctic*
*explorer to another.*

*John C Behrendt*

*SCAR*

*July, 2012*

UNIVERSITY OF NEW MEXICO PRESS

▼

ALBUQUERQUE

Library of Congress Cataloging-in-Publication Data

Behrendt, John C., 1932–
The ninth circle : a memoir of life and death in Antarctica,
1960–1962 / John C. Behrendt.
p. cm.
Includes bibliographical references.
ISBN 0-8263-3425-3 (cloth : alk. paper)
1. Behrendt, John C., 1932– —Diaries.
2. Physical scientists—United States—Diaries.
3. Explorers—United States—Diaries.
4. Antarctica—Discovery and exploration—American.
5. United States Antarctic Research Program.
I. Title.  G850 1960 .B4 A3 2004
919.8′904—dc22
2004021994

DESIGN AND COMPOSITION: Mina Yamashita

# ninth circle

*We passed onward to where the ice roughly enswathes another folk, . . . for the first tears form a block and like a visor of crystal fill all the cup beneath the eyebrow. . . . And although, because of the cold, as from a callus, all feeling had left its abode in my face, it seemed now to me I felt some wind. . . . Then I saw a thousand faces made currish by the cold, whence shuddering comes to me and will always come, at frozen pools. How I became then chilled and hoarse, ask it not, Reader, for I write it not, because all speech would be little. I did not die, and I did not remain alive.*

◆ ◆ ◆

*The Divine Comedy*, Volume 1, Hell [the *Inferno*]by Dante Alighieri

# Contents

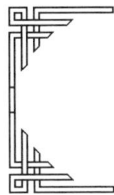 

# To Laura

# Acknowledgments

Many people have contributed to this book. For assistance of various kinds during its preparation, I wish to thank Bob Allen, Charlie Bentley, Dusty Blades, Henry Brecher, Alexandra Brown, Bill Burch, Parker Calkin, Art Ford, Jane Ferrigno, Mario Giovinetto, John Gillies, Pat Hill, Mel Holzman, Tom Laudon, Wes LeMasurier, Barb Mieras, Bob Ruford, Mary Siders, Bob Tingey, Charles Swithinbank, and Igor Zotikov. Susan Baur (who suggested the reference to *Dante's Inferno*, Dian Belanger, Jody Berman, and Mildred Crary provided professional advice at various times. David Behrendt and Faith Rogers, professional editors and writers, freely gave a vast amount of time commenting in detail on several versions of the manuscript. James Syvitski, Director of the Institute of Arctic and Alpine Research (INSTAAR) at the University of Colorado, and the University of Colorado in General, were quite encouraging, as I worked on the project. INSTAAR colleagues Tad Pfeiffer and Diane McKnight provided useful insights for the epilogue. Several people at the National Science Foundation were helpful, in particular Scott Borg and Dave Bresnahan at McMurdo, Antarctica, in 2003; Guy Guthridge and Harry Mahar provided the statistics regarding deaths in the U.S. Antarctic Program. Pat Quilty helped obtain the permission from *Aurora* to quote the Bill Burch material. I would like to thank the scientists, graduate students, technicians, NSF managers, pilots, air crews, and other Navy men (and they were all men) with whom I worked in Antarctica in 1960–62. those who were with me aboard R4D-8 #219 on that fateful 22 November, 1960, in the Crary mountains will never be forgotten. The other members of the Antarctic Peninsula Traverse party, Lee Kreiling, Con Merrick, John Molholm, Perry Parks, Hiro Shimizu, and Pete Wasilewski put up with me, and were each invaluable in making the traverse "go." We seven were together only at one time ever, for the intense seventy-six days from our arrival at Camp Minnesota, until Hiro left us at Byrd. My wife, Laura Backus, and my sons, Kurt Behrendt and Marc Behrendt, and my brother, David Behrendt, were particularly supportive during the trying summer of 2003 when I completed the manuscript. ◆

## Editorial Note

Journal entries are indented, and along with other quoted material, have been edited for punctuation and clarity. A journal entry without a date preceding it is a continuation from the prior entry above it. For ease of reading, some material has either been shortened, incorporated into the main text, paraphrased, or omitted entirely. Brackets are used to clarify syntax, to provide brief definitions, or to give currently accepted names for geographic features (from *Geographic Names of Antarctica,* Second Edition, 1995). Radio messages originally had no punctuation and were all capital letters; punctuation has been added here.

The photographs (most taken by me) are from my personal collection unless noted otherwise. ◆

# Preface

I first traveled to Antarctica in 1956, at the beginning of the "scientific era" ushered in by the International Geophysical Year (IGY) 1957–58. The book *Innocents on the Ice*[1] was an account of my personal experiences as a small part of this ambitious undertaking. The Antarctic Treaty was negotiated and signed in 1959, largely as the result of the peaceful cooperation and scientific success of the IGY and the continuation of the research programs on the continent in the following years. The Antarctic Treaty entered into force after all twelve signatories had ratified it in 1961. No territorial claims are recognized, all pre-existing claims are essentially frozen, and no new claims can be made as long as the Treaty is in force (indefinitely).

Although the National Science Foundation (NSF), along with other federal agencies, provided much of the funding for the scientific part of the U.S. Antarctic Program during the IGY, their staff were not directly active in Antarctica. The entire scientific program then was managed by the U.S. National Committee for the IGY at the National Academy of Sciences (NAS) and operated through the Arctic Institute of North America, which employed many of us then. The big budget was the Navy's and was funded through the Department of Defense. As planned, the US IGY expedition (Navy Operation Deep Freeze I, II, III, and IV) lasted from 1955 through 1959. The numbering system was changed after the IGY period starting with the International Geophysical Cooperation (IGC, one year, 1960) in that the 1959–60 austral summer season was designated Deep Freeze 60. By this time the National Science Foundation had taken over the scientific program (United States Antarctic Research Program [USARP]), which had a budget of about $6 million. The Navy budget for Antarctica was about $20 million. This book covers primarily the Deep Freeze 61 and 62 seasons, in which I had a minor role.

When we young scientists first went to Antarctica to participate in the mission-oriented directed research of the IGY and in the USARP in the early 1960s, the world was quite different from the undirected proposal-driven U.S. Antarctic Program (USAP) of the 1980s–2000 period. The Cold War was at its height and the Navy and participating researchers accepted risks that would not be tolerated today. Risking astronauts' lives to repair the Hubble telescope would seem an appropriate comparison in 2004. The Antarctic air squadron VX6 had an accident rate eight times that of U.S. Naval aviation in other parts of the world at that time.

Because of these risks, and because of U.S. strategic interests prior to the entry into force in 1961 of the Antarctic Treaty with its disarmament and territorial claims articles, we draft age graduate students, and technicians, all male, were deferred from military service. We were also given a 25 percent hazardous duty pay differential for the period we were in Antarctica. However, as Igor Zotikov phrased it in a lecture in 2004, in the early 1960s significant new scientific discoveries in Antarctica were "picking mushrooms in a virgin forest."

This book, written as a memoir, is an account of my personal experiences in Antarctica from October 1960 to March 1962. During these two austral summer field seasons I kept a daily journal, which formed the basis for this account. More than forty years later the United States Antarctic Program has changed dramatically, as has my perspective as a researcher "on the Ice" in each of six decades. I attempt here to describe my third and fourth Antarctic trips as a young scientist leading my first field parties, both from my fresh impressions at the time and from the distance of the twenty-first century. In 1960, we were about as close in time to the heroic era of Scott, Shackleton, and Amundsen as we are now, as I write in 2003, to the period described in this book.

Since the 1950s much has changed in the way Antarctic science and U.S. Antarctic expeditions operate. Most notable are the presence of women, greater safety, availability of reliable maps, and, of course, technological advances—particularly in electronics, communication, computers, satellites, navigation, etc. Large areas of West Antarctica, which we studied in the period described here, were totally unmapped, and had not even been seen from the air. Nonetheless, there were dramatic changes in the U.S. Antarctic Research Program and logistic capabilities during the four years from the time I spent three months on a ship to get to Ellsworth Station on the Filchner Ice Shelf in 1956 to flying in a few hours from New Zealand to the Ross Sea area in 1960. During IGY the only major U.S. Antarctic scientific field activities, starting in 1957, were three oversnow geophysical-glaciological traverses. By 1960–61 there were many geophysical, geological, glaciological, and biological projects, and other field projects as described here. ◆

# ONE

# Near-Miss in the Crary Mountains

## 22 November 1960

*I could see nothing through the clouds from the right-hand seat in the cockpit of the plane, where I was recording the [barometric and radar] altimeter readings. Our height had been varying between 2200 and 2300 feet above the surface of the West Antarctic ice sheet. The radar operator reported on the intercom that there was "a target 13 miles ahead."[1]*

A radar target meant only one thing: mountains! I started to get a little nervous, but said nothing. Lou, the copilot at the controls in the left-hand seat, began to climb as fast as he could, and two minutes later we were at 8300 feet but still only 2250 feet above the snow level. There was absolutely no visibility. A minute later we had pulled up to 8640 feet elevation above sea level, but the snow surface was also coming up and was still only 2300 feet below. Then the radar altimeter (which measured the height of the plane above the snow using a radar pulse) began to unwind. Thirty seconds later we had climbed to 8680 feet, but the ground was now only 1500 feet below.

For the next 30 seconds I could only stare at the radar altimeter, which dropped with terrifying rapidity to less than 50 feet (a red light came on). Meanwhile, Lou was pulling the nose up until we began to stall. The air speed dropped below 80 knots.

The plane would stall at 77 knots and fall toward the ice below.

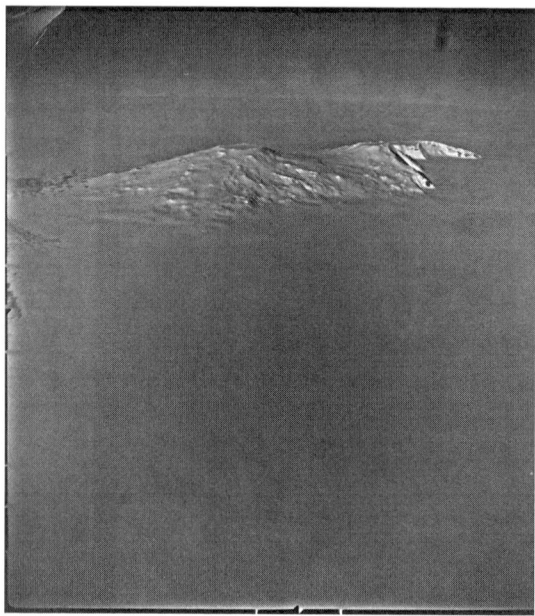

1. Crary Mountains looking northwest from about 25,000 feet (7600 meters) elevation (Official U.S. Navy photograph).

Of course all hell broke loose throughout the aircraft. Joe, the pilot, who had been dozing in a seat on the port side across from the navigator, was startled by a can of orange juice falling off a shelf onto his lap. Andy, the plane captain (crew chief), had come forward into the aisle between Lou and me. Lou was yelling for Andy to "Get Joe!"

Tom was hanging onto the ropes in the main cabin and could see a rock outcrop just to starboard; the wing of the plane was perpendicular to a cliff. Pete had been standing directly behind the navigator in the aisle and saw him put on his helmet and tighten his seat belt. Pete started to run for a seat and was thrown through the air. Art was hanging on and saw an outcrop to starboard. Dick, who had been operating the magnetometer and listening to the intercom, was struggling to keep the geophysical equipment from tipping over. He could see that the magnetic field had been coming up very fast during the preceding minute, and he finally saw the garbled signal from the magnetic sensor (called the "bird") as it bounced along the snow or rock 60 feet or less below. Suddenly, the bird broke off.

Somewhere about this time the tip of our starboard wing hit a rock.

Meanwhile, Joe had rushed forward, pushed Andy aside and took a half-kneeling position between Lou and me. The plane was shuddering violently.

> Joe was yelling at Lou to "Get the nose down! Get the nose down!" Joe finally reached with his left hand and did this himself, by yanking the controls from Lou's hands. We made a vertical bank to the left and dove. With his right hand Joe started to pull the throttles all the way back to kill the two engines. He figured it would be better to crash sliding forward along the surface than flipped over on our back. With the fuel off, we were slightly less likely to burn. He was sure the three of us in the cockpit would go through the windshield, but possibly those in the cabin might survive. Miraculously(?) we picked up air speed and did not plow in! The radar altimeter showed 200 feet.

Through much of this action, I could see the sun glowing feebly through the fog directly in front of us. It was swinging violently from the port side to the starboard and back as we progressively stalled. We all had complete vertigo. We had been flying north, with the sun to our south at this time of "night." Obviously, we somehow had turned completely around. I wished fervently that this would end soon.

There were a few seconds of respite, during which I dove out of the cockpit seat and Joe scrambled in. I went charging back to strap myself into a seat, but could not find the belt. (I hadn't had my seat belt fastened in the cockpit either.) I dropped the data book and felt guilty about it. A note at this time in my data book reads: "Amongst mountains we cannot see and trying to get the hell out. Barely clearing tops."

> The plane staggered around like a drunken man and finally began to climb. We went up to 13,500 feet and could catch glimpses of mountains apparently as high on either side. I felt giddy and exhilarated from the lack of oxygen at this elevation (I thought).
>
> The sun was now shining, and it felt very good to be alive!

I was a twenty-eight-year-old graduate student and was leading my first Antarctic field party. We were flying over the West Antarctic ice sheet in the late evening in a ski-wheel, Navy R4D-8 (DC-3). Marine Capt. Joe Walker, the aircraft commander, was twenty-nine years old. We had headed toward Toney Mountain on a course north from Byrd Station with nothing visible below but the featureless snow surface of the ice sheet, covered by sastrugi (windblown linear ridges). I recorded the barometric- and radar-altimeter readings to measure the snow surface elevations every five minutes. A Navy photographer and five civilian scientists of the

United States Antarctic Research Program (USARP) were observing and operating a magnetometer. They were crammed into the main cabin, which also was crowded with our survival gear, JATO bottles[2] and a 500-gallon internal fuel tank full of aviation gasoline. We planned to land and do several hours of field geology in the unexplored area toward which we were flying.

In reconstructing the incident later, it became clear what had happened. At 2310,[3] a little over an hour and a half out of Byrd, we entered clouds and did not come out. We had drifted off course to the left by about 20 miles and into the volcanic Crary Mountains. This range had been discovered, mapped, and named three years earlier by Charles Bentley's oversnow traverse party, as had Toney Mountain about 90 miles farther on, so they were included on the latest edition of the air navigation chart. However, the Navy air navigation chart (two years older) the navigator was using was obsolete; it showed no mountains in this area.

Consequently, we had tried to fly through a 10,000-foot pass between two 12,000-foot peaks at an aircraft altitude of less than 9000 feet. The pilot tried to climb and bank to the left, but we had insufficient air speed. Because of the drag of a non-retractable tail ski, the maximum air speed was only about 114 knots. The stall speed was 77 knots. In a stall, airflow over the wings is disrupted, destroying lift and causing a plane to fall. The navigator told me that at the time of the crisis our plane had dropped below 80 knots airspeed.

Later, Andy and Joe both said they thought they felt the wing hit the mountain. We were shuddering and banging around so violently that the rest of us thought they were mistaken.

We had made four progressive stalls, first one wing stalling and dropping, then the pilot recovering control, only to stall again to the other side, in continued sequence, each stall more extreme. During this time we turned about 180 degrees and headed to the south, away from the mountains. However, at one point an outcropping came up so close on the right side of the plane that our wing hit the rock. The magnetometer sensor—encased in a fiberglass "bird" normally towed about 60 feet below and slightly behind the plane—dragged along the ground for 17 seconds before it broke off.

When Joe, the pilot, grabbed the controls and dove, we picked up air speed, and because we had turned away from the peaks, we did not crash. All this time the engines were running at full takeoff power. As we tried to clear the hidden mountains, Joe circled and slowly we climbed to the level of the tops of the peaks in our unpressurized plane.

During the incident everyone was doing his job, not because of any particular bravery or sense of duty, but because no one had time to think. Lou and Joe flew the plane. The radar man, who did not know that the pilot had no forward visibility, watched the radar target ahead split into two peaks as we apparently (to him) proceeded between them. The navigator tried to plot the rapid course and elevation changes. Dick operated the magnetometer and I kept recording times and elevations in a data book. The entire incident lasted only about three minutes after the snow surface started to rise fast beneath the plane.

When the crisis was over, Joe called me forward and asked if I wanted to go on. "Sure, if you're willing," I replied. We got the rear door off, pulled in the old magnetometer cable, and put the spare bird out. We civilian scientists barely understood what we had gone through and were quite shaken. Joe, however, was surprised that we carried a spare cable and bird, as though these were normal occurrences. Actually, we had the spare in case there was an electronic breakdown.

At 2352 Joe called me forward and noted that the whole area was clobbered in by clouds. He suggested we go home and try again another day. I heartily agreed. We landed at Byrd, 4 ½ hours after we had left it, a somewhat chastened group, at 0130 (23 November).

We climbed slowly out of the plane, walked over, and examined the right wing. There was a fist-sized dent in the tip. Joe and Andy had been right. Dick and I examined the end of the magnetometer cable where the bird had pulled off after dragging on the ground. I still have this end as a grim memento of the luck that prevailed that day.

Everyone congregated in the chow hall over [Navy issue medicinal] brandy and coffee.[4] The airdales (Navy flyers) were at one table and the USARPs (civilian geophysicists and geologists) at the adjacent. I'm afraid that my notes on hearing the radar operator mention a "target" 13 miles ahead just a few minutes before we hit makes Lou look a bit bad.[5] Dick, also hooked into the intercom, heard this too, and wondered why we didn't turn. He wrote it on the magnetometer record. There were minor sins of commission and omission also. Joe blames himself as plane commander for not being in the cockpit. We should have had the most up-to-date map. And so it went on and on . . .

The brandy took its effect and we began to relax and unwind from our keyed up states of mind. Soon the talk turned to other air accidents near and fatal that had been experienced or witnessed. We all agreed that this was the closest call any had ever been in or heard of. There is no doubt that we all would have been killed if we had crashed.[6]

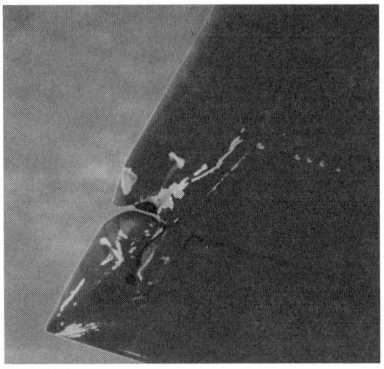

2. Dented wing tip caused by hitting peak in Crary Mountains.

3. Wold holding end of magnetometer cable beneath dented wing of Navy R4D #219. "Bird" broke off from cable after dragging seventeen seconds in Crary Mountains.

4. Behrendt (left) and Wold relaxing in Byrd Station galley immediately after returning from 22 November 1960 flight to Crary Mountains (photograph by T. Laudon).

5. Walker, aircraft commander on R4D #219 on Crary Mountains flight.

[The next day I wrote] It's beautifully clear and calm tonight and seems quite warm. I hope we can fly again in the morning. I wish we had some more flights behind us. I can begin to understand how flyers in wartime count the missions still ahead.

I got together with Fred, the navigator, and plotted our track last night. I found that we were in amongst the Crary Range during the trouble. These mountains are shown on the 5th edition of the SP5 map, which I have, but not on the 3rd edition, which is all Fred had to go on. Just this error could have killed us all.

For several days, I was preoccupied and kept replaying the entire episode over and over in my mind—even in my sleep. My outlook was permanently changed. A minor example: since that near-death experience, I have never to this day ridden in a car or flown in a plane without putting on a seat belt.

We saw the movie *The High and the Mighty* [four weeks later], which I had seen before. I remember the first time I was quite impressed when the radar altimeter dropped below 200 feet and the plane in the movie almost hit the peaks around San Francisco. This time it seemed like a great deal of elevation with room to spare.

This incident in the Crary Mountains, although the most dramatic of my life, characterized the United States Antarctic Research Program and Navy Operation Deep Freeze in the early days of the "Scientific Age." I only gradually came to that realization, while writing this account describing my third and fourth seasons as a geophysicist in Antarctica.

From 1955, at the start of the Deep Freeze operations, through 1961 there were 19 deaths in aircraft accidents, or 3.8 per year. According to the National Science Foundation, since 1970 there has been only 1 fatal aircraft accident, a helicopter crash in 1992 that killed 3 people, a rate of 0.1 deaths per year. In other words, during the early years of the Scientific Age of Antarctic activities, including the period covered by this book, the death rate due to U.S. aircraft accidents was 38 times the rate during the past three decades.

Back then we took for granted the "routine" aircraft and crevasse incidents that occurred from time to time. From the IGY beginning in 1957 until 1966, we few Americans (with a small number of other researchers from the Soviet Union, France, Australia, Argentina, New Zealand, and the United Kingdom carried out a successful geophysical reconnaissance of the Antarctic Ice Sheet. But our accomplishment had a grim price. ◆

# TWO

# Off to the Ice

I had dreamed of being an Antarctic explorer since I was a small boy reading about Admiral Byrd's expedition in *Life Magazine*. My parents, both Wisconsin natives like me, were the son and daughter of immigrants from Germany and Norway, respectively. They brought me into a climate of cold winters and introduced me, at an early age, to vigorous outdoor activities. I used to go camping in the snow just for the fun of it.

So I'm sure my parents were not surprised that, by the time I graduated with a BS degree in physics in 1954 from the University of Wisconsin (UW) at Madison, I had abandoned any thought of spending my life in a laboratory. In fact, that summer after graduation opened a new and formative period of my life. Madison Professor George Woollard offered me a summer job as a geophysical field assistant and convinced me to enroll in graduate school that September as his student.

By the following summer, I was a field assistant for a newly-minted Ph.D., Edward Thiel. We collected gravity and magnetic data in the Uinta Mountains of Utah (data I used for my master's thesis, completed in 1956). Ed became my mentor over the next several years, serving as a fine role model for how a young scientific researcher works under difficult conditions.

My work with Woollard and Thiel led me directly to Antarctica. My first trip, from 1956–'58, was as an "assistant seismologist" (the job's official designation during IGY) on the Filchner Ice Shelf Traverse under Ed's leadership.

Also of considerable influence on me at that time was Albert P. Crary, who had overall responsibility during the IGY for the three main U.S. Antarctic field projects, called oversnow traverses.[1] As a geophysicist-glaciologist, Bert Crary was a scientific inspiration to all of us traverse people. He was the first person to set foot at both the North and South Poles. During his career he survived crevasses, near plane crashes and, most harrowing, a fall into the Ross Sea in 1959 from the 100-foot-high ice shelf at Little America.

The primary objectives of the U.S. oversnow (and airborne) traverses, along with Soviet and French traverses, were to measure the thickness of the Antarctic Ice Sheet primarily using seismic reflections, and to determine snow accumulation and other glaciological parameters. The ultimate objective was to ascertain whether the Antarctic ice sheet was increasing or decreasing; this is still a subject of strong disagreement.

Unlike today, carrying out Antarctic research under the U.S. program (and probably others) was viewed by all scientists as a duty and obligation, rather than a privilege. From its start with the IGY (1957–58) there were never enough experienced American geophysicists and glaciologists to man (there were no women participants) the U.S. oversnow traverse program and other field research programs. Many scientists (including graduate students) were recruited during the period 1956–66 from other countries.[2] Some of these made outstanding reputations later in either the United States or their original countries; one went to jail.

After returning from Antarctica in 1958, I resumed graduate school in geophysics under Woollard back at UW. I also worked on Filchner Ice shelf data. Woollard had arranged that the geophysical data reduction and interpretation from the three oversnow traverses of the IGY would be carried out at Madison. Soon the effort was designated the Geophysical and Polar Research Center of the Geology Department at the University of Wisconsin.

During the summer of 1958 there were three other former "assistant seismologists" at Madison: Ned Ostenso, Hugh Bennett, and Edwin "Robbie" Robinson from the IGY traverses. Crary remained in Antarctica at Little America, Bentley stayed at Byrd Station, and Mario Giovinetto, a glaciologist, moved from Byrd to the South Pole for their second consecutive winters. Bentley returned from Antarctica to Madison in 1959 to join us, where he has remained to this day. He and Ed Thiel were the only ones at the Geophysical and Polar Research Center who had Antarctic experience and a Ph.D. degree.[3]

Ed Thiel and I shared a rustic cabin for several months in 1958 on the west side of Madison. We had no running water and an outdoor privy. Ed soon moved out, and after a year, so did I. Thiel, Bentley, Ostenso, Bennett, Giovinetto, and several of the others from time to time shared a house near Lake Monona while I shared a basement apartment with an old college roommate a block away. There was much socializing amongst us all, as we dated various women. Ed was the first to marry, in 1960, and eventually all of us did. This group went on to become well known in polar research circles over the coming years.

I returned to Ellsworth Station on the Navy Wind-class icebreaker *Edisto* for the 1958–59 field season to make gravity measurements and do a bit of field geology on unexplored nunataks (rock peaks exposed through the ice) by heli-copter. Meanwhile Ed Thiel led the first airborne traverse party working with Ned Ostenso. Robinson returned to work with Crary on the Victoria Land traverse and spend the following winter at McMurdo.

Thiel led another airborne traverse in West Antarctica during the 1959–60 Antarctic summer season approximately along the 90°W meridian north of the Thiel Mountains, which he visited for the first time and sampled geologically (with geologist Campbell Craddock, of University of Minnesota).

After returning from Antarctica, I spent the spring and summer of 1959 tieing in gravity base stations throughout North America, completing my scientific visits to every U.S. state. During the 1959–60 academic year I finished my last course, passed my German and Spanish language exams, and studied intensively for my "preliminary" doctoral exam.[4] The "prelim," given orally for three hours in 1960, was required for admission to candidacy for the Ph.D. It was frightening to contemplate (worse than the prospect of Antarctic crevasses), as a significant number of students failed this test. During this year, I was also work-ing full time on my research for my thesis on the Filchner Ice Shelf.

Fortunately, the graduating senior I was in love with also had to put in many hours a week studying. Sara left Madison for an internship in physical therapy, in Nashville, about a week before my oral exam in May. This would give me an uninterrupted week for study—or so I thought.

On a warm spring Sunday three days before the exam, my brother David and his fiancée, Mary, visited my study site at the Geophysical and Polar Research Center, located on the idyllic fifteen-acre Brittingham estate on the west side of Madison. They brought along a picnic lunch and a twenty-year-old nursing student friend, Donna Ebben. After lunch, it seemed like a good idea for me to take a break with Donna to see a movie, *Black Orpheus*.

Most of my friends in Madison and my family were unaware of my impend-ing exam, so when I celebrated my twenty-eighth birthday on 18 May with Dave and Mary at dinner the night before, they found me uncharacteristically silent and preoccupied.

The intense studying paid off; I easily passed the prelim. Reid Bryson, a member of my committee from the Meteorology Department, delighted in watching me squirm over questions he posed about continental drift. One of the geologists on my committee was quite opposed to this controversial theory, which we Antarctic researchers had to use as a working hypothesis to explain the new geological and geophysical results from the IGY research.

Throughout the summer of 1960 I worked, writing my thesis. I also prepared, with others at UW, for our coming Antarctic field season. Bentley would lead his fourth oversnow traverse from Byrd Station to the Bellingshausen Sea. Bennett planned detailed seismic measurements on snow for his Ph.D. thesis. Robinson and Giovinetto would assist Crary on the McMurdo–South Pole traverse. Forrest Dowling, another graduate student, would make gravity and magnetic measurements accompanying a D-8 tractor train from Byrd Station to the South Pole.

As for me—at twenty-eight, tall (over 6 feet 3 inches), thin (about 185 pounds), and very nearsighted, with thick glasses—I was about to begin my third trip to Antarctica. I would lead a three-man airborne geophysical traverse over the West Antarctic Ice Sheet, making aeromagnetic, gravity, and seismic measurements and doing some field geology on the ground at unexplored nunataks.

Our primary objective was a transect of seismic ice thickness measurements south of the Amundsen Sea in the Pine Island–Thwaites Glacier area and a series of aeromagnetic and snow surface elevation measurements using "flights of opportunity." Graduate students Richard Wold (geophysics) and Thomas Laudon (geology) were the other two members of the party. Ed Thiel and Ned Ostenso "tended the store" in Madison during this season.

In September all scientific participants who were headed for Antarctica traveled to Skyland, a resort, in Shenandoah National Park a few hours' bus ride west of Washington D.C., for a week of orientation. We stayed in small cabins and the new men had many hours in a relaxed setting at Skyland to get to know those of us with several years of Antarctica experience. Our Antarctic clothing was also supplied to us at the orientation.

NSF staff, Naval officers, and senior scientists lectured us on various issues to prepare us for the coming Antarctic experience. I recall Bert Crary joking that the U.S. Antarctic Research Program was the largest unemployment bureau around. This seems less funny in 2003.

One particularly memorable lecture was by the chief Antarctic Navy Medical officer Captain Earland Hedblom. This gruff, jovial, heavyset man, with much humor, and graphic descriptions of horrific accidents illustrated with color slides, made us realize what we might be getting into and how to take common sense precautions that could save our lives. One of many vivid examples was the account of a small tracked vehicle (Weasel) that broke through the sea ice at McMurdo and sank in about 10 feet of water with five men on board. One man, riding jammed on top of the engine to the right of the driver, got out across the driver onto the sea ice without even getting his feet wet. He was there to pull three others out as they bobbed to the surface of the freezing water. When divers recovered the body of the fifth man, they found that he had been trapped with the radio microphone cord wrapped around his neck. If he had not panicked he could have reached out and unplugged the mike.

Another cautionary story Hedblom told was of the crash of a C-124 Globemaster while making an airdrop of supplies at Hallett Station. The plane hit a peak and the lumber on pallets inside the cargo cabin exploded, killing six people. The copilot was only knocked unconscious and lay on the ice for several hours, while rescuers tended to the more severely injured. However, he had been wearing only street shoes and froze both feet before anyone came to his aid. Hedblom showed graphic slides of his frostbitten feet, which had had to be amputated. I came away from this lecture with the strong lesson that one needs to be prepared to be unconscious in the cold or deal with a fire (i.e., be able to tear hot metal with gloved hands or jump to the ground from a crashed and burning plane).

"Doc" Hedblom also recommended carrying a little whisky with one's personal survival kit to sip before going to sleep after surviving a crash or other field disaster. Modern field safety experts strongly advise against this, but it still seems like a good idea to me.

On 20 October, 1960, after months of planning and weeks of anticipation, I left Madison as the first member of my field party. I carried a small portable gravity meter to make very accurate measurements of the differences between the main UW base station at Science Hall, and other sites along my way, and in Antarctica. I planned to continue around the world making gravity base station connections at the end of the field season.

I also took an airborne magnetometer in six large blue steel boxes totaling about 800 pounds. I flew uneventfully to San Francisco, and drove to Travis Air Force Base. All of the U.S. scientists en route to the Ross Sea area of Antarctica, until about 1980, flew on various types of U.S. Air Force Military Air Transport Service (MATS) or U.S. Navy planes to New Zealand.

My journal continues:

*22–23 Oct. Sat.–Sun.* I waited around until 1000 on Saturday before we got into the plane. The crew members were helpful about letting me plug the meter in.

The small LaCoste and Romberg gravity meter (G-1), the first of its type, needed to be kept at a constant temperature. A gravimeter, or gravity meter, is a weight on an extremely sensitive spring. Very slight variations in gravity can be measured by adjusting the spring length with a delicate screw to keep the "stretch" the same. The number of turns of the screw is the measurement of the change in gravity. Because the instrument is so sensitive, the internal temperature must be kept constant by a thermostat and a battery-powered heater.

I joined others en route to Antarctica in a U.S. Air Force C-118, the military version of a DC-6 configured with backward facing seats. This prop-driven airplane had limited speed and range compared to modern jet aircraft.

These long, long flights in slow military planes, which I made in January 1960, October 1960, October 1961, and February 1962, with stops at several places, made me realize how really big the Pacific Ocean is. Since the late 1970s, on nonstop jet flights from Los Angeles to New Zealand, one leaves about 2200 and lands in the morning about ten hours later, allowing one to sleep through the night. The Pacific seems much smaller now.

We landed at Hickam Field, Honolulu about 1930. It was quite warm. When I got over to the officers club the dining room had just closed; I got a steak in the snack bar.

*23 Oct. Sun.* We took off about 1414 and flew over the monotonous Pacific towards Canton Island, a small coral atoll, where we landed at about 2030 for an hour to refuel.

*24 Oct. Mon.*—didn't exist (dateline crossing about midnight).

*25 Oct. Tues.* Our plane landed to refuel again at Nandi in the Fijis about 0200. We arrived in Christchurch, New Zealand, on South Island about 1030. After making a precise gravity observation, I got my gear stowed away out at the airport headquarters U.S. Navy Task Force 43.[5]

The four of us USARP personnel who had just arrived, came in to the Gainsborough Hotel, which provides a bed for 25/ [shillings] or about $3.50 per night. The furnishings are Victorian-era style and about that old. Large worn overstuffed chairs and sofas in the living room down-stairs. Of course there are no rooms with private bath, as is true for almost all of New Zealand. Breakfast is furnished in the cost and tea is brought around at 0700.

Everything is way behind schedule due to bad weather at McMurdo. Only 9 USAF C-124s (Globemasters) have gone down so far with no air drops to the Pole yet. Some people, like Bill Long [Ohio State geologist] and Robert Nichols and George Denton [Tufts University], have been here for nearly two weeks.

Nichols was the geologist on Finn Ronne's private Ronne Antarctic Research Expedition (RARE) 1946–48, at East Base on the Antarctic Peninsula. He was a great admirer of the British Antarctic explorer Robert Scott and was a strong advocate of man-hauling sleds in field work. Denton, an undergraduate assistant of Nichols, went on to become a prominent Antarctic geologist. A graduate student, Parker Calkin, another member of Nichols's party, is today a well-known glacial geologist.

Ed Thiel and I had worked with Bill Long in Alaska in 1956 on the Juneau Ice Field Research Project.

Eddie Goodale, the USARP representative, and his assistant really have their hands full with all the people and high priority cargo waiting to go in.

Goodale, whom I got to know pretty well, was a dog sled driver on the first Byrd Antarctic Expedition, based at Little America I on the Ross Ice Shelf from 1928 to 1931.

*26 Oct. Wed.* I went into town in the evening and ate a tough venison steak at a small cafe on the square. I wandered around for an hour or so by myself before ending up at a movie, *Let's Make Love* with Marilyn Monroe.

This was my last opportunity to be alone for some months, although I did not appreciate it at the time.

*27 Oct. Thurs.* A flight arrived from the U.S., with Dick Wold, Forrest Dowling, Tom Laudon, Tom Berg, Jim Sullivan (all University of Wisconsin geology grad students), Ken Moulton (National Science Foundation), Cam Craddock (head of the University of Minnesota geology field party), and others.

We all went out to dinner at Milando's, the only good restaurant in Christchurch [in 1960], and had a fine meal. This is one of the most expensive places in town. My bill ran over 1 pound ($2.85 US).

*28 Oct. Fri.* We checked in early in the morning at a regular counter marked ANTARCTIC FLIGHTS. I took my gravity meter out to the plane (named Phoenix) and got it hooked up. I dressed up in my longjohns, field trousers, and USARP shirt for a go at the Ice.

In 1960 there were none of the elaborate departure procedures such as drug-sniffing dogs for baggage and sequestration of the personnel prior to boarding that have been standard since about the 1980s. We just walked out to the plane and got on. Then, as now, all passengers on the flights to McMurdo from Christchurch dressed for Antarctic climatic conditions, even on a hot summer day in New Zealand. In case the plane had to land on the ice sheet in an emergency, at least people would be dressed properly.

> The "Connie" started down the runway on the takeoff run at 0945. The engines suddenly slowed and we taxied back to the grass parking lot over near headquarters. No. 4 engine was overheating. By the time everything was checked over, word had come for a 12-hour postponement.
>
> We went back to town. I took my room at the hotel again, although we were told to report back at 2000 for a flight out tonight. The hotel people weren't very surprised to see me. They assured me that I would-n't get out tonight either. "Once the weather is bad down there it takes 48 hours to clear up," I was told. These Kiwis [slang for New Zealanders] know all about Antarctica, so it seems.
>
> Today there were five aborts [abortions, i.e., flights canceled after takeoff]. Four C-124s and ourselves. Some were several hours out on their way before turning back because of bad weather at McMurdo.

All of our flying from this time on was with Navy air squadron VX6, which was attached to TF-43. In 1960–61, VX6 had a variety of planes, including four new ski-wheel C-130s (Hercules, or "Hercs," designated LC-130s since the 1970s), one R4D5, three R4D8s (DC-3 Dakotas), three P2V Neptunes, and five Otters (UC1, single engine). Non-ski-wheel planes in VX6, were one R7V (Super Constellation), one R5D (DC-4), and four HUS1 helicopters. The UH1B (Huey) turboprop helicopter was introduced into the Antarctic program later in the early 1960s.

In addition to the Navy aviators, an Air Force Squadron comprising C-124 Globemasters operated from the sea ice runway at McMurdo to air drop heavy supplies, mostly fuel, to Byrd, South Pole, and Hallett Stations. ◆

# THREE

# McMurdo

**O**n the evening of 28 October we found that the weather was pretty good at McMurdo. Five C-124s, an R5D, a Hercules C-130, and the R7V Super Constellation flew out.

> When we arrived at the airstrip, planes were taking off for Antarctica right and left. The R5D used JATO, and looked spectacular as it roared into the darkening sky.
>
> We took off in the R7V at 2145. Our estimated time to fly the 2092 miles to McMurdo is 9 hours 18 minutes. A picket ship, the *Wilhoite,* is on station at 60°S, 170°W to fish us out of the drink if we ditch. The plane flew about half way at 10,000 feet and then went up to 18,000. It's now 2225 and I'm going to try to get some sleep . . . [We were very crowded in with our survival gear and scientific equipment jammed in around us.] We crossed the edge of the pack ice at about 65°S.

This was a very hazardous flight in planes that passed a "point of no return" (called more euphemistically "point of safe return" in 2003) a little over half way down. We were each provided a "poopy suit" (insulated immersion suit), which would only have protected us in the Southern Ocean for a very limited time in near freezing sea water. A few trips and several years later I heard the wry question: "In case a plane ditches at sea is it better to grab a life preserver or a tool box when leaving the plane?" You would go down fast with a tool box. Fortunately, the air operations for this flight are extremely conservative, which is why I have experienced so many turnarounds ("boomerangs," as they were called in the late 1990s). No U.S. plane has ever ditched on the way from New Zealand to McMurdo. However, there have been several crashes due to poor weather while landing at McMurdo, resulting in a number of deaths. The concept of "point of no return" gives one pause to think.

6. Glaciers and mountains in Transantarctic Mountains between Hallett and McMurdo. Photograph taken December 1984 from *Polar 3* (Dornier 228) aircraft flying at elevation of about 11,000 feet (3400 meters).

*29 Oct. Sat.* About 0300 it got light, and about 0600 we passed by Cape Adare and Cape Hallett. The view of the Admiralty Range in northern Victoria Land was quite superb. These beautiful snow-covered peaks are largely unexplored. Eventually the Royal Society Range hove into view and we landed on the sea ice runway at McMurdo Sound. The USARPs were taken in tow by George Toney.

Toney had spent the first winter at Byrd Station (1957) as Station Scientific Leader. He continued with the National Science Foundation when it took over USARP. George was well liked and competent. He was the NSF representative in Antarctica during the 1960–61 austral summer, and was stationed at McMurdo.

It was about 0°F with a little wind. The sky was clear, and we were surrounded by a beautiful view.

7. Glaciers flowing through Transantarctic Mountains between Hallett and McMurdo. Small linear glaciers are probably flowing through fault-controlled valleys. Photograph taken December 1978 from C-141 aircraft flying at elevation of about 41,000 feet (12,500 meters).

On my previous two trips to Antarctica, I had traveled comfortably by ship. This gave me the opportunity to observe the gradually changing climate, see icebergs, sea ice, seals, whales, penguins, and many other birds. Tourists pay a lot of money for a cruise to Antarctica so they can have this experience. In December 2002 I traveled on a scientific cruise from New Zealand to the Ross Sea in the U.S. research ice breaker *Nathaniel B. Palmer* and again had the pleasure.

Flying to McMurdo in a cramped military plane with roaring engines and little or no visibility is a quite different experience and distinctly less pleasant. The payoff, however, comes when stepping out of the plane on a clear, blue-sky day and being overwhelmed by the spectacular view of the Royal Society Range of the Transantarctic Mountains rising up over 4300 meters (about 14,000 feet) about 40 miles across McMurdo sound. Towering above the lower peaks of Ross Island is Mt. Erebus, an active volcano 3794 meters high (over 12,400 feet), which frequently has a cloud of steam (condensed water vapor) trailing downwind from the summit crater. Even though I had already spent about two years in Antarctica, I got a real thrill on that day in 1960.

From the sea ice runway, we could see McMurdo, a spread-out cluster of one-story buildings on Hut Point Peninsula, on volcanic Ross Island.

8. C-130 on sea ice, Williams field. Active volcano, Mt. Erebus, in background.

Robert Falcon Scott had moored his ship *Discovery* there on his first expedition (1902–04) in what he called Winter Quarters Bay, next to Hut Point. There his men built a hut, but they lived for the winter on the ship.

The airstrip, called Williams Field in 1960,[1] was on sea ice at least 6 feet thick. At the beginning of each summer season the ice is thick enough to support wheeled aircraft. By mid-December, the weather has warmed to the point that melting is occurring and the sea ice is unsafe. After that time ski Hercules C-130 aircraft land on an airstrip on the Ross Ice Shelf about an hour drive by tracked vehicle from McMurdo Station. This strip has also been called Williams Field (Willy Field for short) since about the 1980s. As there is little institutional memory at McMurdo, today people do not know that the sea ice strip was once called Williams Field.

By 1995, the Pegasus, so-called "blue-ice" strip, about another hour farther away on the Ross Ice Shelf, was developed; it can take landings of wheeled aircraft at any time. This strip, however, is not a true blue-ice area caused by wind, which removes the snow and/or sublimates the snow and firn down to the underlying ice. Rather the Pegasus strip is ice at the surface equilibrium line between snow accumulation and melting.

In contrast to Pegasus, there are many areas of naturally occurring blue-ice requiring no maintenance, that can be and are now being used for heavy wheeled aircraft operations directly from other Southern Hemisphere continents. This concept, pioneered by Charles Swithinbank and Giles Kershaw elsewhere in Antarctica,[2] has revolutionized Antarctic aircraft operations. Because large aircraft, such as the C-141 Starlifter, used since the late 1970s, can carry a payload into as well as sufficient fuel to fly out of Antarctica, the continent has been opened to the outside world as never before. Many "adventure tourists" are being routinely flown into blue ice landing areas by wheeled aircraft from South America, Australia, and Africa. They are then delivered to the South Pole or some climbing or ski trekking starting point by twin-engined, small ski aircraft such as Twin Otters.

During the IGY the U.S. had operated seven Antarctic bases and/or scientific stations around the continent and in the interior. The official name of the base on Ross Island at McMurdo Sound during IGY was Williams Naval Air Operating Facility;[3] there were no civilians on the base except summer personnel en route to the South Pole. The name was soon changed to McMurdo Station, and the name Williams applied only to the sea-ice landing strip by 1960. Little America Station on the Ross Ice Shelf, the center of American science operations during the IGY, was closed at the end of the 1958–59 summer. The headquarters of U.S. research in Antarctica was then transferred to McMurdo.

By 1959, Ellsworth Station, on the Filchner Ice Shelf at the south end of the Weddell Sea, had been given to Argentina. I had spent the 1956–58, and 1958–59 periods in this area. Wilkes Station, closest U.S. station to Australia, was turned over to Australia.

Hallett Station, on the west coast of the Ross Sea about 400 miles north of McMurdo, was jointly operated by the United States and New Zealand. Amundsen-Scott Station, as it still is officially known, at the South Pole, was and still is completely supported by air. Byrd Station, in West Antarctica at 80°S, 120°W, had been built and supplied by tractor train from Little America and by air support.

Palmer Station, on the Antarctic Peninsula, was not established until February 1965. Therefore all U.S. operations were concentrated in the McMurdo, Hallett, Byrd, and South Pole Stations areas in the early 1960s.

We drove into McMurdo in a Sno-Cat [described below]. George Toney took me to Jamesway J1, where I would be staying. Hugh Bennett, Charles Swithinbank,[4] and Jack Tuck[5] were the only people I knew. Swithinbank and Tuck are just leaving for a few days on a glacier they will be studying.

A Jamesway hut is an ingenious structure first used by the U.S. Army. The hut, which can be quickly assembled and taken apart, consists of wooden, hinged arches covered by four-feet-wide insulated fabric panels and fabric ends equipped with wood doors and covered vestibules. There is a wooden floor, of boxlike panels about six inches high. When warmed by a diesel fuel space-heater, the hut is quite comfortable.

A bearded fellow came in and I puzzledly tried to figure out why he

looked familiar. When he spoke, I immediately recognized Edwin
Robinson (Robbie). He will be going on the McMurdo-South Pole
Traverse and has just finished the winter here.

McMurdo in 1960 would be almost unrecognizable to a first timer at the
beginning of the twenty-first century. The base was built in 1955–56 during Deep
Freeze I with the prefabricated Clement huts standard at all of the US IGY
stations. These huts were constructed of four-by-eight-foot insulated panels,
about five inches thick, painted red on the outside, light blue-green on the
inside, held together by metal clips. The buildings were heated by diesel fuel
furnaces called jet heaters; fans forced the hot air through ducts.

By the summer of 2000–01 all of the original Deep Freeze I and II buildings had
been replaced. Unfortunately none of them was saved for historical purposes. The
politically correct view today (with the exception of a preserved Australian station)
is that bases or buildings built in Antarctica before World War II are "historic," (such
as the U.S. East Base on the Antarctic Peninsula and Scott's Hut at McMurdo) and
those built later are trash and must be destroyed and the debris removed.

In 1960 there were also the above-mentioned Jamesway huts, and some
corrugated metal Quonset huts. The various huts were lined up on either side of
a street, with a metal-arch Quonset hut built into the "Chapel-of-the-Snows" at
the end nearest Observation Hill.

McMurdo had 150 people in the winter and by now has 500. There are
200 more in the camp at the strip.

By December, McMurdo would be so crowded that everyone not needed there
was sent somewhere else. More than 1000 men were housed there at peak times
during that summer. I recall about 1400 maximum in these years, but cannot find
a good reference for this. Part of the confusion lies in the great number of personnel just passing through McMurdo and staying only a few days.

Robbie and I went out to the large Butler Building, a recently constructed
two-story-high metal building, which UW mechanics[6] were using as a
garage to work on the two huge model 843 Sno-Cats,[7] scheduled for the
McMurdo-Pole oversnow traverse.

This building is where Berg field center was located from the 1970s through
the 1990s.

9. "Main street" McMurdo, October 1960; view toward Observation Hill. *Chapel of the Snows* at end of street. Robinson at left.

10. View of McMurdo, October 1960, from Observation Hill. Garage (later called Berg Field center) in foreground.

# CHAPTER THREE

11. View of McMurdo from Observation Hill, January 1995. Crary Building in center.

The smaller Tucker Sno-Cats used on the three oversnow traverses during the IGY[8] and IGC years were painted orange and had a streamlined appearance, with no windows except for the driver and right-hand front passenger. Unlike the Weasels[9] and D-4 and D-8 Caterpillar tractors, Sno-Cats have a steering wheel like an automobile. Because of the mass of the vehicle and because of the separately articulated forward and rear pairs of pontoons, hydraulic steering is essential. Although the engine was actually inside the cab, it was insulated from it so there was no heating of the vehicle by the engine in the IGY Sno-Cats.

The IGY Sno-Cats were powered by 185-horsepower gasoline engines, but the 743 and 843 models purchased by the UW (with NSF funds) about 1960 had diesel engines. They and most of the other vehicles at McMurdo in 1960–62 used ether cartridges fired directly into the cylinders to turn the engines for one or two cycles to start them. However, my mother, a teacher at a school in central Wisconsin at the same time, used an electric heater plugged into a 110-volt cable provided by the school for each of the teachers' cars in much lower Wisconsin winter temperatures than those in McMurdo in the summer. Eventually the Antarctic program adopted this method also at McMurdo. The ether cartridges used with the diesel Sno-Cats on the oversnow traverses worked well, of course, and were quite useful.

I set up the magnetometer in a small room in the garage, which is the electronic shop. [During the next several days I checked this out but Dick

Wold finally got it operating.]

After supper, Hugh Bennett and Robbie went out to record a seismic refraction shot, which Charlie was going to fire. I was going to go with Charlie, but when I realized this would take all night, I decided to sleep until 2300 when he was scheduled to leave. I had been up about 37 hours by this time and I don't even know if Charlie ever tried to wake me.

Of course the sun was up for 24 hours a day and had been for a week or more at McMurdo. All day it moved from east to west and all night from west to east. New arrivals forget to sleep—until they crash as I had just done. The temperature at McMurdo was in the low 20°s F at this time. There was no melting and it was not unpleasant working outside in the sun.

> *30 Oct. Sun.* Up at 0700 and just missed breakfast. They serve four meals
> a day, two hours each from 5–7, 11–12, 17–19, 23–1.

In 1960 the mess hall was a large building constructed of Clement hut panels. There was a segregation of officers from enlisted men, and each stood in separate cafeteria lines. All civilians were given officer status and expected to eat in the officers' mess. By the turn of the century, the Navy had phased out of the USAP, the mess hall had been rebuilt, and there was only one central eating area. This is a very attractive group of tables of various shapes scattered throughout an aesthetically pleasing sunlit room.

In the 1960s, evening movies were shown in the enlisted mess (I recall). By the late 1980s movies at McMurdo were no longer shown in the mess hall. They are now available as video tapes and shown on TV sets throughout the living quarters. This is convenient, but it does not provide a common place for all of the various groups to congregate for relaxation as we did in the 1950s and 1960s. By 2003, one of the bars (formerly the officers' club), now designated the coffee house, shows "art films" (or what pass for "art films" at McMurdo) on weekend evenings.

> I took a couple of hours off this afternoon to climb up Observation Hill with
> Charlie Bentley and Mario Giovinetto. This is a small 500-foot peak
> composed of volcanic rock. From the summit I got a good look at our base,
> New Zealand Scott Base, McMurdo Sound, Mt. Erebus and Mt. Terror on
> the other side of the island. There is a large wood cross on the summit
> erected in memory of Scott and his lost party by the other members of
> that expedition in 1913. To the south the Ross Ice Shelf stretches off in the

distance. To the south and west is the Royal Society Range with Mt. Lister and other peaks looking quite beautiful covered with snow. Mt. Discovery, an extinct volcano, is quite prominent across the sound.

As we climbed up Observation Hill, we passed the site of a nuclear power reactor on which construction was just beginning. The Navy was very enthusiastic about this project in 1960. The Deep Freeze 61 Cruise Book[10] described it as "the first power reactor that will be making a profit. Because of high transportation costs, diesel oil in a remote area like the Antarctic is more expensive than the nuclear fuel required to produce the same amount of electricity."

Not necessarily. A couple of years later Phil Smith of NSF told me that a careful calculation of the additional fuel delivery costs to McMurdo by tanker, after the ice breaker had broken a channel and the first barrel was delivered, was about 9 cents a gallon. In 2003 dollars that still can't be more than about 40 cents a gallon additional delivery cost. "The reactor system is designed so that it can be put together by Navy Seabees within 60 days after arrival at the site and readied for full power generation only 15 days later."

The reactor, which was affectionately called "Nukey Poo" from its Navy designation, NNPU, never was cost effective. It "went critical" in March 1962, but never produced power efficiently because of operational problems. Nukey Poo was eventually decommissioned in October 1973, and dismantled and prepared for return to the U.S. during the 1973–74 and 1974–75 summer seasons. However, disposal of nuclear waste in Antarctica is prohibited by the Antarctic Treaty. "In all, 365 metric tons of radioactive waste or radioactively contaminated components were removed from the . . . site. . . . The effort was completed on January 24, 1975, when the last of the radioactive waste prepared during the summer was loaded aboard the resupply ship."[11]

Sometime in the 1980s, additional dirt and rock at the former reactor site on Observation Hill were removed and brought to the U.S., where a controversy erupted regarding importing nuclear waste into California. Eventually it was deposited at a Navy facility on the coast north of Los Angeles.

No other power reactor has ever been built in Antarctica, although the former Soviet ice breaker, *Lenin,* which operated in Antarctica during the IGY period, was nuclear powered. There was never any controversy among environmentalists during the period that the reactor at McMurdo was under construction, in operation, or being dismantled. If fact, there were few, if any, environmentalists then. There was never any legal problem under the Antarctic Treaty in building a nuclear power reactor in Antarctica. Until 1993, the U.S.

12. Cross erected by Scott's men in 1913 at summit of Observation Hill. Mt. Erebus in background.

13. Bentley on summit of Observation Hill.

National Environmental Policy Act (enacted in 1969) did not apply to the National Science Foundation program in Antarctica. The Environmental Protocol to the Antarctic Treaty, which requires stringent Comprehensive Environmental Evaluations (CEE), did not enter into force until 1998.

I assume that American and Soviet nuclear submarines routinely transited Antarctic waters, submerged, throughout the Cold War and most likely they still do. This "innocent passage" of warships underway is legal under the Antarctic Treaty.

Robinson, Bennett, and Bentley shot a seismic refraction line on the sound tonight.

They were conducting an experiment to measure the velocity of sound in the rock beneath the approximately 700 meters of (about 2100 feet) sea water in McMurdo Sound. By firing a series of several-hundred-pound charges of explosives in the water at ever-increasing distances they would make this determination, and thus infer the underlying geologic structure. No one gave any thought to the possible effects of the explosions on any seals, whales, fish, penguins, or other life in the water. About this same period Soviet geophysicists fired a large explosive

14. C-124s on sea ice, Williams Field, 1960. New Zealand dog team from Scott Base in foreground.

charge in a small meltwater lake near one of their bases in East Antarctica for a similar seismic experiment. Again no one considered the impact on the fragile and possibly unique biota in this pond. In later years, the use of explosive charges for geophysical work in the sea has been essentially terminated for environmental reasons, not only in Antarctica, but in most of the world's lakes and oceans.

> *31 Oct. Mon.* I drove out to the air strip on the fast ice of McMurdo Sound with George Toney about 1900, to meet incoming people from New Zealand, as several planes were due to land. The sky was overcast and there were near whiteout conditions.

A "whiteout" is a common optical phenomenon in Antarctica, resulting from an overcast sky over the featureless snow surface. This results in multiple reflection and scattering of the light so that no shadows or definition of the snow surface or horizon are visible. The air, however, is clear; there is no fog or falling snow, and distant people or vehicles are visible.

> Just about the time we started out to the strip the Project Magnet[12] Super Constellation, called a WV (or Willie Victor) because of a dome for anti-submarine warfare instruments rather than an R7V, came in from Christchurch. Because of poor visibility, the plane undershot the runway and crashed. Two people were seriously injured and six others suffered minor injuries. There were 23 people aboard.
>
> As we drove out we met a stalled Sno-Cat with one of the injured men.

15. Phoenix 6, Super Constellation (R7V) at Williams Field. Most U.S. scientists flew into Antarctica on this aircraft in 1960–62 period.

16. Project Magnet Super Constellation (WV) crashed at Williams Field (31 October, 1960).

We were going to take him in, when a helicopter came in right beside us and picked him up. The chopper pilot was in such a hurry landing that he almost hit us. We all ran behind the Sno-Cat to get out of the way.

We got a look at the wreckage when we arrived at the strip. It wasn't pretty. The left wing was torn off and the body broken in two. There was a Globemaster (C-124) circling around and the R7V came in from Christchurch and started waiting overhead also. The runway had to be cleared of the snow piled up in the crash. The smashed plane itself was clear of the runway.

As the runway was on sea ice, which eventually broke up, the wrecked Super Constellation sank to the bottom of McMurdo Sound, as did a P2V, which had crashed there, killing four people in 1956, also because of poor visibility. There is a bit of confusion about the two Super Constellations wrecked at McMurdo. An R7V (Super Constellation), the same type of aircraft as that circling above at the time of this 1960 crash, called the *Pegasus,* crashed on 10 October 1970 on the Ross Ice Shelf several miles away. There were 80 people on board on that date, but they were not hurt. This wreck is still visible from an aircraft flying across McMurdo Sound. The "blue-ice" field on the Ross Ice Shelf is called the Pegasus strip because of the nearby wreck. When I was at McMurdo in 1978, no one even knew about the crash of the WV Super Constellation on this evening in October 1960.

When news of the Project Magnet crash reached the papers in the United States a day or two later, people in Madison thought it was our group, because of our planned aeromagnetic surveys. We did not know this at the time, and made no particular effort to reassure our friends and families.

Finally the planes landed and we met five USARP scientific personnel. Back at McMurdo, several of us sat around Robbie's room telling crevasse stories for a while.

I find it interesting that even though we had just spent a couple of hours involved with an airplane crash my journal only notes that we told "crevasse stories." I think now this was bravado or we were repressing our emotions—probably both.

*1 Nov. Tues.* I helped Robbie, Charlie, and Ralph (a UW mechanic) change a pontoon on a Sno-Cat. We finished about midnight and I drove it up to the blasting cap magazine for Robbie. It was the first time I'd driven a Sno-Cat in two years, and I was a bit rusty on the sharp turns, much to the amusement of the other three, who offered much constructive criticism and many helpful suggestions, such as,

Ralph: "Give her hell straight ahead!"

Charlie: "Better back up."

Robbie: "What's that growl in the gear box?"

The explosive magazines were placed well up on the hill behind McMurdo. Closer in was the dump, filled with old and not-so-old broken-down vehicles. During the previous winter the Kiwis at nearby Scott Base had salvaged a discarded Weasel from this dump and rebuilt it. Jack Long, the head UW mechanic, had managed to get a discarded D-4 Caterpillar tractor running again. When the

Seabees needed a part, they occasionally would go up to the dump and cut a piece off an abandoned vehicle with a torch, and bring it into a warm building to unbolt what was needed. This kind of premature disposal and scavenging didn't make the Navy look very good, so Admiral Tyree eventually ordered all of the scrapped vehicles and other non-burnable trash to be hauled out on the sea ice. There it all sank to the bottom of McMurdo sound when the ice broke out at the end of the summer. This later became the routine method of disposing of heavy trash at McMurdo.

Today, not only is this not done, but all of the trash in the old garbage dump has been put in cardboard containers or metal drums (for hazardous waste) and shipped out of Antarctica. There are no more skuas (birds) around the McMurdo dump site because no food garbage is disposed of there. Today, all garbage and trash (but not sewage) is shipped out of Antarctica.

*2 Nov. Wed.* Overcast and blizzard all day, clearing in the afternoon. I estimated the winds about 50–60 knots. I tried to walk out to the garage at one time, but it was impossible to see across the hundred-foot space. Visibility was about 25 feet at the worst. It was quite warm however, and I just wore my windbreaker parka.

I got Robbie to show me where all the seismic gear I will use for ice thickness measurements is, and packed it ready to ship out to Byrd Station.

*3–4 Nov. Thurs.–Fri.* Dick Wold, Forrest Dowling, and Tom Laudon flew in on the Connie (R7V).

*5 Nov. Sat.* After supper George Toney told me I was going to Hallett in the morning. My cough is worse.

People wintering over have essentially no communicable diseases. However, when the summer people arrive with colds, etc. these go through a station such as McMurdo like wildfire. This is the reason influenza vaccinations are required for all people deploying to Antarctica each year. I'm sure some suffered because of my bad cold, which I have not described here. The base was full of upper-respiratory infections—as is common at the start of every summer season.

The weather became overcast and there was a raw cold wind in the evening when Dick and I walked over to Hut Point and looked at Scott's Hut. After 50 years it was still in good shape, although the inside was full of snow.

17. McMurdo area from Observation hill, October 1960. Hut Point in background. Vince's Cross is on top of point at left end of peninsula. YOG (Fig. 19) and Scott's Hut (Fig. 18) are barely visible at Hut Point. Nuclear reactor site under construction is visible on flat volcanic rock area immediately below photographer.

Leslie B. Quartermain, an old New Zealand Antarctic buff whom I met in Christchurch in February 1960, stirred up enough interest and funds to refurbish the old huts that Scott and Shackleton used between 1902 and 1916. He started his actual work in Antarctica in the 1960–61 summer. The hut at Hut Point, where McMurdo Station is located, has been cleaned of ice and restored essentially as Shackleton's ill-fated Ross Sea support party for the Transantarctic Expedition left it in 1916. It is kept locked, but is open for visitors by special arrangement. Inside are old supplies, seal carcasses, a primus stove, etc.

I managed to visit the other two huts on Ross Island, several tens of miles away, at Cape Royds (Shackleton's 1907–09) and Cape Evans (Scott's 1911–13) in 1984 via helicopter. These and the hut at McMurdo are managed by the New Zealanders at Scott Base. Both have also been cleaned up and the Cape Evans hut is arranged just as in a famous photo from Scott's last expedition.

Two small Navy ships called YOGs (escort tankers) are frozen in the ice and abandoned next to Scott's Hut at McMurdo.

Also on Hut Point is a cross commemorating the death of a man killed on Scott's first expedition (Vince's Cross). It stands on a little knoll

18. Scott's Hut as it appeared in October 1960.

overlooking McMurdo Sound. As we stood there looking out, the bleakness and awful desolation of this continent was brought home to us by the cold grey aspect of everything. One doesn't get the impression so easily when surrounded only by ice and snow as at Ellsworth on the featureless Filchner Ice Shelf. It's the expanse of exposed rock with only a few lichens that gives it such an appearance of death.

Actually there is quite a lot of life in the area. There are of course the seals, penguins, and skuas with which most are familiar, but also there are lichens, algae, and insects. The USARP biological program is quite extensive in 1960, and divided mainly into terrestrial and marine life studies.[13] D. E. "Curly" Wolschlag of Stanford University is in charge of a large share of the marine studies. Others are studying insects and bacteria.

One of the scientists about this time cultured viable bacteria from the Scott party's old privy half a century earlier. In 2002–03 season, a scientific team cultured viable anthrax bacteria from 90–100-year-old dung from Scott's ponies.

A Seabee was killed here the other day when he tried to cut an empty

19. Auxiliary tanker (YOG) frozen in sea ice. Mt. Discovery in background.

antifreeze drum with an acetylene torch. It exploded in his face. The incident is being kept rather quiet.

There have been a number of fatalities over the years at U.S. and other Antarctic stations in "industrial" types of accidents like this.

*6 Nov. Sun.* I was ready bright and early to fly to Hallett, but the weather there was bad so we didn't leave until about 1230. It was overcast with fairly good visibility when we took off in an R4D-8.

The twin-engined Navy R4D-8, described in chapter 1, was a Douglas DC-3, designated C-47 by the U.S. Air Force, Dakota by the British, and by the slang expression of Gooney Bird by many. The last of these aircraft was built in about 1944. I believe some are still in service in the early twenty-first century. The Navy R4D on skis was one of the several types of aircraft called "workhorse of the Antarctic" by the press over the years. The R4Ds used extremely flammable, high-octane aviation gasoline (avgas),[14] as did all of the other aircraft in VX6 except the C-130s.

We taxied out to the end of the runway and revved up each engine as the pilot and plane captain (crew chief) checked everything out. All of us passengers were seated on canvas bucket seats along the sides of the cabin, buckled into our web seat belts.

I set up the magnetometer [instrument rack] in the after part of the cabin just forward of the door. At one point the paper take-up for the magnetometer record started binding, but that was easily fixed by jamming a screwdriver into the works. We flew over the Ross Sea at an altitude of about 2000 feet.

The plane captain was familiar with Ed Thiel's aeromagnetic work the year before and after takeoff took charge of deploying the "bird" partially described in chapter 1. After we were airborne and I was readying the instrument, he removed the door, inward, including the entire frame, and secured himself to a tie-down on the deck with a web belt arrangement. He let the bird out in its fiberglass aerodynamic exterior case. It flew well a few feet outside the door so he let the 100-foot cable out hand over hand and we got a good signal recorded on the instrument. The cable dragged in a catenary about 60 feet below the plane. A woven fiberglass sheath protecting the wire cable inside it was tied down to a fitting on the deck of the plane.

The magnetometer measured the earth's total magnetic field by using the precession of protons in a bottle of a hydrocarbon, such as gasoline, in the bird that had been "set" by a short pulse of current in a coil. The current was shut off and the precession "signal" was counted. The variations in the earth's field produce a different precession count. One cycle of counting took about 0.75 seconds. In 1960, this count was recorded on a 2-inch-wide paper tape in the instrument package inside the plane.

The aircraft 28-volt power was connected to the instrument unit by inserting bare wires into a socket in the plane (we used various planes and outlets, so we did not have plugs to fit). The wires were secured to the power socket for each flight using filament tape. It only took us a few minutes to install the magnetometer for any specific flight, so we could use any available airplane with about an hour's notice. The accuracy of the magnetometer readings was about the same as similar instruments in 2003.

Navigation was the largest source of error. When we landed I would get the air navigation chart, used by the navigator during the flight, to plot our track, with times noted along it. He would determine his positions by dead reckoning supplemented by sun shots taken with a sextant. The navigator would also peer at the snow surface if it was visible through a drift meter to estimate the side slip off our course heading due to winds. When there were visible (by eye or radar) landmarks whose positions were previously known, the navigator's locations could be fairly accurate, such as on this flight to Hallett. However, over the usual

20. Adelie penguin rookery at Hallett Station, October 1960.

featureless ice sheet, we could easily be in error by 50 kilometers at the far distance of a flight from the base.

By the 1990s, when a very sophisticated aerogeophysical operation was started in the USAP, several weeks of wiring, testing, and test flights were necessary before routine flights on a predetermined grid to an accuracy of a few tens of centimeters using a GPS (Global Positioning Satellite) system were possible.

The objective of the aeromagnetic flights was to acquire a profile of the Earth's magnetic field. Slight variations in magnetite (a magnetic mineral) in the underlying bedrock produce "anomalies" in the observed magnetic field. We would interpret the magnetic anomalies to help understand the unknown geology beneath the ice or sea. On our flight over the Ross Sea continental shelf to Hallett Station and back this day, we acquired the first two profiles over the very-high-amplitude Polar Three anomaly, rediscovered in 1984.[15]

> When we landed at Hallett it was snowing slightly. The station is about a
> 20-minute drive by tracked vehicle from the airstrip on sea ice. The ice is
> getting quite thin and the field will be closed in a few days. The station is
> on a little spit of land covered with penguins and guano, with mountains
> to the west. The weather cleared a bit and I shot a lot of pictures. Two
> wildlife biologists showed me around.

21. Adelie penguin incubating eggs at Hallett Station, October 1960.

There are about 120,000 adelie penguins all around the base, which is built on a rookery. The birds have mostly finished their courting, although male birds are fighting and copulating all over the place. Many eggs could be seen in the nests made of pebbles. The males could be told from females in some cases because the females had footprints on their backs. When the chicks come the skuas will get many of them.

I heard a saying about this time: "Seabees at McMurdo hate skuas because they kill little baby penguins, but Seabees at Hallett love skuas because they kill little baby penguins." The Adult adelie penguins are about 1 1/2–2 feet tall. Skuas have a wingspread of about 6 feet.

This was my first and only experience in a penguin rookery. I shot a number of color slides using Kodachrome 25, which I still use in presentations. This short walk among the adelies was one of the highlights of my 48 years of Antarctic work.

Hallett Station was closed and abandoned a few years later. Tourist ships visiting in the 1980s complained about the environmental mess. New Zealand and U.S. workers cleaned it up and removed all the waste except for one hut left as a refuge. The Antarctic Treaty now prohibits people from walking in a penguin rookery or approaching these birds too closely.

The buildings were of the usual red Clement-hut variety and were largely free of snow. I measured the gravity on the ground at the front door of the science building with penguins clustered around.

We ate supper in the dining room where everyone sits at one large table. During the winter there were 17 people including three New Zealanders and three U.S. scientists.

There was a crashed R4D5 with bent propellers on the fast ice next to Hallett Station. About 30–40 penguins were clustered around and beneath the wreck.

We were on the ground from 1600 until 2200. We flew back to McMurdo, and again I ran the bird. On the way up the door was partly open to protect the cable and everyone got quite chilled. On the return, however, the door was closed as there was enough space beneath it to let the cable through.

George Toney met us on our arrival about 0130. He told me to be ready at 0700 to fly to Byrd. It was 0300 before I got to bed after packing up the magnetometer and gravity meter.

[A week earlier] George Toney and I took my maps over to VX6, where we talked to two of the pilots about my airborne program using an R4D-8 operating out of Byrd Station. These include 8 seismic landings to measure ice thickness along a traverse between the Hudson Mountains and Mt. Murphy about 100 kilometers south of Thwaites Glacier and Pine Island Bay on the Amundsen Sea Coast and about 2200 kilometers from McMurdo, and two landings for geology at these ranges. We also want magnetometer flights [of opportunity]—and miscellaneous gravity ties. A C-130 can carry all our stuff out to Byrd.

I had been in Antarctica nine days and all of our people and equipment were collected together. Although McMurdo was (and is) stimulating because it is the center of U.S. Antarctic activities, it can be a very frustrating experience to spend much time there. For a field researcher the lab is out there on the ice sheet. We were eager to leave for Byrd Station and start our summer program. ◆

# FOUR

# Old Byrd Station

**7 Nov. Mon.**

*I was up at 0545 and crammed my personal stuff into the ubiq-uitous orange USAP bags [These canvas bags are still used by personnel in the USARP program in 2003]. It was clear and cold (I'd guess about −5°F) at the strip. After many delays, we took off about 1530.*

This was my first flight in a C-130 Hercules. We were strapped in along the sides in red canvas bucket seats similar to those of the R4D8 with backs made of one-inch red web strap. The cabin interior is huge compared to the R4D8: 40 feet long by 10 feet wide by 9 feet tall inside. The noise of the four turboprop engines is deafening. Soft plastic ear plugs are supplied to cut the sound. The only way to communicate, unless one is plugged into the intercom system, is to shout in someone's ear. On most flights, our feet are propped up on cargo that occupies the center of the plane. On a long flight the experienced folks quickly leave their seats and find places to stretch out and sleep on the cargo. On the port side aft is a urinal and an elevated toilet next to the unloading ramp. There are a few small circular windows along the bulkheads, but it is difficult to see out from the main cabin. With special permission from the load master, one can climb up into the large cockpit and get a fine view of the terrain. At the dawn of the millennium some of the same planes flown by VX6 in 1960 were still being flown by the New York Air National Guard, which replaced the Navy crews in 1998.

In the course of my Antarctic career I have made many flights over the ice sheet in C-130s including some on which I managed to ride in the cockpit. On that day's flight, however, Admiral Tyree (whom I met for the first time on this

22. Bowman Glacier in Transantarctic Mountains at south end of Ross Ice Shelf (out of picture at lower left). Polar plateau on horizon. Photograph from LC-130 at about 30,000 feet (9100 meters, Official USGS photograph by Behrendt).

flight) rode up there on a bench on the flight deck behind the two pilots, the navigator, and the flight engineer.

I got a good view of the mass of crevasse fields throughout the Ross Ice Shelf through a small circular side window.

We crossed Ice Stream D (Bindshadler Ice Stream), one of the fast-moving (300–800 meters/year) ice streams A-E, which drain the West Antarctic Ice Sheet into the east side of the Ross Ice Shelf; these had not been recognized in 1960.

Along the way, the plane crossed the 180° meridian, so we gained a day and lost four hours. Consequently it was about 2230 on

*6 Nov. Sun.* when we arrived at Byrd Station on the featureless ice sheet.

As our skis touched down, we caught a glimpse of a wrecked plane (an R4D), partially buried, its tail in the air near the end of the runway. This plane had stalled and crashed on Christmas Eve, 1959. "The plane was coming in for an instrument landing because of poor visibility and the altimeter read 40 feet instead of 70. The pilot dropped the required 40 feet and felt a jerk. . . . He thought that was the snow surface so he cut the power."[1] Because he was still 30 feet in the air, the plane stalled. "One wing hit the snow, recoiled to the other wing, and the whole plane turned violently and skidded forward. Both wings were severed instantly, and when the fuselage finally came to a stop, only the pilot had sustained a minor injury to his head."[2]

The temperature was –33°F and the wind was at about 20 knots as we quickly scrambled out of the plane. The noise of the engines was deafening. Charlie and I got our gravity meters into heated Sno-Cats quickly and everything was soon inside the tunnels of Byrd Station about 10–15 feet below the snow surface. This is more like the Antarctica I knew at Ellsworth Station.

I was amazed at the quickness with which the plane was offloaded. The deck was covered with rollers and the 10 tons of cargo on plywood pallets slid quickly out onto big sleds backed up to the lowered rear ramp by Caterpillar tractors. The engines could not be shut down and easily restarted again so speed was essential. Everything was out in about ten minutes.

The introduction of the Hercules C-130 truly revolutionized the USARP. The C-124 parachute drops of supplies were discontinued a few years later. However, by the 2002–03 season there were insufficient experienced air crews to operate all of the LC-130s (ski equipped) that were available (two were left in the U.S.) and a route for an oversnow tractor train to resupply the South Pole was again being explored.[3]

Byrd Station was established in 1955–57 at the center of Marie Byrd Land (by definition) at 80°, 120°W. This was before the Antarctic Treaty; therefore the United States wanted an inland station in the only unclaimed sector of Antarctica. Scientists assumed that bedrock was shallow beneath the 1500 meter -(about 5000 foot) -high snow surface. On his 1928–31 expedition, Commander Byrd had claimed the territory east of 150°W (the edge of the British- and now New Zealand-claimed area) first seen from the air from west of 150°W. Lincoln Ellsworth had claimed this general area of Marie Byrd Land for the U.S. on his flight across West Antarctica in 1935. Neither of these claims was ever officially made by the United States.

Like almost all of Antarctica, the area surrounding Byrd station is a feature-less, crevasse-free snow surface marked only by windblown sastrugi. Charlie Bentley's traverse from Little America to Byrd Station in early 1957 had first shown that the ice beneath Marie Byrd Land is about three kilometers thick there. This surprising thickness led to the naming of the Byrd Subglacial Basin for the vast subsea-level area directly beneath Marie Byrd Land.[4]

During the 1955–56 season one Navy man (Max Kiel) had been killed in a crevasse accident working with a field party trying to find a route from Little America to the site of Byrd Station. Eventually, in spring of 1956 (Deep Freeze II), a small party using Weasels located a safe route through the crevasses at the edge of the Ross Ice Shelf. "Army Lt. Philip Smith and his team of crevasse specialists were brought up. With dynamite they blew the tops off"[5] of the snow bridges. After a safe route was established, a tractor train comprising six D-8 Caterpillar tractors each pulling two 10-ton sleds arrived at Byrd with the first load on 23 December 1956.

Byrd Station consisted of Clement huts of the same type as used at McMurdo. The buildings, food, and fuel caches at Byrd and the other under-snow stations were connected by an elaborate system of tunnels constructed of frames covered over with burlap. Snow drifted around and over these frames.

Byrd Station at the end of 1960 was on its last legs, although one more winter was scheduled.[6] Because of the high snow accumulation of about 15 centimeters water equivalent (or about 1.5 feet of actual snow), and drifting through the previous four winters, the tunnels were slowly being crushed and the 4-inch-by-8 inch wood beam floors of the tunnels were buckling. The overhead snow load was held up by used fuel drums supporting wooden beams and about 6-inch-diameter steel

23. Entrance to "Old Byrd" station October 1960.

pipes, which were bowed. The main access to the station was down an about 8-foot-wide ramp into main tunnel. There were one or two narrow vertical access shafts connected to the surface by built-in wood ladders.

The original plans were for, at most, two years of operation, and the four undersnow bases (Byrd, Pole, Ellsworth, and Little America V) worked very well during that period.

The station scientific program at Byrd in 1960 continued work started during the IGY. The winter projects included operation of a seismograph, which detected earthquakes in Antarctica (very few) and elsewhere in the world. A station magnetometer measured time changes in the earth's magnetic field, which we used to correct our aeromagnetic surveys. There was an aurora tower with three plexiglas domes through which the aurora observer operated an all-sky camera and other instruments to study the aurora australis ("southern lights") during the Antarctic winter. An ionosounder measured the height of layers in the ionosphere from reflections of a sweep of radio frequencies.

The meteorological program called for launching hydrogen-filled balloons carrying small instruments connected to radio transmitters to measure pressure and temperature. The data were recorded as a time record, which gave wind speed and direction at all elevation levels of the ascent.

Shortly after we arrived, the cook had a big turkey dinner ready in the chow hall. It helps to travel with an admiral. They have only about 21

24. Offloading cargo from C-130 at Byrd. October 1960.

25. Inside tunnel at "Old Byrd" (official U.S. Navy photograph).

26. Rear Admiral David M. Tyree.

people here in winter, but more have come in this summer.

This is a much nicer place than McMurdo, as everything is less hectic. Also, there are more facilities for work. I found a place in the science building to set up my seismic gear and check it out. There were several familiar faces around. Perry E. Parks Jr. of our UW geophysics crew is here as well as Walter Davis, now a CPO (chief petty officer), who wintered at Ellsworth with me, and Dale Reed, who was at Ellsworth the second winter (1958). Davis is going to the South Pole with a tractor train, which is planned to bring two D8s there.

I was told they had a good winter with bad weather. Not too cold (about –60°F) but lots of wind. Right now I imagine all of us new people are creating a lot of confusion in their previously peaceful existence. I haven't detected any xenophobia, although I suppose they do resent us a bit.

As expected, things are quite crowded at this time and most of the USARPs including Tom Laudon and Dick Wold were put in a 16-bed Jamesway built for the summer on the snow surface above the buried Byrd Station. Charlie and I are sharing a double-deck bunk in a room in one of the barracks buildings. I won the toss, so I am on the bottom. I turned in at 0200 after a short phone patch home [on the ham radio] with the folks (through Jules Madey K2KGJ in New Jersey).

The ham procedure was to make a radio contact, on the state-of-the-art, single-side-band, 1000-watt transceiver, with a ham operator in the States. That operator would connect the radio using a "phone patch" to a telephone and place a collect call to a particular individual, who paid only U.S. domestic long-distance charges. These phone patches at the U.S. stations were purely a volunteer effort by the hams in the States. Jules Madey, a young student at the time, was particularly conscientious and helpful during the early years of the U.S. program. Unlike in my winter at Ellsworth Station in 1957, where Finn Ronne strictly controlled all ham radio communication, at Byrd in 1960 I learned to operate the system myself and usually did so during the 1960–62 period.

*7 Nov. Mon.* I was pretty shot last night by the time I got to bed. I tried to get up at 0930, but didn't make it until 1145.

I had only about two hours' sleep the previous night and I was suffering a little jet lag from the four-hour time change from McMurdo, although this was not well understood in 1960.

The wind was high with much blowing snow. Dick and I spent the afternoon and evening checking out the seismic gear and running test records. The science building is really crowded with gear, but is still much preferable to McMurdo. It has a small library room with a hi-fi set, many records, and a typewriter.

There was a Monroe mechanical calculator, which was the state-of-the-art in Antarctic computing capabilities in 1960. This machine, nearly one cubic foot, whirred and chattered as it ground out only arithmetic calculations to many significant digits.

Right now I am sitting in the library listening to a record of Rossini Overtures. There are several art prints on the wall and a big easy chair made of a mattress and a box. I am reading Mark Twain's *Autobiography,* which Sara gave me before I left home. It's delightful stuff for down here.

*8 Nov. Tues., Election Day.* Dick, Tom, and I did seismic work all day. I got a mechanic to help me warm the engine of a Sno-Cat with a Herman-Nelson aircraft preheater.

This four-foot-long gasoline-powered heater was used for aircraft and surface vehicles of all types and provided heat as needed through flexible ducts to specific locations.

Meanwhile Tom and Dick were getting ready. It was −25°F with a 20 knot wind and clear. We hauled the seismic gear out in an akio.

Akios, now known as banana sleds, are still in common use in the U.S. Antarctic program. This very useful piece of Army equipment, about five feet long by two feet wide, is made of white fiberglass and has a white canvas "skirt" to cover cargo.

We loaded the equipment aboard *Carole,* one of Charlie's old Sno-Cats of several years ago, which had no heater. We drove out a few hundred yards, and while Tom and I hand drilled a 6-meter hole. Dick laid out the spread.

We drilled all of our shot holes with a hand-operated SIPRE (Snow Ice and Permafrost Research Establishment) coring auger, which took about a 3-inch-diameter core and a 4-inch-diameter hole. We had to pull up the 1-meter-long core

27. Behrendt firing explosive charge for seismic reflection ice sounding. Case of Nitromon explosive primers in foreground (photograph by T. Laudon).

barrel three times per meter because the snow and firn (slightly hardened snow at shallow depths beneath the surface) cuttings filled the barrel. As we could only lift about three or four of the aluminum rods over our heads in removing the core barrel, we had to take the drill string apart this often. Two of us could drill an 8–10-meter hole, but we needed three to drill about 15 meters for our deepest shot holes.

In our standard seismic operation, as planned for the airborne survey, we laid out a 1200-foot cable and attached geophones (miniature seismographs), or "jugs," to each of 12 pairs of wire connectors at 100-foot intervals; this was called the "spread." We shot off explosive charges in the hand-drilled hole and anywhere from about 2–15 meters deep. Charge size generally was a pound or two for a reflection (echo) from the ice-rock interface. When the geophones on the snow surface vibrated in response to the reflected sound (seismic) wave, a small voltage was generated and received at the recording instruments. Half the measured time from the shot to the recorded reflection, multiplied by the velocity of sound in the ice and snow, which we measured independently, gave the ice thickness.

The seismic equipment was state-of-the-art in 1956, when sent to Antarctica, but is quite primitive by early twenty-first-century standards. Because each of the 12 amplifiers had about 10 vacuum tubes, each aluminum case of 6 weighed about 50 pounds. Another 50-pound case contained the control unit; still another converted 24 volts, from a heavy-duty truck battery, to high voltage. We did not have digital recording equipment or even tape recorders, but used an oscillograph camera weighing about 70 pounds and photographic recording paper.

The photographic solutions developed each seismic record as soon as it was measured. We would record for several seconds after each shot usually at 36 inches/second. A miniature darkroom on which the camera rested was used to develop the records. Access to the darkroom was through an opaque sleeve into which the developing hand and arm were placed to reach the three developing tanks. This in turn required plenty of water (preferably warm), chemicals, etc. After they were developed and fixed, the 8-inch-wide, 4–10-foot-long paper records required careful washing and drying.

I showed Tom how to make up explosive charges. I did the shooting.

I unwound the 20-foot lead to a blasting cap from a small reel and inserted the cap in a hole in the one-pound metal cylindrical shaped high-explosive primer. I secured the cap to the charge using a half hitch tied in the cap lead wire. If I needed a bigger charge I would screw on one or more one-pound cans of Nitromon (ammonium nitrate—essentially fertilizer). When detonated by high explosive, ammonium nitrate will also explode, but needs no special care in shipping and handling, unlike the blasting caps and primers. I then attached the two leads of the cap wire, by twisting the ends, to two-conductor shot line (common electrical cord). I always was careful to short the ends of the shotline by twisting the ends together so no stray electric current from a radio transmitter or other source could be induced into the wired charge and fire it off in my hand. I would then lower the charge dangling from the wires, into the four-inch-diameter shot hole.

When all was ready with the instruments, I would connect the two leads to the blaster in its approximately 10-inches-cubed wooden case. I knelt on the snow with the blaster a "safe" distance away, depending on charge size and depth of hole. In turn, the blaster had a wire connection to the camera of the seismic system to record the shot instant. When Dick was ready, I would check to see that anyone else was well away and then twist a spring-loaded switch and hold it until a small bulb lit, show-ing a capacitor in the blaster was charged. I then loudly called out "Charge!" and held everything. When Dick yelled "Fire!" and started the photographic paper running in the camera, I threw a spring-loaded toggle firing switch, and there was a not very loud "bang" and a plume of ice and snow blew out of the hole.

The unheated Sno-Cat was quite cold and the records froze as Dick, who

28. R4D-8 takeoff at Byrd using JATO.

was operating, pulled them out of the hypo so we could examine them. By afternoon the developer was so cold, even though we had started with it hot in a thermos, that Dick was developing for 10 minutes. We got no reflections, which isn't surprising as no one has ever observed any here this early in the season.

The snow (firn) was so cold at this time of Antarctic spring near the surface from the low temperature of the previous winter, that long chains of shot generated incoherent noise that did not die out soon enough to observe an echo from the bottom. The main purpose of the day's work—to show Dick and Tom how the operation proceeded and check out all the equipment under field conditions—was accomplished.

We missed lunch, but the cook gave us some sandwiches. I listened to election returns for a while this evening on *Voice of America*. It seems that Kennedy is winning.

*9 Nov. Wed.* Dick didn't feel well all day and went to the doctor with a 100.6°F fever and sore throat.

No wonder, after being exposed to my cough a week earlier, and spending the previous day in an unheated Sno-Cat developing record with his hand in cold water for 10 minutes. It took Dick about a week to recover fully.

Charlie Bentley and his crew have been working hard getting last minute

29. P2V takeoff at Byrd using JATO.

details squared away for the Bellingshausen Traverse (which became known in reports as the Ellsworth Highland Traverse). All they need now is a recon flight. One of their Sno-Cats has "Bellinghausen Sea Expedition 1960–61" painted on the side. I pointed out the misspelling of "Bellingshausen," which somewhat disconcerted Charlie.

*10 Nov. Thurs.* We saw an interesting optical phenomenon tonight. The sky was partly overcast although it was clear around the sun. There was a "rainbow" like a pair of sun dogs with a bright pillar of light extending vertically down to the snow surface.

*11 Nov. Fri.* I was up at 0600 and took a turn at washing dishes for breakfast. Tom did noon and night. As he had another man to work with at night, and I had to swab the deck, we considered it even.

The recon flight for Charlie's traverse was planned for tonight. I got the magnetometer out to the plane and the plane captain hooked me into some power.

At about a quarter to midnight we started our takeoff run. I was startled by a loud roar as the JATO were fired off. In a blaze of smoke and flame we launched into the air. A JATO takeoff in a ski-equipped plane was quite dramatic, and to the uninitiated—terrifying! I would make many JATO takeoffs in ski-equipped planes in the next two years, and always waited with baited breath for the rocket ignition. When the rockets fired, the plane would abruptly lurch forward. Flames spurted out beneath (on an R4D8) or along the sides of the fuselage (on a P2V). Fortunately for our peace of mind, in the R4Ds we could not see this, as the JATO bottles were hung beneath.

For ski takeoffs in Antarctica, JATO was usually used because the friction of the skis on the snow was so great that it was generally not possible to get up to a safe takeoff speed without this assistance. JATO bottles, small solid-fuel rocket engines weighing 175 pounds, were hung in pairs from brackets beneath the fuselage of an R4D. Each JATO bottle provided 10,000 pounds of thrust and burned for 10 seconds. Various numbers, from 2 to 8 of them, would be fired in an R4D takeoff depending on snow conditions. After firing, the JATO bottles were released; they are now littered around Antarctica. A P2V usually required 16 JATO rockets to take off on snow, attached on each side and bottom of the fuselage.

The flight that night was a major reconnaissance intended to cover the entire planned route of the Ellsworth Highland Traverse. It would also be one of our longest magnetometer flights.

> *12 Nov. Sat.* As soon as we were airborne, I got the bird out the door. I immediately found that things weren't working with the magnetometer. One trouble I traced to broken wire in the bird. Another problem was low voltage. We had to move everything over to another 28-volt outlet near the rear and opposite the door. Then something else went wrong in the equipment. I managed to get everything going in 15 minutes or so.

Many of the flights we made during this and the following field seasons were over totally unexplored terrain. There was no GPS, nor even inertial navigation available in the 1960s. The method of navigation employed then was essentially the same used by the early pioneers of Antarctic flying, except for gyro compasses, and radio-time signals received from the United States, which allowed the chronometers to be set accurately.

On the aeromagnetic survey flights we would make during this season there was always a man, usually me, sitting (after takeoff) in one of the seats in the cockpit. I recorded altimeter readings by hand in a data book at five-minute intervals (about 18 kilometers distance). The air-pressure elevation minus the radio-altimeter elevation gives the snow surface elevation. Because not even the most rudimentary knowledge of the elevation of most of the ice sheet was available at the time covered by this book, these snow surface elevation measurements, and the results of the 1957–60 oversnow traverses, were allowing us to map the topography. I also took notes on surface features and any mountains we might discover or use as navigation control. However, on this flight Bentley rode in the copilot's seat and took notes and recorded elevations for me.

> Hiromu "Hiro" Shimizu [a Japanese glaciologist who would go on Charlie's traverse] took notes and pictures. Occasionally I took pictures with a Polaroid camera as well as my 35mm Alpa 7 using Kodachrome 25 color film.
>
> We flew northeast until we could see the majestic Sentinel Mountains, the highest in Antarctica, [5140 meters (about 16,000 feet) at the Vinson Massif] about 125 miles away.

On 22 November 1935 (only 25 years previously) Lincoln Ellsworth and his pilot Herbert Hollick-Kenyon first saw these mountains. Ellsworth wrote: "We came abeam of a solitary little range . . . with peaks rising to 13,000 feet. . . . I named it the Sentinel Range."[7]

Ellsworth named the most prominent peak near the north end, Mt. Louise Ulmer, after his wife. Mt. Ulmer, actually only 9107 feet (2776 meters) high, is about 110 kilometers north of the high Vinson Massif. The next people to see this range and make the first scientific observations there were the members of Charlie Bentley's and Verne Anderson's Sentinel Mountain Traverse in January 1958. Throughout the period covered in this book, as we flew across the West Antarctic Ice Sheet, the Sentinel Range provided a landmark that could be seen for several hundred miles.

> We swung northwest and flew over the Hudson Mountains, where we plan on doing some geology. The area was badly crevassed and disturbed. From the Hudsons the plane turned northeast and headed for Mt. Tuve and Mt. Peterson, which Finn Ronne reported in 1947. They must be somewhere else, because we didn't find them.

Ronne's reported positions[8] for Mt. Tuve and Mt. Peterson were, however, about 160 kilometers farther southwest (about 5° of longitude) than the position determined by the Antarctic Peninsula Traverse (APT) of 1961–62 from accurate USGS surveys from the snow surface. Early flights in Antarctica were frequently off in dead reckoning and sextant locations. This caused us problems in our work in the area in 1960–61 and 1961–62. We expected mountains where there were none and found others where none had been previously reported.

Although we did not realize it at the time, no one had ever flown over or seen the eastern area we covered on this flight.

We swung back northwest toward the Bellingshausen Sea and the Jones Mountains, which were barely visible in a fog. At one time the navigator said to the pilot [I was hooked into the intercom system and could follow all the conversation]

"Do you see anything ahead?"

"Negative."

"Do you have any visibility ahead?"

"Negative."

"Turn 90° left and climb fast! There is a mountain dead ahead on radar!"

We did and caught a glimpse of it as the fog swirled in and out. Icebergs were visible, protruding through the fast ice of the Bellingshausen Sea, before we turned back. We examined the Jones Mountains again along the steep north side. A plane could land here easily at the low base of the mountains with a geology party. In contrast, the gentle south side was overridden by snow [ice].

The Jones Mountains had been discovered by Ed Thiel and Campbell Craddock only ten months earlier on a reconnaissance flight, although they may have been seen from a distance on two different flights in 1940 and 1946.

We headed south to the Hudson Mountains and Pine Island Bay along the Amundsen Sea coast. The plane missed Byrd Station and had to spend 30 minutes looking for it. We finally landed about 1400. The pilot, Joe Walker, figured, counting everything, our flight was about 1800 nautical miles [3300 kilometers]. We had been in the air more than 14 hours.

I sacked out for a couple of hours and then had a steak for supper. I went to bed at 2200 with a stomach ache.

*13 Nov. Sun.* About 0430 I woke up after a restless sleep. My stomach still hurt. I went back to bed, but got up to vomit once. At lunch, I had only a few sips of soup and a glass of orange juice. After lunch, I went to the doctor. My white blood count is up (about 10,000–13,000), and I have pain in the lower right quadrant of my abdomen. Nausea, vomiting, and diarrhea complete the list. My temperature is below normal. Seems like appendicitis.

Although my journal notes below treated my situation lightly, it was relatively serious. Fortunately I was young and healthy. I have often wondered if the severe cold I had just recovered from, combined with the stress of the long flight just completed, might have triggered my appendicitis attack.

In bed all day. Radio blackout. No flying (without radio communication).

One of the longest, most intense magnetic storms in recorded history up to this date was just starting. No flights were possible without radio communication, so I could not be evacuated to McMurdo for surgery.

Doc has everything sterile to operate on me, but would prefer to send me to McMurdo as they have better facilities. [I doubt he had ever performed an appendectomy.] Watchful waiting.

*14 Nov. Mon.* Chloromycetin shots in the tail and IV feeding, as I vomited up my fluid the previous day. Sort of a limbo existence. Pain always there, but not too bad. No sharp twinges. Still radio blackout; no flying.

I finished Mark Twain's *Autobiography*. It was very enjoyable reading for the sick room until the part wherein his wife and two daughters died.

Charlie Bentley, Perry Parks, Hiro Shimizu, Herb Meyers, John Molholm, the mechanic George Widich and a meteorologist left on the Ellsworth Highland Traverse in three Sno-Cats sometime this morning. I envy them.

Art Ford moved into Charlie's bunk above me.

Arthur Ford has been a long-time colleague and friend. A few years after this he was influential in my starting work at the U.S. Geological Survey, where we both stayed until retiring in 1995. We met under rather adverse conditions, when he replaced Charlie in the bunk above my sickbed.

*15 Nov. Tues.* I was awakened about 0700 by the Doc and corpsman (a Navy medic). I was shot the third time with streptomycin and penicillin as they have run out of chloromycetin. Four times a day now. I'm getting sore! My stomach feels better. It took all morning to get 1500 cubic centimeters of dextrose 5 percent [Dextran] pumped into my vein. It was facetiously referred to as "breakfast." I figure they are giving me 1200 calories/day, which is plenty.

Dick, Tom, and a USGS geologist came in about 1600 and played bridge with me. I convinced the doctor that I could drink my fluid, so he let me try pineapple juice, bouillon, and eat some Jello. This may not seem exciting to an outside reader, but it is to me! I don't need the IV tonight. This treatment of appendicitis seems to be working all right.

I am reading Will Durant's *Age of Faith*, a medieval history. I definitely feel better and my temperature was down to 99.2°F. I even felt hungry today.

I was not as coherent as these notes imply. Someone (probably Art Ford) told me that I was groaning in my sleep on occasion. The reason I was saved from a probably rather crude appendectomy was that the Navy physician at the South Pole the previous winter had removed an appendix successfully. However, back in the States at the time, the Navy physicians reconsidered the risks of surgery in Antarctica and recommended antibiotics as the preferred treatment. In my case, it worked.

*16 Nov. Wed.* My temperature was down to normal today. I had two pieces of toast for lunch—the first food since Saturday. For supper I had some toast and a slice of cold meat. I've been getting 2,400,000 units of penicillin per day. Tomorrow the Doc said I could get up for a while. The pain in my stomach is almost gone. Still a radio blackout; no flying. Byrd Station, and I suspect none of the other bases have had any radio communication with the outside world since Saturday.

I'm still plowing through Will Durant, but when a fellow brought me a few *Playboy* magazines, I thought I'd take a break from Moslem Civilization for a while. I walked over to the head and back tonight. I'm pretty weak.

*17 Nov. Thurs.* I got up as my temperature was normal and there was no pain in my belly. I felt pretty weak at first, but gained strength throughout the day. The Doc stopped the antibiotic in the morning. Now we'll see if I can make it on my own. It sure felt good to be around again, even though I was only in bed a few days. I was surprised at how many people told me they were glad to see me up again. I guess Doc has been sounding various people out to find helpers in any operation on me he had to do.

One of the fellows saw five sun spots tonight, so I guess we will have at least a few more days of no flying.

An associated solar flare had caused the magnetic storm and radio blackout. This would have been a particularly bad period to collect aeromagnetic data.

*18 Nov. Fri.* The weather was good for flying today, but still no radio, so no flights. The ham radio is working now, and Jules Madey (K2KGJ) in New Jersey told us that there had been no flights from ChiChi to McMurdo for a week. Two planes started yesterday, but turned back. Our Navy radio contacted McMurdo, but was just able to get two messages through before the band faded.

*19 Nov. Sat.* I was awakened by Joe Walker at 0630 and told we were going to fly the recon for the airborne traverse today. We got all the paraphernalia out to the plane and ready to go by 0900. This was my first time outside and it felt good. The temperature must have been up to –5°F. While we were waiting a cloud cover came up and the flight was canceled.

Doc Bartlett sent a message about my appendicitis,[9] which was the first information out of Byrd about my illness, caused some consternation back at McMurdo and in Madison.

*20 Nov. Sun.* A beautiful clear day (about 0°F), but the communications were out again so no flying.

During the three months we spent at Byrd Station, when we could not fly, we worked routinely on various geophysical tasks, which I do not generally describe here. We also helped out occasionally with general base work.

About midnight a geologist outside saw an aircraft approaching. He came in and told people. Ken Moulton, the NSF representative, woke up a radio operator, who got on the air and found it was a C-124 ready to make an airdrop.

Because of the extended radio blackout, apparently the Navy operators at Byrd had stopped keeping a radio watch.

*21 Nov. Mon.* There were five C-124 airdrops and three C-130 loads for the day. Mail and more people. I received a letter from Bert Crary, who is at McMurdo.

By 1959 Albert P. (Bert) Crary, a geophysicist, was Chief Scientist of the USARP at NSF in Washington, D.C. However, persuaded by Charlie Bentley, he had come down to McMurdo to lead the McMurdo-South Pole oversnow traverse this season.

Crary wondered about my appendix. He hopes to get off by 28 November and put in 12 major stations before reaching the Pole. Apparently they have a good route up the Skelton Glacier thanks to the recon by Bill Long, Mario Giovinetto, and others.

Byrd now houses 80 people. All of us in the USARP barracks had to give up our rooms for the new wintering people, who have just arrived. I moved a cot and mattress into the traverse office in the Science Building. Art Ford and another man set up cots in the tunnel near the barracks.

*22 Nov. Tues.* Bill Long got out his two motor toboggans [snowmobiles], and was put-putting around camp. [A few days later] Dick, Tom, and I took turns at driving them. They are about seven feet long, three feet wide, and weigh 300 pounds. Ohio State University paid $1300 for each complete with spares. They will drive 30 miles per hour theoretically, but no one has driven them very fast. [These days snowmobiles reach speeds over 100 miles per hour.] No one knows how durable they are nor how they behave on a steep slope.

I believe these were the first snowmobiles used by the U.S. program in Antarctica. They were generally not available in the U.S. in 1960. The motor toboggans revolutionized field work over snow in Antarctica in the next few years. They completely replaced dogs in the Antarctic field programs of countries such as the UK, Australia, Argentina, and New Zealand.

At lunch Joe Walker told me we would probably take off on our recon about 2100.

This was the flight (described in chapter 1) on which we hit our wing tip on the peak in the Crary Mountains. It was my first flight out after recovering from appendicitis five days earlier.

"What has been the hardest in my life I have told first in my narrative. . . . I needed to tell those terrible things first, to pass through Scylla and Charybdis early in my voyage of telling." That quote from *Ahab's Wife*[10] is a bit strong, but it seems appropriate. Although I had just recovered from appendicitis, this plane incident was obviously the more stressful event, particularly because it involved all of the others on the plane that had dented its wing on the mountain peak. As discussed previously, we flew from Byrd toward Toney Mountain and encountered the Crary Mountains hidden in a cloud bank. My wan look in the photograph (figure 4) just after this flight is probably partly the result of only five days out of my sick bed. A few days later I received a friendly note from Bert Crary at McMurdo telling me to keep my magnetometers off his mountains!

I went to bed after the flight about 0600 and slept until noon. After dinner I called Ed Thiel, in Madison on the ham radio and asked him to send a new sensing head and cable. I didn't tell him about the near accident as VX6 hasn't reported it yet. I talked to George Woollard also. They were more concerned about my appendicitis than anything else.

Dick and I walked out to the plane and took some pictures of the wing. Jim Cornwell [Officer in Charge (OIC) of VX6 at Byrd] asked Dick and me to write up statements of the incident. I wrote five pages.

*24 Nov. Thanksgiving, Thurs.* Buildings in camp are sagging [under the weight of 10–15 feet of snow overhead] and water is dripping in various places. One of the bunks in the recreation hall got soaked today.

Jules (K2KGJ) comes in strong every day; I'll call the folks again one of these days.

I had not told my parents about my appendicitis and the near fatal plane incident, nor did I intend to while in Antarctica. Now, as the father of two grown sons who frequently travel to and live in dangerous parts of the world, I wonder at my judgment about this in 1960. Perhaps I was correct.

We had a big turkey and ham dinner today as is typical of the Navy. This is my fourth Thanksgiving on Deep Freeze.

I really had a lot to be thankful for this holiday, but I did not make any mention in my journal of my recovery from appendicitis and the near miss in the mountains in relation to Thanksgiving. ◆

# FIVE

# Exploring the West Antarctic Ice Sheet

The remote flight operations out of Byrd Station continued to be delayed for weather and other reasons through the summer. The C-130 operations continued regularly from McMurdo to Byrd.

> *25 Nov. Fri.* I got up at 0645 hoping to fly. Instead I found Joe Walker was planning to take a load of Bill Long's geologic gear out to the Horlick Mountains.

During the IGY, geology and topographic mapping were not a part of the Antarctic program because of the unrecognized and overlapping territorial claims and the possibility of mineral resource disputes. The Antarctic Treaty, signed in 1959 and entered into force in 1961, has no mention of mineral resources, but does set aside the claims issue.

Some of us geophysicists and glaciologists on the oversnow traverse program during the two summer seasons of the IGY had geological background. Naturally we made geologic observations and collected rock samples at nunataks and mountains in the unexplored areas we visited. By the time the IGC program started in January 1959, geologists from the United States and other nations were hard at work in Antarctica. Three remote geologic field parties were planned out of Byrd in early November, 1960, in addition to geology scheduled for our airborne traverse party and possibly by Bentley's oversnow traverse.

> Bill Long, graduate student and field party leader, his professor Richard Goldthwait, head of what is now the Ohio State Byrd Polar Research Institute, and Larry Lackey, another geology graduate student, went out on the initial flight.

Bill had spent a few days during the 1958–59 Horlick Mountains Traverse doing the initial geology in the Horlick Mountains. After that season, Long had examined the geology of South Africa and found striking similarities in rock strata, fossils, and geologic ages. These early results helped convince some of us working on our Ph.D. theses that Antarctica truly was a key part of the several-hundred-million-year-old megacontinent, Gondwanaland, as had been proposed several decades earlier. However, U.S. geologists and geophysicists were very skeptical of this hypothesis in 1960. Long's research party was setting out to study the question in the Horlick Mountains.

Dick, Tom, and I went out right after breakfast and unloaded all our stuff out of the plane. We cleaned every nook and cranny of binoculars, cameras, ice axes, etc. and joked about not wanting to leave any of our stuff in such an unlucky plane as this. It has a name besides a number, *Semper Shaftus*; all the crew except the copilot are Marines. It was a beautiful day when the plane took off about 1000. Sometime after 1300, Doc Bartlett came in to the Science Building and said we could scratch one R4D. Joe Walker had crashed on landing on a 9000-foot plateau in the Horlick Mountains. The landing gear had collapsed and therefore the engines were also probably damaged when the props hit. The wing was damaged to some extent also. No one was hurt. The P2V [already airborne on a photo mission] went over to have a look.

The P2V was not a suitable plane to make an "open field landing" at a totally unprepared snow strip, particularly one with a crashed plane on it.

*26 Nov. Sat.* George Janulis and his R4D-8 got in from McMurdo about 0030. After an hour rest and refueling, they took off for the Horlicks. The boys out there had smoothed a runway and the pickup was made without incident. Everyone was back in camp by breakfast. Joe Walker had landed in very bad sastrugi about 12–24 inches high. They didn't realize the gear had collapsed until they had stopped. I gather that the crew are getting a bit depressed at the events of the last two flights [the Crary Mountains incident and this one].

Thus far the record isn't too good for flights out of Byrd. Counting the P2V there have been three successful flights [including the one on which we hit the mountain, where we did measure two magnetic profiles], four

30. Behrendt at Byrd.
IGY Sno-Cat at right.

aborts, one crash and one SAR [search and rescue].

*27 Nov. Sun.* It was more or less clear with 10–20 knots wind at –2°F. We loaded up [the seismic gear] in *Hectori 2* and Tom, Dick, and I drove out about five miles toward Little America on the marked Army-Navy trail.

The route from Little America to Byrd Station, originally used by tractor trains and Sno-Cats starting in the 1956–57 season, was marked by trail flags.

At Mile #640, we fired about 10 shots with good reflections on most. I calculated that the ice thickness there is about 2500 meters.

I felt my appendix twinge a bit today.

*28 Nov. Mon.* Major Havola [U.S. Army, the leader of the Byrd-Pole tractor train of Caterpillar D8s] arrived at Byrd last Friday. Before my program can begin, Havola's recon of their planned route must be accomplished. I managed to get Forrest Dowling scheduled on it with the magnetometer. This recon flight took off tonight about 1900. It was a beautiful calm and sunny evening.

*29 Nov. Tues.* I got up at 0830 and cornered the navigator from the R4D that made the recon. They flew out around the east end of the Horlicks [Thiel Mountains] and up onto the plateau. Havola found a good route up beyond the Horlick Mountains, which extend about 60 miles farther east than mapped [It is this eastern range that later was named the Thiel Mountains].

No plane had ever flown into this area before, although a P2V flight from McMurdo in 1956 had discovered and photographed the Pensacola Mountains about 300 kilometers still farther to the east, including the spectacular Dufek Massif, about 600 kilometers to the northeast of the Thiel Mountains.

This extent of the mountains is quite interesting as the trough is narrower than anyone had known previously. This is where I believe most of the ice of the Filchner Ice Shelf comes from.

This area between the Thiel and Pensacola Mountains is the route routinely taken since the 1980s by adventure tourists skiing to the South Pole from the Berkner Island area of the Filchner-Ronne Ice Shelf system. In 1957, I, with four others led by Ed Thiel and Hugo Neuburg, had explored the Filchner-Ronne Ice Shelf. We drove in Sno-Cats as far as the area just south of the Dufek Massif in December, 1957.[1] We had wanted to continue the traverse up this route to the west of the Pensacola Mountains, on the South Pole, and be the first to take oversnow vehicles there. However, this was not possible because of our difficult relations with Finn Ronne.

Dowling got magnetic data and snow surface elevations as well as air photos.

At lunch George Janulis asked me if we were ready to go on our recon. I answered "Yes!" At 1600 we took off. We flew northwest toward Mt. Murphy.

I sat strapped in to the right-hand seat in the cockpit with my data book in hand. Through the intercom, I could communicate with the pilot and Dick Wold, who was operating the magnetometer aft. I had as good forward visibility as the pilot, in the left-hand seat, and peered ahead at the ice sheet.

About half an hour after we took off we could see the Crary Range, which we had hit on 22 November. Mt. Takahe[2] soon appeared just to the left of our course. This massive, solitary volcano extends for 20 miles in diameter and is over 11,000 feet high. We could see Toney Mountain far to the west and ahead, the looming snow-covered volcano, Mt. Murphy.

We tried to land and do field geology in the Mt. Murphy-Kohler Range area for the next two months. The flight that day was the first of three to these ranges, all with the magnetometer and snow surface elevation measurements. Here I have combined and shortened our observations made on 29 November, 17 and 30 January.

The sastrugi are rough on the south side of Mt. Murphy, and the snow comes up nearly to the summit. On the north side of the peak we could see some vertical faces, which were quite impressive. The area to the north appeared to be nearly at sea level and is very crevassed. [On 17 January] I opened the escape hatch on the port side and shot K20 and 35mm pictures as we circled the massif. Small, frozen-over meltwater ponds and possible cirque glaciers give evidence of melting and glacial action. Several smaller peaks could be seen between us and the ice shelf bordering on the Amundsen Sea. We saw no open water.

[On 30 January] we flew past the east end of the range and out over the ice shelf for about eight miles. The Kohler Range to the west of Mt. Murphy consists of a low ridge separated from Mt. Murphy.

We had seen the 8023-foot-high [2446 meter] Mt. Murphy and the east-west-trending, 2600-foot [800-meter] -high Kohler Range in the distance on the 12 November traverse reconnaissance flight.

We turned east and flew over the route of our planned seismic landings. To the left were many crevasses in the near-sea level snow surface. Probably we were over floating ice shelf. Further out icebergs could be seen in the solid pack ice of the Amundsen Sea. Eventually we could see Pine Island Bay with open water.

All along here to the right (south) the ice could be seen rising in rolls up to about 3000 feet. There were crevasses near the probable grounded ice contact as well as farther up the slope. We reached the point shown on the navigation chart for the southernmost of the Hudson Range and found nothing there.

Janulis refused to fly to the position of the Hudson Mountains, as we had located them on the traverse recon (12 Nov.). Obviously he could not accept or understand that we were operating in an essentially unexplored part of the world, and needed to do reconnaissance. He was just intending to fly to the coordinates on the chart, based on very superficial knowledge of the area.

Our radar went out on the return leg to Byrd and we deviated to the left of our course so as to fly to Byrd on a sun line-of-position.

The normal procedure was to locate Byrd Station using radar from a distance as we approached.

I recall sitting in the cockpit in the left-hand seat on one of these flights while copilot Bob Farrington sat in the right-hand seat reading *Don Quixote* with the plane on autopilot.

About an hour out of Byrd we came upon Charlie's traverse track and followed it in to camp, landing about six hours after takeoff.

A movie was just completing as we arrived in the mess hall—*The Adventures of Happy Babba*. It was a lousy show, but it had lots of thinly clad girls and lots of sex [tame by 1970s–2000s standards], so it is the most popular movie in camp. It seems a bit ludicrous to be out exploring unmapped areas of Antarctica one hour and watching a movie the next.

*2 Dec. Fri.* Joe Walker flew in from McMurdo last night in another R4D to replace the damaged one in the Horlick Mountains. I showed Jim Cornwell a message, which I received from Charlie on the traverse, which included: . . . Possibility exists connection above sea level between Sentinel [and] Woollard Mts. and 78.5°S, 115°W. Does any chance exist for airborne soundings particularly in western part this region near Byrd. Urge consideration . . .

This is quite interesting and I wonder where this leaves Charlie's channel from the Ross to the Bellingshausen Seas.

In an early paper after the IGY, Bentley and others had suggested that there was a deep sub sea-level-channel from the Ross Sea to the Bellingshausen Sea. As more data were collected we were finding that the bedrock beneath the West Antarctic Ice Sheet was more complicated than we had first thought.

Kieth Marks, Neil Brice, and two others are working with Stanford University studying very low frequency radio (VLF) noise and plan to make several landings between the Kohler Mountains and Beardmore Glacier. Brice is a Stanford graduate student from Australia. [We became good friends over the next two years in Antarctica.] The Stanford people are paid quite a bit more than we are at University of Wisconsin.

I was paid $6500/year on a full time basis plus 25 percent for the days spent on the Ice.

We had fresh milk again today. The planes have been bringing in lettuce, tomatoes, milk, fruit, etc. since the first flights in October. Now that the wheeled C-124s have gone home [because the sea ice runway at McMurdo became unsafe] flights from ChiChi will be few and far between.

*5 Dec. Mon.* Ken Moulton [NSF representative] left last night, so now I have the responsibility of seeing that everything Bentley needs gets out there. I flew out in *Wilshie Duit*, George Janulis's plane [#853] to talk with Charlie. After about two hours' flight, we saw the two trailing Sno-Cats of Charlie's traverse. [The oversnow traverses traveled four miles apart to carry repeated barometric altimeter measurements.]

The plane landed a few miles ahead near the lead cat. Our tail ski broke on a very smooth landing. Janulis radioed in, but they were unable to get out to us today as the clouds came in at Byrd about 2000. We were stranded with the traverse party, which did not trouble me at all.

Charlie Bentley drove up in Sno-cat *Hootmon*. I took a gravity reading upon landing and plugged the meter into the seismic cat, *Sallie-Jean*, to keep the internal temperature high.

The traverse mechanic, who doubled as a cook, fried steak for the lot of us and we ate in two shifts in their wanigan. This is a small building on a sled and contains the dining room/galley.

This wanigan had been made at Ellsworth Station on the Filchner Ice Shelf during the winter of 1959.[3] Built on the base of a 2–1/2-ton sled from the same wall panels as the Clement huts used at the IGY stations, it provided effective insulation against the cold.

We sat around chatting until quite late. We discussed the high area in the bedrock topography [where I intend to make seismic soundings]. I slept

# CHAPTER FIVE

31. R4D-853 after losing tail ski on open field landing.

on the floor of *Hootmon*. There were plenty of sleeping bags for everyone. The VX6 men slept in the plane.

The black Sno-Cat was quite comfortable even though not heated. I am sure
that the shiny aluminum plane was very cold. The air crew could have put up
tents, which they carried for just this type of situation, and slept much warmer.
But aviators in Antarctica go to great lengths to avoid camping out in the snow.

*6 December Tues.* We had a breakfast of pork chops and blueberry
pancakes. I helped Charlie and Perry Parks on a seismic refraction profile
all day. After a supper of spaghetti, we worked some more until Joe
Walker flew in about 2030. We were back at Byrd by 2300, where we
enjoyed a snack of soft boiled eggs fresh in from New Zealand. They
hope to fix the tail ski tomorrow.

Although I treated this incident as just another day's work, and a vacation for
me from Byrd Station, it could have been quite serious. The tail ski was easily
replaced this time, but more severe damage, even with no injury to people, could
have been the end of this plane and most of our programs for the season. At this
point, two of the three R4D-8s were out of commission in the field.

This short visit was the only opportunity I ever had to work in the field with

Bentley, although we were in the same program together in Antarctica and at Madison for eight years.

7 Dec. Wed. Dr. Walk, the OIC, assigned me to a top bunk in the Navy barracks. Now that we have an office to work in things are much improved.

I had been sleeping on a cot in the seismic office in the Science Building.

*8 Dec. Thurs.* VX6 flew out [yesterday] with parts and the damaged plane at the traverse was fixed. Both planes flew back to Byrd, getting in early this morning.

Major Havola and his tractor train left for the South Pole this morning about 1100. They took two D8s and two Weasels. The Major wore a multi-colored hat with tassels that was quite indescribable. Dave [Walter Davis], a Navy mechanic and Chief Petty Officer, was smoking a big cigar and seemed in a great happy mood. The two wanigans labeled *Hellava Mess* and *Cathouse* were painted up.[4] Various flags were flying, including the U.S., Confederate, Army Transportation Corps, and a pair of pink panties.

We now have 64 people here, down from 104 last week. Jim Cornwell talked to me about the subject of washing dishes. He wondered if the USARP people would contribute a man per dinner and supper for a week or so to help VX6. I thought we could try it for a while at least. I assigned Dick for tonight, which made him very unhappy, although he didn't complain. I plan on taking a turn tomorrow noon.

Perhaps I should give a quick character sketch of my team at this point. Richard (Dick) E. Wold, twenty-three, is slight of build, medium height, very bright, generally easygoing. He seems the sharpest of our group. He got his BS in physics at UW last June and has nearly enough geology credits for a major there too. Very competent especially in electronics, which is the main reason I picked him to be the assistant seismologist. Reads a bit and is a sensitive and religious person. I could not think of anyone whom I would want to replace him with. Dick was married on 4 September this year.

Thomas (Tom) S. Laudon, twenty-nine, tall (about 6 feet 2 inches), heavyset, easygoing, BS and MS geology at Wisconsin and is currently working on his Ph.D. Spent two years in Japan with USAF. Tom is married with three girls. Loves the party life. Dick disapproves of this aspect of Tom's character but hasn't said so. Tom gets along very well with people,

32. Laudon at Byrd.

and is a good and willing worker at any task. He was picked as a geologist, but hasn't and won't have much time on rock. He doesn't complain although he gets most of the unskilled work with the seismic program. Tom has done gravity meter work for Woollard in Asia, South America, and Pacific area. Spent a year in Brisbane, Australia on a Fullbright. He is also very intelligent, but this is not as readily apparent at first acquaintance. A definite asset to the party and a great moderating influence.

On 1 December Campbell Craddock, the leader of the University of Minnesota geology group, had arrived on a C-130 flight. He had done geology with Ed Thiel on the airlifted geophysical traverse the previous season.

Craddock and the Minnesota group will fly out to the Jones Mountains in an R4D tomorrow, lay out a runway, and receive their equipment by C-130 from McMurdo.

I went in about 1430 to see Jim Cornwell about getting Tom aboard the R4D flying Craddock's group out to the Jones Mountains to make a gravity tie. However, Janulis' plane would be too heavily loaded. It occurred to us to send Tom, with the gravity meter, to McMurdo on the C-130 due in here at 1500 and then let him fly out to the Jones Mountains

33. Wold at Byrd.

with the C-130s from McMurdo. This gave Tom only half an hour, but with help he had his things down at the strip when the plane arrived.

*9 Dec. Fri.* This morning Janulis took off with Craddock and his bunch. About two hours out they lost radio contact and when they still had heard nothing by noon, Jim Cornwell took off in the P2V on a SAR trip to search for the plane. An hour or so out he managed to contact them so he relayed word back to launch the two C-130s from McMurdo for the approximately 2300-kilometer flights.

Farrington Ridge in the Jones Mountains was later named for Lt. Robert Farrington, copilot on R4D-8 #853, which made this first landing in the Jones Mountains.

Everything went off successfully and Tom was back at Byrd in the R4D about 2130. Tom got his gravity readings at Camp Minnesota in the Jones Mountains. He got a look at the Hudson Mountains and thinks we will have no trouble landing there. The C-130s flew at 30,000 feet so he could see the whole area. The C-130s did the job as though they had been making open field landings all summer. The snow was very smooth, and after landing about six miles out from rock on the north side of the range, they taxied to within a half a mile.

These were some of the first (perhaps in fact, *the* first) "open field" landings the C-130s had made in Antarctica to support remote field parties. This procedure soon became routine, although several of the Hercules planes crashed or were stranded for various periods of time while carrying out open-field landings in Antarctica during the coming four decades. By the 1998 season the Navy was out of Antarctic operations and the New York Air National Guard was flying LC-130s in Antarctica. After dropping a Hercules partly into a crevasse in 1998, the Air Force became very conservative about open-field landings.

I washed dishes this noon with two men from Joe Walker's crew.

The pilots, being officers, did not share in kitchen duties. Although all civilians had officer status, I did not want to differentiate between me and the other two in my field party.

The roof leaked in on Dick's bunk. The panels in the roof have unsealed cracks through which the melted snow from overhead drips. To combat this, gutters of aluminum foil channel the water off into a basin or out into the tunnel.

*10 Dec. Sat.* The planes flew Ohio State University gear into the Central Horlicks all day. Bill Long and three other men from his party will go in tomorrow.

After these men were delivered, for the next eight days there were no completed flights because of weather problems.

*12 Dec. Mon.* I had a beer with my Navy roommate, the station electrician. I didn't particularly feel thirsty at that moment, but he offered me a can from his case so I acquired a thirst.

There was a real shortage of beer at Byrd that summer, which was low on the priority list of cargo. One of the Navy men had hidden a case of beer away. He wanted to take it with him when he flew out to McMurdo, which caused a lot of resentment. But because he had paid for it and carefully rationed himself during the winter, he felt it was his to use as he wished. After several messages between McMurdo and Byrd, he was allowed to fly out with his beer.

*13 Dec. Tues.* The wind blew about 40 knots all day and visibility was reduced to about 100 feet.

*15 Dec. Thurs.* The Byrd-Pole tractor train is 150 miles out and has been delayed 2 1/2 days by the weather. Bert Crary is on the Skelton Glacier, the route from the Ross Ice Shelf to the high East Antarctic Ice Sheet.

In contrast to the traverse and the field parties, we barely noticed these storms other than as a delay to flying. It may have been dripping on us under the snow at Byrd, but we certainly were protected from the weather.

*18 Dec. Sun.* Jack Tuck and two others, who recently arrived, will drive a Sno-Cat out 40 miles to mark a site for an auroral sub-station. He has been trying to get me to go along and help nurse *Hectori* those 80 miles, as he knows nothing much about Sno-Cats. However, I'm sure the flying for us would start as soon as I'd leave camp.

*19 Dec. Mon.* VX6 flew some cargo to Little Rockford, a weather station at mile #240 on the Army-Navy drive. I went along for a gravity tie. We got off at 1830 and arrived a couple of hours later.

Little Rockford (population six) was one of two Auxiliary Air Facilities. Little Rockford and Beardmore, at the foot of the Beardmore Glacier, had as their primary responsibly providing three-hour surface weather observations and upper air and wind soundings using balloons. Since the early 1990s unmanned automatic weather stations have been sending in surface measurements from all over Antarctica by satellite.

The men at Little Rockford posted a sign reading: "I'm dancing with tears in my eyes because the girl in my arms is a boy."

*20 Dec. Tues.* It was nearly whiteout. We ate about 0300, and I got two hours sleep. The horizon opened at 0600 and two hours later, we landed at Byrd under a clear sunny sky.

Jim Cornwell agreed to send #188 out for three seismic stations about 100 miles out. Joe Walker, the pilot, got a finger slashed pretty bad [working at the plane], requiring five stitches. We loaded our gear and took off around 1130 after banging the tail against some fuel drums as we jockeyed around.

In addition to our geophysical equipment, we carried a case of Nitromon primers (high explosive) and a case of ordinary Nitromon (ammonium nitrate). I carried the electric blasting caps separately (i.e., about ten feet away) in my small climbing pack secured to the bulkhead of the cabin by a carabiner. Of course, we carried JATO bottles in the cabin and used JATO to become airborne. In the 1990s the VXE6 Navy squadron (as it was then known) did not want to fly explosives into the field at all, and never knew about these routine operations in the 1960s.

We found a way down through a cloud layer and landed in very soft snow at 1253 [at Station A]. Tom set up the transit to determine the surface slope. The plane crew helped hand drill the 4-meter shot hole. While Dick laid out the spread, I got the gear ready.

The approximately 500 pounds of electronic cases and batteries had been secured to the deck and bulkhead during our flight. I untied these to the minimum extent possible and hooked up the cables. The photographic solutions were carried in one-gallon thermos containers. I emptied the solutions into the developing, washing, and fixing tanks mounted beneath the oscillograph "camera." I then connected the wire from the blaster, which supplied the shot instant, and we were ready to go.

We began shooting about 1245. After some delay due to instrument problems, we got a good reflection on the first try. After another shot to confirm this, we rolled up the spread.

At 1630 we tried to take off, but found the skis buried so deep that even two JATO couldn't budge us. A little digging and four more JATO got us going, but we didn't get airborne the snow was so soft. We got out and hung on the last eight bottles of JATO and this time got up using six. As we didn't have enough JATO for another landing and takeoff, we had to come home.

I had supper back at Byrd at 1900, which was my first meal since 0300 at Little Rockford. By this time I had passed the point of being sleepy and so watched Kirk Douglas in *The Indian Fighter*.

After the movie, I made a quick calculation of the ice thickness where we shot today.[5] I went to bed about 2230 having been up all but two hours since yesterday at 1300.

However, we waited until 10 January for our next seismic flight.

[On 10 Jan.] George Janulis and I decided to finish up the two remaining seismic stations near Byrd. We took off at 1221 and, wonder of wonders, used no JATO. About an hour later we landed at 79°05'S, 110°00'W and put in [Station B]. It clouded up and snowed a bit while we were on the ground. The snow surface was very soft.

Dick laid out the spread with Bob Farrington, the copilot, helping by watching the unwinding reel at the plane to see that it didn't backlash and tangle. It backlashed and tangled. I had been getting things going with the instruments, but had to spend 15 minutes straightening the reel out. I helped Tom drill the fourth meter of the shot hole. Our first shot was full of electronic noise. I found the trouble, a loose connection, and we tried again. This time we ran out of paper and the timing motor quit. I loaded paper and noticed smoke coming out of the tuning fork assembly. There was a short circuit due to a broken wire. I fixed this with a piece of tape and a match stick.

We got a good reflection, with a one-pound primer. We shot another reflection with five pounds and rolled up the spread.

In spite of the difficulties, we were ready to go in 2 1/2 hours after landing. Unfortunately we couldn't go because we were stuck in the soft snow. After much shoveling and roaring of engines, to no avail, we finally blasted off with 10 JATO.

Our next landing [Station C] was at 78°55'S, 113°45'W at 1713. The weather closed in immediately. This time everything went smoothly and we got the station completed in one hour ten minutes. We waited for the weather to clear, but after some time with everyone in the plane sitting and reading, George finally took off anyway. It was a total whiteout with snow falling. The surface was quite hard, but not wanting to mess around without forward visibility, George fired off the last JATO and we climbed rapidly. We flew almost to Byrd completely on instruments.

[The next day] I scaled the records of the seismic shots.[6]

These stations [called A, B, and C only here] are in a 1996 aerogeophysical survey area over the relatively high bedrock topography beneath the divide of the West Antarctic Ice Sheet.[7]

*23 Dec. Fri.* A single engine Otter (UC-1) crashed, near Minna Bluff about 60 nautical miles [111 kilometers] south of McMurdo. No one was injured as far as I know. Engine trouble necessitated landing in a crevassed area and the ski was damaged. They flew out in a helicopter and picked up the crew. The plane will be abandoned.

*24 Dec. Christmas Eve, Sat.* Overcast off and on all day. R4D-8 #853 launched to the Horlicks to pick up #219 [the repaired plane]. They lost radio contact with the base. The weather closed in here. The planes took off anyway and a patch of blue opened up at Byrd just in time for them to land.

Bottles of various sorts began appearing around supper time as people started relaxing and absorbing some Yuletide spirits. A small party got going in the Science Building after supper. Jack Tuck, who got back this afternoon from his Sno-Cat trip, Tom Laudon, Joe Walker, a few others, and I shot the breeze, and told tall tales about previous military or Antarctic experiences. We got to talking about the first winter (1957) at Ellsworth Station, when I was there and Tuck was at the Pole. They used to listen to our radio conversations and got a good picture of the trouble we were having with Finn Ronne.[8]

During the movie, everyone was pretty high and was attempting to make humorous remarks. It was a gay evening.

"Gay" had a different connotation in 1960, from 2003; so did "high."

*25 Dec. Christmas, Sun.* A plane came in from McMurdo today with a Catholic priest from ChiChi and a Protestant chaplain from McMurdo. They conducted services after the usual large and delicious Navy Christmas dinner.

This brief note on the chaplain's visit and the Quonset hut "Chapel-of-the-Snows" at McMurdo are the closest to a comment on religion in my journal of experiences in Antarctica during the 1960–62 period. In an online book[9] by Marty Sponholz of his experiences with the U.S. program in the 1960s in Antarctica he wrote: "I was stunned at the almost complete lack of interest in religion of any kind by so many of these scientists who were now my friends established through

34. Behrendt working in science building at Byrd.

frostbite, risk and survival." With the exception of the first few weeks at Ellsworth, when a lay preacher tried to interest the station in Sunday services (unsuccessfully), I do not recall in my 13 trips to Antarctica any mention ever of any religious thoughts, or participation of any of the scientists in any religious service. Obviously, the devout Sponholz noted this as an anomaly.

> *26 Dec. Mon.* Joe Walker took #188 out to Bill Long in the Central Horlicks. Dick Wold went along with the magnetometer and gravity meter. Dick talked to Bill Long and the Ohio State gang. They have only had 2 days out of 16 when the weather was good enough to work. Their little motor sleds [snowmobiles] are working excellently. They can pull 600–700 pounds and climb 3/4 of the way up the mountains.
>
> We ate canned hamburgers for supper. Our food supply is exhausted of good stuff.

Probably there was "good stuff" in the new supplies that had been air-dropped earlier by the C-124s or delivered by the C-130s. We (many) summer people would have eaten a lot of the winter food if given a chance at it.

> *27 Dec. Tues.* We now have 30-odd JATO left. Jim Cornwell figures our

program alone still needs about 180 bottles. A C-130 can carry about 100 JATO at 175 pounds each.

The JATO limitations held up all of the flying out of Byrd for the entire season.

*29 Dec. Thurs.* I got on the ham set and put in a call to the research center at the University of Wisconsin in Madison. I talked to Ed Thiel, Ned Ostenso, and George Woollard. Ed will move to Minnesota in a few days to start his new job as an assistant professor in the geology department. George wanted to know if I still planned on going across from Perth to Johannesburg with the gravity meter; I told him I did.

*30 Dec. Fri.* George Janulis took Art Ford and Pete Bermel with a load of the USGS cargo out to the eastern Horlicks [Thiel Mountains], found a site, and landed [on 26 Dec.]. Ford and Bermel returned with the plane.

This afternoon, Art Ford and two others flew out [with Janulis] to set up the USGS field camp. [Two days later] Joe Walker flew out with their last loads and three people. Ford and his party had been waiting at Byrd since 14 November.

Janulis left the USGS party 10–15 miles from the rock outcrops, and they had no motor toboggans. Janulis Spur was later named for Lt. George Janulis, USN, and Walker Spur was named for Capt. Joseph Walker, USMC, both in the Thiel Mountains as proposed by Ford and Bermel.

It's now 2330 and I'm sitting in the library in the Science building listening to *Rigoletto*, and reading *Hawaii* by Michener. One of the [scientists] is sitting at the table doing some last minute sewing on his clothes before leaving for the field. It is a beautiful, clear, sunny night out with the temperature about −5°F.

*31 Dec. Sat.* Clear and cold today. Joe Walker took off for Bill Long's party in the Horlicks this morning using only four JATO, but barely staggering up. The plane was loaded so heavily and far aft that they needed maximum power most of the flight. The starboard prop was running in surges, which added to the difficulties. When they got out to the mountains there were clouds in the area where they wanted to land. After searching for a hole and waiting 45 minutes they came home.

35. Sir Charles Wright at Byrd.

A P2V came in about 1900 with Sir Charles Wright, one of the men from Scott's last expedition. He and [an assistant], Don Evans, are with Pacific Naval Laboratories, Victoria, B.C. They are working with ELF (Extra Low Frequency radio noise studies) and will set up in a Jamesway here to make simultaneous observations with a station at the conjugate northern geomagnetic latitude at Fort Churchill, Canada.

Six of us drove over to New Byrd in a Sno-Cat about 2000. We had some coffee and headed back, arriving about 2330.

A New Year's Eve party had been going on for some time on 190 proof alcohol flavored with peppermint. Many were high and four passed out cold, including Joe Walker and the cook.

At least it was ethanol. A year earlier a man had died at Marble Point near

McMurdo from drinking (mislabeled) methanol. During the winter of 2000, a scientist at the South Pole died of unknown causes. The rumor around the program in 2001 was that he had methanol poisoning, because he had been making alcohol in a homemade still. ◆

# SIX

# End of the Summer at Byrd

Our morale was a bit low about this time because of the long delay due to continuous bad flying weather, which I do not mention in most cases.

*1 Jan. 1961, New Year's Day, Sun.* Steak for New Year's dinner. Many people are hung over.

A group of us got talking with Sir Charles [who was 74 in 1961] about the second Scott Expedition. He was on the support party that man-hauled supplies with Scott to the top of the Beardmore Glacier on the final run to the South Pole. His sense of humor is quite keen. He told of a splendid argument they had up there (about 8,000–10,000 feet) as to whether they could make strong tea by boiling it. As no one knew anything about it, it made a fine argument, which couldn't even be resolved by experiment (apparently they had no tea at the time).

The following summer Wright was on the sledge party that found the bodies of Scott and his companions in the tent where they had died on the return from the Pole.

He told me that he was shocked a few days earlier at McMurdo, when he was asked whether they contemplated bringing the bodies back rather than burying them in the tent where they were found. They had never considered it, and in 1960, he thought the question morbid and in bad taste.

*4 Jan. Wed.* A message came in from Havola telling us that the tractor train is in crevasses[1] and requesting an air recon. This was quite a surprise, as they are up on the plateau over 8000 feet in elevation and we expected crevasses lower down.

36. Hanging JATO bottles beneath R4D-8.

The Byrd-Pole tractor train was in an unnamed ice stream that our group defined only at the end of the season from our flights and Dowling's altimeter measurements on the tractor train.

*5 Jan. Thurs.* When Havola requested a recon, the powers that be at McMurdo loaded up a C-130 with 128 JATO, which arrived at Byrd about 0500.

A message from McMurdo this morning ordered the flight to Havola [the tractor train] and requested that the "U. of Wisconsin group" take the magnetometer along. I guess George Toney is still in there plugging for us. I only got an hour sleep, before Dick and I got up to go out to the tractor train with the magnetometer. Janulis took off in #853 about 1000.

The weather was clear the whole flight except in the vicinity of the Horlick Mountains, where we flew in a fog. Fortunately the mountains were visible on radar, so we managed to stay well clear of them. Eventually, we came out into the clear and saw some of the peaks in the distance. As we continued south the elevation dropped off again before rising to the plateau elevation of 8000–9000 feet.

About 1355 we picked up the trail of the tractor train. About five minutes later we crossed crevasses perpendicular to the trail. At 1430 we passed over the tractor train. They had crossed about six crevasses unbeknownst to

37. Crevasses about 140 nautical miles (260 kilometers) from South Pole.

them and many more lay in front. We flew back and forth for a while and I took several pictures including a couple of Polaroid shots. We dropped a bag of mail, in which I enclosed the Polaroid pictures.

It looked like they could get out by turning right and running parallel to the crevasses for five or ten miles. These crevasses are large, about 100 feet wide, and miles long. Dick saw crevasses trending east for quite a way. It is interesting to speculate as to the causes so high on the plateau.

These are the widest crevasses on a grounded ice sheet I have ever seen or heard of. If they were 100 feet wide they must be several hundred feet deep, because the walls appeared vertical. Our estimate of width was probably fairly accurate because we had the D-8 tractors and sleds for scale.

After flying on south for a few more minutes and seeing no more crevasses, we turned back about 60 miles short of the Pole. I tried to talk George Janulis into going to 90°S, but the carburetor was malfunctioning and he wanted to head for home. We ran into clouds again, which caused icing on the wings. Consequently, we flew most of the way back at 12,000 feet.

Since our incident in the Crary Mountains (chapter 1), the sound of full takeoff power when we were just flying was unnerving to Dick and me; Janulis had to use it to get above the clouds. We landed at Byrd about 1830.

The flight that day was the first into this unexplored area of the Antarctic ice sheet. No plane had ever flown from Byrd to the South Pole. I assume that has been accomplished several times since, but probably never recorded. The pilots who flew the R4Ds and C-130s in 1960–62 generally did not appreciate that they were operating in unexplored areas. This was not the case during the IGY period (1956–1958) when Admiral George Dufek, Capt. Finn Ronne, Capt. Edwin McDonald, and our oversnow traverse parties were well aware that they were making new geographic discoveries each season. We were also exploring new territory during the period described in this book just a few years later, but only the scientists on the oversnow and airborne geophysical parties realized it.

Unlike the Lewis and Clark or Fremont expeditions into the American West in the early 1800s that "discovered" what native Americans had explored crossing the Bering land bridge from Siberia at least 12,000 years previously, no humans had ever been to the areas of Antarctica we visited in the late 1950s and early 1960s.

There will be no flying tomorrow because #188 is down [i.e., not in operating condition] for a check, and now #853 needs a new carburetor. The P2V is down too, with a hydraulic leak.

6 Jan. Fri. Havola followed our suggested route out of the crevasses and is now on the way to the Pole, in the clear along 82°W.

Doc Walk came to tell me of a message he had received from McMurdo. There has been some concern about the Atlas Petrogel, a 60 percent nitroglycerine gelatin dynamite [used for seismic work], which is stored out in the magazine with the other high explosives. The dynamite wasn't intended for use below −50°F. There is some question as to whether the stuff has decomposed, with the nitroglycerine becoming concentrated in pockets. This would make it likely to detonate by a slight jar. I personally don't think it has reached this stage [On what basis, I wonder now?]. None of the Seabees has been to demolition school and consequently none is qualified, or paid, to handle explosives.

If there were a large explosion at the magazine, which was just a pile of boxes not far from camp, the very unstable Byrd Station, being slowly crushed by the weight of snow, might collapse.

The Navy wants to know what and how much explosives we have here. George Toney suggested that I take an inventory since I am the only qualified person (supposedly) here. Tom, Dick, and I went out and counted and dug up around the cases. We found 18,200 pounds of explosives.[2] [On 15 January] Tom, Dick, and I went out to the magazine and unloaded a ton of Pelletol from a sled.

*7 Jan. Sat.* Clear, sunny and windy today. A C-130 came up to new Byrd tonight and brought a new carburetor for #853. The generator on #188 was ready to fall off and spare parts are needed for that.

I moved some Nitromon over to the magazine from where we had left it near the runway after the last seismic flight. [No one is that casual about explosives these days.]

*9 Jan. Mon.* George flew #853 about 140 miles south with the Stanford group. We saw *The Trouble With Harry* tonight, an excellent Hitchcock film with Shirley MacLaine.

*10 Jan. Tues.* Joe and crew flew #219 (the repaired plane) back to McMurdo this evening. They plan to carry it back to the States by ship and rebuild it. There are no more R4D-8s in existence, so the Navy has to keep these three operating. [The next day] Joe and his men flew back to Byrd in a C-130.

*11 Jan. Wed.* The tractor train arrived at the South Pole this morning about 1100.

*13 Jan. Fri.* Charlie Bentley sent a message in on 9 January, saying he needed resupply immediately. I got Jim and Joe to agree to take me and the magnetometer on the last (of four) resupply trip to Charlie. Dick and I loaded the magnetometer into #188 after supper. We planned to take off about 2000 but the weather had moved in and we were in a near whiteout. George was instructed not to come back yet from the traverse in #853. There was a light snow falling.

*14 Jan. Sat.* The sky had scattered clouds when we took off in #188 about 1030. I sensed something was wrong as we were on the takeoff run. We got airborne with only four JATO, but were just a few feet off the deck for a long time. We slowly climbed to about 200 feet, but every time Joe tried to pull up, we shuddered and nearly stalled. For some reason we were too heavy. The controls weren't just right. With difficulty we banked and returned to Byrd.

A crew member came running back to check that I was still strapped in. I certainly was! We came in to land, but missed the approach. Joe had to bank radically at a very low altitude. When we finally did come in on the right track, the plane stalled and fell the last couple of feet. We had been flying at only 95 knots. Aside from a slightly rough bump there were no ill effects.

When we had taxied up to the fueling site and stopped, it was evident what the trouble was. The light snow we had last night had melted due to radiation and refrozen on the top of the fuselage and wings. This was visible before we took off, but most blew right off and it was assumed that all had. There was also ice in the control surface joints.

This was one of the most dangerous incidents of this dangerous field season, as we had a full load of avgas on the plane and were overloaded. In a similar incident in early 1966, a USGS party on the Ross Ice Shelf was waiting for a field pickup and the arriving R4D-8 stalled out on landing in poor visibility. The plane crashed spectacularly into the snow. The men on the surface raced out in their snowmobiles and made a quick check into the wreck as a fire started. They told me that everyone appeared dead, and the flames drove them off. As they watched helplessly in horror, the fire raged for more than an hour and melted a hole deep into the snow.

The crashed airplane at Byrd, which also had stalled out on landing (see chapter 4), mostly drifted over with snow at the edge of the runway, was sobering to see each time we took off or landed.

Meanwhile George Janulis was coming back through a total overcast above which he could not fly even at 13,000 feet. He reported heavy icing.

Fortunately he was able to break most of the ice loose from the leading edges of the wings, rudder, and stabilizer by pumping air into the rubber boots that cover these surfaces, changing pitch on the props, and squirting alcohol out on the prop blades.

George made it in and landed without incident.

*15 Jan. Sun.* Today, a message came in from the U. Minnesota party in the Jones Mountains stating that the weather is clear, no sastrugi, and one of their party has four broken teeth and should see a dentist.

The injured man was Robert Rutford, graduate student, who broke several teeth out when digging out a tent collapsed by drifting snow. The metal rod of the external frame sprang up and hit him in the mouth.

Bob Rutford, whom I had first met a few weeks earlier at Byrd, went on to a prominent career in geology and geopolitics. He later served a stint as Director of Polar Programs at the National Science Foundation, and still later was President of the University of Texas at Dallas. In 2002, he was a geology professor and president of the Scientific Committee on Antarctic Research (SCAR). He and I spent time in Antarctica together en route to our various field projects over the years and served together on many U.S. delegations to Antarctic Treaty Consultative Meetings from the 1970s to the mid 1990s. As he worked in the McMurdo area during the 1959–60 season, Rutford and I are possibly the only men to have worked in Antarctica as part of the U.S. Antarctic Program in six successive decades.

*17 Jan. Tues.* I had a long talk this morning with Jim Cornwell about the flying situation. He finally agreed to use just one R4D to evacuate Craddock and party and keep the other one for us.

Jim told me they were flying the Stanford from south of Byrd VLF group out to Mt. Murphy. He said Tom and I could go along and recon the area for our geology landing there when they came in to refuel.

We took off about 1550 and flew out past Mt. Takahe to Mt. Murphy in about two hours and ten minutes. It was a beautiful clear day and we could see the Crary and Toney Mountains quite plainly. We flew about 1500 feet above the deck because we were very heavily loaded. When we reached the three-peaked snow-covered massif of Mt. Murphy, we again examined the black rock outcrops [as described on 29 November].

We wanted to land near Mt. Murphy but Janulis did not like the surface. We finally landed, about 12 miles away from the rock about due south and in line with Takahe. The elevation was only 2500 feet and the terrain slopes down to the east in the direction of our planned seismic profile.

They had late chow for us at Byrd about 2230, which tasted pretty good, even if it was only beans and wieners.

38. R4D-#853 at VLF camp. Mt. Murphy in background.

Craddock sent in a message: Request evacuation. Party confined to camp since 7 Jan awaiting plane. Please advise asap date of evacuation.

Later, Jim Cornwell told me we would go out with #853 tomorrow to try for four seismic stations. I heard him telling Bob Farrington in the ionolab next door, which he also uses as an office, that he only had JATO for either me or Craddock, but not both. He wants to fly our group and keep Craddock out a while, so he can get weather reports from him.

I am sure Bob Rutford, who had the broken teeth, and was out in the field with Craddock, would not have appreciated this conversation.

(We were delayed a day by weather.) It finally cleared and it was decided that George would take us out for seismic landings. The wind kept blowing the heat away from the aircraft engines faster than the Herman-Nelson heaters could supply it, but the engines finally started. We tried to taxi out to the south end of the runway for takeoff, but the wind was so strong they couldn't turn the plane. We kept getting farther north on the runway. Finally we took off across the open snow without using the runway, which forced us to use eight JATO. We flew about five hours, but had to abort the flight because of weather.

*18 Jan. Wed.* A C-130 came in with 11 JATO plus Forrest Dowling and Hank Rosenthal [Brecher].[3] I talked to Hank and Forrest about their trip

39. Sentinel Range. Highest peaks over 16,000 feet (Vinson Massif 5140 meters, photograph by R. Rutford).

on the Byrd-Pole tractor train. Forrest got a gravity station every mile, a magnetic reading every two miles, and altimeter every half mile. He fell into a crevasse up to his waist, which shook him a little. They only had two climbing ropes for the 11-man group. I don't believe anyone in the party had any mountaineering experience.

The Byrd-Pole party passed through sastrugi up to ten feet high in at least three places. Their temperatures ran in the −20°F range. The party located many peaks in the Eastern Horlick [Thiel] Mountains.

Names of some of the party are now attached to these peaks in the Thiel Mountains.

The tractor train party was surprised to find that they had already crossed six of the big crevasses, amongst which we found them on the flight of 5 January.

*21 Jan. Sat.* At 1900 the Minnesota party reported clear skies, and George Janulis took off about 2100 to pick them up. Although the plane had generator trouble on the way in, a few hours later, the Minnesota party arrived uneventfully back at Byrd. Cam Craddock (and the injured Bob

Rutford) took the first C-130 flight in to McMurdo to plead [to no avail]
for the Sentinel Mountains work.

By choosing to go out to his lower priority Jones Mountains objective on 9
December rather than the Sentinel Range, Craddock and his party had removed
themselves from Byrd, the place where flight decisions were being made.

However, this University of Minnesota party found the first evidence, in the
Jones Mountains, that glaciers had been active in Antarctica for at least 12
million years. Up to this time geologists had interpreted sparse evidence in the
McMurdo area to indicate that Antarctic glaciation was contemporaneous with
that in the Northern Hemisphere, or 1–2 million years old at most. Craddock
and his students had found glacial striae (scratches) on a smooth rock surface
partially overlain by volcanic rocks that were dated by radioactive decay at 12
million years. This very significant finding altered the way geologists and
glaciologists considered the history of the Antarctic Ice Sheet.

This accomplishment illustrates the serendipity that frequently happens in
Antarctica, when trained field scientists are put in an essentially unknown area.
Several years ago, a volcanologist-petrologist friend, David Elliot, of Ohio State
University, found a significant dinosaur fossil on an outcrop he had gone to
study for other purposes. During the 1961–62 season, on an oversnow geophysical-glaciological traverse, I, a geophysicist, found significant fossils in an unexplored area as described below.

*22 Jan. Sun.* Our crew got our seismic gear, explosives, etc. loaded into
#188 and took our climbing equipment and rock hammers also. We took
19 JATO, which left 11 for SAR. The plane finally took off at 0052, with no
JATO, and headed in the direction of the Hudson Mountains.

We were headed for the primary objective of the airborne seismic program
this season. We planned to determine the bedrock configuration beneath the ice
south of the Amundsen Sea coast in the catchment area of the Thwaites and Pine
Island Glaciers. This part of the West Antarctic Ice Sheet is now known to be
changing the most rapidly of any area in Antarctica.

About two hours later we finally broke out of the clouds and could see
the blue water of Pine Island Bay ahead in the distance. We continued
north and could see the low snow-covered knolls of the Hudson
Mountains. The snow surface below was exceedingly rough and Joe

didn't want to land, so we gradually worked west, looking for a better spot. He finally landed right in the middle of our profile [at 75°53'S, 104°12'W] between the Hudson Mountains and Mt. Murphy.

It was clear and sunny but with a strong wind from the north-northeast. Dick laid out the spread, while I got things ready at the plane. Joe Walker and Tom Laudon drilled the four-meter hole and then Tom surveyed the slope with the theodolite. We got a reflection on the first shot and then tried a second at five pounds to look for a multiple reflection.[4] It took one hour and 15 minutes to complete the station, including picking up the spread.

Joe and I decided to fly back east and a bit south of our previous track for the next two stations. We took off without JATO. The new skis make a big difference.[5]

The wind was quite strong, so at our next landing, which we thought was 50 miles farther on, we found we had only come 25 miles. This station was at 75°44'S, 102°15'W. The position shot by Fred Streitenberger, the navigator, on the snow surface was quite accurate, compared to the air navigation. Fred took sunshots while on the deck; his positions are estimated to be better than 2 kilometers.

The wind was much stronger here, about 30 knots. This time we were done in 50 minutes with a reflection on the first shot. We again used no JATO on taking off over the hard, low sastrugi surface.

Our third landing [75°46'S, 99°35'W] was about 25 miles farther east. This was the windiest of all, probably 40 knots. I could barely see the plane from the end of the spread 1200 feet away. The cable bowed way out as I dragged it along and I could only try to get it in a straight line. This station also took 50 minutes and required only one shot for a reflection.

These last two stations were just south of the Pine Island Glacier.

The ice is fairly thin here. In spite of the wind, the records aren't too bad. We filtered everything out above 215 hertz to remove wind-generated noise. It was 0820 when we finished here. Again no JATO for takeoff.

The plane headed west now, and overflew the first two stations. When we reached the next station [75°44'W, 105°40'W], we could see Mt. Murphy in the distance before we landed. The wind was much less here and Tom managed to do some surveying. This station took one hour 15 minutes.

We took off without JATO, and landed at the fifth and last station [75°52'S, 108°50'W] at 1055. We could see Mt. Murphy and Mt. Takahe. I laid out the spread for my fourth time today. Joe drilled the hole by himself and dropped the auger down it when a pin pulled out. Fortunately, Dick could just reach the end and managed to slip the pin back in and retrieve it. I got the line all tangled up and had to spend some time straightening this out.

The pace was beginning to tell, as all of us had been up about 24 hours. I had eaten only a sandwich before the first station. [And we were shooting explosives and flying an airplane!] We finally got our reflection on the first shot and rolled up the spread. The wind was hardly blowing here.

These last two stations are upstream from the Thwaites Glacier, named for Fredrik T. Thwaites,[6] University of Wisconsin.

When we took off, again with no JATO, the escape hatch by the plane captain's seat popped open and blew off, so we had an open window all the way back to Byrd. A seal on the fuel pump for the starboard engine broke and started leaking gas and lost fuel pressure. Fortunately the R4D-8 has a cross-feed fuel system. This means that we could pump fuel to the starboard engine with the port fuel pump. We flew uneventfully[!] back to Byrd through clouds most of the way, landing at 1445.

I went to bed about 1600 after a snack of cold chicken.

I had been up about 32 hours.

I got up in time for the movie at 1930 and stayed up until 0100. That nap apparently cut the edge off my fatigue. I could feel my leg muscles stiffening up when I woke up. I guess I haven't been getting enough exercise lately.

*23 Jan. Mon. and 24 Jan. Tues.* I worked up the elevations of our seismic stations and calculated the seismic results in a preliminary fashion.[7] The seismic reflections show a trough about 700–1000 meters (2600–3300 feet) below sea level extending between Mt. Murphy and Hudson Mountains upstream of Thwaites and Pine Island Glaciers. There is about 3400 meters (11,000 feet) relief from the top of Mt. Murphy to the bottom of the trough nearest these mountains. The depths will still all be below sea level after allowing for isostatic rebound if the ice were removed.

These results were published in a paper in 1962[8] and shown on an American Geographical Society map of 1963. They are significant because a number of papers in the late 1990s suggested that the West Antarctic Ice Sheet might collapse (or be collapsing), in the vicinity of Pine Island Bay and the Thwaites Glacier, into the Amundsen Sea directly north of this profile. Our 1961 data were "lost" to the late 1990s scientific community because they were not used in a compilation of bedrock elevation of Antarctica published in 1983.

No other seismic or radar ice sounding data were collected over this area of the West Antarctic Ice Sheet bordering the Amundsen Sea from our work in January 1961 until 2000. At a meeting about the West Antarctic Ice Sheet in 1998, I pointed out the existence of this seismic profile, so the results are now "found." I made the suggestion that remeasuring the seismic thickness at the same locations might provide evidence of significant thinning along this profile, if it had occurred during the subsequent four decades after the data had been collected.

In 2002 Andrew Shepherd and others from the British Antarctic Survey published a paper[9] showing that the ice in the area inland from the Amundsen Sea upstream from the Thwaites and Pine Island Glaciers is thinning at the turn of the century by as much as 2.6–4.8 meters per year and that the thinning has extended as far as 150 kilometers inland. Conservatively this means that there would be about 100 meters of thinning along our 1961 profile if this high rate can be extrapolated back 40 years. If this much thinning were not measured by repeat seismic soundings (at the locations of our 1961 stations), it would mean that the high rate of thinning reported over the decade from 1991–2001 indicates a significant acceleration in the rate since 1961.

Prior to the 1960–61 season Bentley and others had published a paper suggesting that the deep bedrock beneath the West Antarctic ice sheet extended from the Ross Sea to the Bellingshausen Sea. The results of Bentley's Bellingshausen Traverse, in 1960–61, showed a high bedrock ridge blocking the proposed channel to the Bellingshausen Sea. Our seismic profile collected on 22 January apparently showed that the channel continued through to the Amundsen Sea instead.

In 1961 we assumed that the high topography of Sentinel Range of the Ellsworth Mountains continued as a ridge beneath the ice to the Antarctic Peninsula. During the next season I would lead a traverse into the unknown area northeast of the Sentinel Mountains to determine whether this interpretation was correct.

Because the University of Minnesota party led by Campbell Craddock had not been able to do any geological field work in the Sentinel Range that season there was no knowledge of its geology. It was generally assumed by geologists at this time that the Sentinel range was geologically and topographically continuous with the Antarctic Peninsula. However, no one had made any geologic observations in the southern Antarctic Peninsula in 1960.

*25 Jan. Wed.* Joe Walker flew out to Bill Long tonight in the Horlick Mountains to pick up a load of rocks. When Walker got back to Byrd a ground fog had moved in and his radio altimeter was defective. He could not see the base although he flew right over it and the people outdoors could see him. He flew around for about an hour before he found a hole in the clouds about 40 miles northwest, whereupon he landed and spent the night.

As always, the planes carried tents, food stoves, and other survival supplies, so camping out was no problem.

*26 Jan. Thurs.* Jim Cornwell planned a high-altitude flight to photograph the Sentinel Mountains tonight and offered to take a man and the magnetometer. I asked Dick to go.

We hauled the magnetometer down to the P2V and loaded the sensing head into the fiberglass nonmagnetic tail [designed to house a magnetometer for submarine detection, the primary mission of the P2V.][10]

*27 Jan. Fri.* It was clear and about −8°F when Tom and I watched the P2V off shortly after midnight. Jim Cornwell got off without firing any JATO.

Normally, the P2V fired 16 JATO spaced approximately equally on each side, and beneath the fuselage, which made a quite spectacular takeoff to watch and photograph.

Upon taking off something failed in the hydraulic system of the bow ski, and the plane could not retract it all the way. There were a few tense moments immediately after takeoff, when there was a certain amount of danger of crashing, as they did not have a safe air speed and the ski was creating drag and slowing them.

When we all got out to watch them land, we could see the plane circling as they burned up 6000 pounds of scarce avgas to lighten the load within their allowable landing weight. We could see that the skis were all down, but the bow ski was cocked upward. There was a certain amount of concern, as it was unknown whether this ski would lock into position, or would collapse on landing.

About 0115 they made their final approach. Everyone in the plane had his crash helmet on except one crewman, who was ordered to give his to Dick Wold. The doc and the corpsman were ready with the combination ambulance–fire truck Sno-Cat, which is always present at every takeoff and landing. Just before coming down, the pilot [Cornwell] radioed to the doc, "For your information, there are nine people aboard." When they touched down the nose ski righted itself and held.

When they stopped about 100 yards from the fuel site, hydraulic fluid was running out and around the port ski (not the damaged one).

VX6 made temporary repairs to the P2V and flew it to McMurdo a few days later.

*28 Jan. Sat.* Many of the USARPs and Navy men have been swapping clothes on the basis that the grass is always greener, etc. Now there are many Navy men wearing colorful orange parkas and red shirts, and civilians with olive drab military clothes. I left my USARP parka in the States and have been wearing an old mountaineering parka and Navy sweater I've had for years.

The USARP-issue parkas in 1960 (Deep Freeze '61) and the following were the worst I ever encountered in 13 trips. Those who wore them regularly found they tore to shreds. On the other hand the black wind pants patterned on Army field trousers (cargo pants) were excellent and durable. The same white rubber thermal boots used in the IGY (1956–1958) were then and still are excellent, if one doesn't mind clammy feet. We were allowed to keep all this clothing, but the much higher-quality civilian clothing issued since the 1980s is now carefully checked in at Christchurch after return from Antarctica.

*29 Jan. Sun.* The very warm weather is causing a great increase in the number of drips around the buildings. As I write, I'm sitting in the USARP library listening to the splashing of water into two pails in front of me and several others in the next room.

*30 Jan. Mon.* The temperature reached another new high of +30.5°F. [The next day] we got a message from the Pole mentioning that they have a limited supply of salt tablets if we need them.

Forty years ago people took salt tablets in the U.S. for health reasons when working in very hot weather.

Water is dripping through the Science Building in streams and the tunnels stink something awful as this warm weather doesn't cut the smell from the head.

The heads (toilet and washing facilities) at Byrd, South Pole, Little America, and Ellsworth Stations were all the same, built for the IGY. As I wrote in my IGY journal:

We have the most elaborate pit privy I have ever seen. Jet heaters keep the building—which also contains the laundry—quite warm, and one doesn't quite expect the blast of cold air that comes up from below.

Obviously at the end of the fifth summer at Byrd (buried beneath 15 feet of snow) it was not a "blast of cold air" that was coming up from below.

Joe Walker decided to try a geology flight. We took off about 1830. The runway was very sticky and it took about six JATO. One of these burned a hole in the starboard elevator of the plane about five inches across, which wasn't noticed until we landed.

Several years later a JATO rocket broke loose and "shot down" a C-130. Another burned a hole in the stabilizer of a C-130. Eventually, use of JATO in Antarctica was discontinued for safety reasons. However, in 2003 the USAF (New York Air National Guard) was again using JATO on LC-130s.

A high overcast, about 12,000 feet, covered the area north of Mt. Takahe, and as we approached Mt. Murphy we had no surface definition, although we could see the mountains and crevasses all right. Visibility was now too poor to chance a landing, however, and we headed for the Hudson Mountains.

We flew across our seismic profile at 1500 feet and when we could see the Hudson Mountains at about 2240, we knew we probably wouldn't be able to land here as the overcast continued. I was in the right-hand seat of the cockpit and got a good look at the terrain. The surface dropped down to sea level and we flew over very crevassed ice shelf for 20 minutes [Pine Island Glacier area] before rising slightly as we flew over the south-western-most nunatak. We flew a circuit over four nunataks of the Hudson Mountains, the highest of which was 2100 feet.

Our magnetometer showed that these outcrops of black rock were quite magnetic, which indicated to me that they were probably volcanic.

[On 10 February], Tom Laudon, accompanied by two USGS men, Art Ford, and John Aaron, finally made a trip to the Hudson Mountains, without me. I was not a geologist, but was the leader of the airborne party, so of course I wanted to go. However, I had to return to McMurdo earlier.

The geologists spent nine hours on the ground in the Hudson Mountains, and climbed one of the higher nunataks. Coming down after the sun had set behind the mountain, they leaped a *bergschrund* [a large crevasse located at the head of a mountain glacier separating the ice from the rock] before discovering that visibility was too poor to proceed safely down the steep snow slope. They had to proceed a long way around to get back to the plane. John Aaron took a slip, but Tom Laudon stopped him without difficulty, with a rope. Laudon in turn broke into a crevasse, but only went in with one leg to the waist. All in all they had a great time. Pete Bermel, USGS topographic engineer, stayed at the plane and surveyed.

All the boys found in the Hudson Mountains was volcanic rock, as we had expected.

I sound disgusted about the volcanic rock. However, I later became very interested in this late Cenozoic volcanism (less than about 30 million years old). Based on the field geologic evidence of volcanic rocks (which contain high amounts of the magnetic mineral magnetite) in the Hudson Mountains and other exposed volcanic peaks such as the Crary Mountains and Mt. Takahae that we had crossed with magnetic profiles, we were able to account for their very high-amplitude magnetic anomalies.

The sparse rock exposures in these peaks are indicative of a vast volcanic province associated with the West Antarctic rift system underlying the West Antarctic Ice Sheet as shown by our aeromagnetic surveys. We used the interpretation of unexposed but very magnetic rock at the base of the ice sheet from high-amplitude magnetic anomalies as evidence for volcanic rocks in the adjacent ice-covered areas, as well. The volcanism and the ice sheet have both been active during the same period of time, and their activity is probably related.

[Back to our flight of 30 January.] We headed across ice shelf south of the Hudson Mountains, which is of greater extent than we had previously thought.

However, there is no ice shelf shown on the USGS map[11] made from 1980 AVHRR satellite images in this area. Perhaps the ice shelf we observed in 1961 has disintegrated, as other small ice shelves in West Antarctica have. We were crossing the Pine Island Bay area. In 2001, glaciologists using satellite data[12] reported greater than 40 meters per year bottom melting, the greatest rate in Antarctica, at the grounding line where Pine Island Glacier meets the Amundsen Sea.

About 2320 we set a course towards Mt. Takahe, as I had persuaded Joe to fly over it.

*31 Jan. Tues.* About 0045 the plane commenced climbing to gain enough altitude to safely cross the massive volcanic peak, 11,145 feet (3398 meters) high. We reached an altitude of 12,000 feet but could go no higher without emergency power. Consequently we flew over to the north of the high circular crater [recording a very high amplitude magnetic anomaly], clearing the 10,000-foot-high snow slope by 2000 feet. We returned to Byrd, about 0255.

On the flight we had fried chicken several times. It was excellent, and the best food we've eaten in flight. Usually there is bread and maybe some baloney. Tom always brings a pack full of goodies so we don't starve.

There was a small galley on the port side just aft of the cockpit, with a hot plate, coffee pot, etc.

*1 Feb. Wed.* It cleared tonight and both R4Ds took off for the two field camps in the Horlick [and Thiel] Mountains.

*2 Feb. Thurs.* It was too poor visibility for the R4Ds to come in to Byrd tonight. As a matter of fact, Joe Walker had to land at New Byrd and taxi in to old Byrd [about six miles] when he brought Bill Long's crew in.

The OSU party took the long way home and made a recon flight along the western Horlicks range. The peaks there are about 13,000 feet high [this had not been previously known] and the ice on the south side is too high to fly over at 12,000 feet.

Bill Long's OSU party looked healthy and happy, when I saw them this noon. They found an 800-foot-thick bed of tillite [a metamorphosed glacial deposit], in a Permian formation. This indicates that there were glaciers here about 200 million years ago, which ties in well with evidence from India, Africa, Australia, and South America of similar, simultaneous glaciation, and lends support to the theory that these continents were, with Antarctica, once a supercontinent called Gondwanaland. They also found much petrified wood, and whole logs were abundant.

Although we who worked in Antarctic geology at this time were quite prepared to accept the idea of Gondwanaland, the U.S. earth science community was not. However, as far back as 1916 when Griffith Taylor wrote about it,[13] Antarctic geology in the Royal Society Range was being interpreted in the context of Gondwanaland in the McMurdo area.

Art Ford's USGS party found themselves in igneous rocks entirely. Both the USGS and OSU parties lived in Jamesway huts, which were left up in anticipation of next year's return.

The USGS party had a difficult season. None of the members had been to Antarctica before, in contrast to Bill Long and Cam Craddock, who had one or more seasons each under experienced Antarctic field geophysicists before they led their own geologic parties. The USGS men had to man-haul their akios 10–15 miles to rock outcrops from the Jamesway base camp where the R4D had left them. This distance from their scientific objective greatly limited their work.

In the coming few years, use of snowmobiles and helicopters improved the efficiency of geologists tremendously.

The small radio with which the USGS party was supplied in 1960 never worked, so, as Ford told me in 2001, "we had no radio contact for a whole month and we were never checked on." The fact that there was no longer a USARP representative at Byrd meant that there was no one responsible for the remote parties or to check on radio contacts. But as Art said, "we stayed alive and even collected a few rocks." The following season he returned to the same area and serendipitously discovered the first large meteorite recovered from Antarctica.

In 1999 Ford described their 1961 takeoff "with so many rock samples we were still bouncing from sastrugi to sastrugi after the second batch of JATO rockets were fired. Finally got off after about 10 miles. The pilot, [Janulis,] had said 'sure, put it on (for every rock box we were questioning). We can do it!' What a great spirit in those days!"

*3 Feb. Fri.* Byrd Station put up a new 50-star flag today, replacing the old one with 48 stars. [Alaska and Hawaii had just been admitted as states.]

Dick Wold left for McMurdo with all the seismic gear and the magnetometer. Leonid Kuperov, a Russian ionosphere physicist, arrived at Byrd on the same flight.

Kuperov speaks hardly any English, but seems a friendly fellow.

During the following winter, Kuperov became very ill and was evacuated by a heroic C-130 flight from the U.S., through Christchurch and McMurdo. This was the first fly-in to Antarctica and into an inland station during winter in the dark at very low temperatures. This historic flight has been largely forgotten.

My brother Dave is getting married tomorrow, and I tried from 2100 until 0400 before I got a phone patch.

*4 Feb. Sat.* The movie tonight was filmed in Christchurch. *Until They Sail* is the title of the story, from Michener's book *Return to Paradise*. It's all about the loves and proclivities of American military men in WWII with New Zealand girls. The situation is quite similar to that existing today and some of the lives hit pretty close for some of the fellows here. I wonder how the people in Christchurch liked it?

ChiChi was the Navy slang for Christchurch, usually abbreviated ChCh on the flight manifests. A common expression in Antarctica at this time was: "It's nice on the Ice, but it's peachy in ChiChi."

*7 Feb. Tues.* I decided to return to McMurdo on the next C-130. Tom and I loaded [geophysical] gear plus the data and my bags into Sno-Cat *Hectori*. A new emergency brake set the wood floor on fire underneath when Tom drove me out to the C-130. I hopped out and put the fire out with an extinguisher, which was fortunately on the dashboard. The plane was on the ground unloading. Tom backed up the load ramp, while I held the antenna down to keep it from getting snarled in the tail of the plane. I don't know if the brake caught fire again or not as we immediately took off.

I am certain the air crew would not have been happy to know there was a Sno-Cat burning near the plane. Because the C-130s did not shut down engines when unloading at Byrd, the noise was deafening when up close, so we could not warn the air crew.

I hate leaving without getting to Mt. Murphy and the Kohler Range. I wanted that more than anything else. Oh well. I've got to get the gravity meter to the South Pole.

No one got to Mt. Murphy until January 1968.  ◆

# SEVEN

# South Pole

On 5 February George Toney had come out from McMurdo to inspect Byrd Station deterioration. He thought I had better get back to McMurdo soon if I wanted to get any Pole flights.

*8 Feb. Wed.* We landed at McMurdo about 1800. I asked George Toney when the next flight to the Pole is and he said at midnight. Dick Wold took 12 minutes from leaving the plane to returning, during which time he made a gravity observation at the Pole earlier today.

The objective was to see if the gravity at the Pole was changing. We measured, extremely accurately, repeatedly, the difference between a base on rock at McMurdo and another base at the South Pole. On this night I made a gravity tie to the Pole and again, with Dick and two gravity meters, we made ties on Sunday, 12 February.

*9 Feb. Thurs.* We landed at the Pole about 0247. The C-130 was only going to stay on deck 15 minutes and I was told they would leave without me [as soon as they unloaded 10 tons of cargo]. I huffed and puffed my way lugging the 20-pound gravity meter, through the 9600-foot air [but a pressure altitude of about 12,000 feet], freezing my nose en route. The temperature was −37°F. I went from building to building along the deserted tunnel looking for the science building, before I finally found the right place and read the meter. I was sure the plane had left, but I hurried out and managed to get aboard at 0300.

This was my first visit to the South Pole and I didn't even have time to take a picture. Red-painted Clement huts were connected by tunnels as at Byrd Station. There was much less snow load over the drifted over tunnels and buildings than at Byrd, because there is only about 5 centimeters water equivalent of snow (about 6 inches of snow). At an average yearly temperature of about –50°C the snow doesn't become ice for many years and at a depth of about 300 meters (about 1000 feet). Nine scientists and nine Navy men wintered over for the first time in 1957. In contrast, the third Pole station, completing construction in 2003, will have a winter capacity of 50 people.

The original South Pole station was eventually abandoned and ultimately replaced in 1975. The second South Pole (officially Amundsen-Scott) Station, consists of buildings sheltered beneath a metal dome and adjacent storage tunnels. Over the doorway is a sign: "United States Welcomes You to the South Pole." This station was built for 30 men and now in the summer the population reaches 220 men and women. "Men" is the operative word, as Alexendra Brown, one of the summer managers at the Pole, said in a talk in 2001 in Boulder. There is only one unisex bathroom and a woman finds it disconcerting while occupying a stall, to have to listen to a man at the adjacent urinal.

Jamesway huts on the surface for sleeping are crowded during the summer and there is little or no privacy in the small cubicles. "You pray your neighbor doesn't have a partner you have to listen to all the time," as Brown put it.

The original IGY station is now buried beneath the snow and has moved about one kilometer away from the original location. It is hazardous and off limits to visitors. However, over the years some of the 50 men and women wintering over have visited it, after the summer people have left.

The second winter (1958) of the IGY, there was some irritation with the station scientific leader at the Pole and an old friend, Mario Giovinetto, who, spending his second successive Antarctic winter, thought of a great practical joke. He suggested it would be amusing to put blood on a fire ax and creep into the leader's room and suddenly awaken him with: "You're the last one!"

An Antarctic myth grew out of the story and over the past 40 years I have been told in all seriousness that the hypothesized joke was actually carried out. Mario, a volatile Argentine glaciologist, was the strongest man I ever met. On one occasion that same winter, he had punched his fist through a door at the Pole. The myth had a certain credibility.

I went to bed at 2015.

With the exception of a few hours sleep in the Herc on the way to the South Pole and back, I had been up since morning of 7 February on the other side of the date line at Byrd, about 50 hours.

40. Beardmore Glacier in Transantarctic Mountains. Ross Ice Shelf at left. From C-130 aircraft at about 30,000 feet (9100 meters).

*12 Feb. Sun.* Sir Charles Wright [who had returned from Byrd], Dick Wold, and I hurried down to the strip at 1230 and waited until 1300 for C-130 #320 to take off for another gravity tie to the Pole.

I flew to the South Pole in C-130 #320 in 1995. By this date some of the Hercs were older than some of their pilots.

We got a good look at the Beardmore Glacier and the Queen Maud Range. I wondered how Sir Charles felt looking down on the area he man-hauled over 50 years ago with Scott. We landed at the Pole about 1700 and hustled to read the gravity meters. I saw the two big black #843 Sno-Cats sitting there and realized that Bert Crary and his traverse party had arrived. The temperature was about −40° to −50°F, and I froze my nose again. We landed about 2100 at McMurdo.

Sir Charles commented on how remarkable it seemed that here we had gone to the Pole and back in 7 1/2 hours, while their party 50 years ago had taken 5 1/2 months and hadn't got back at all.

*13 Feb. Mon.* Sir Charles sat down opposite me at supper tonight and we got talking about glaciology. We discussed various theories of freezing

41. South Pole (Amundsen-Scott) Station, 12 February 1961. McMurdo—Pole traverse track visible in foreground.

42. South Pole (Amundsen-Scott) Station, 12 February 1961. Two Tucker #843 Sno-Cats, which had just arrived, visible on horizon.

43. Dome at South Pole (Amundsen-Scott) Station, December 1978. Sign over entrance reads: "United States Welcomes you to the South Pole." Note U.S. flag on dome.

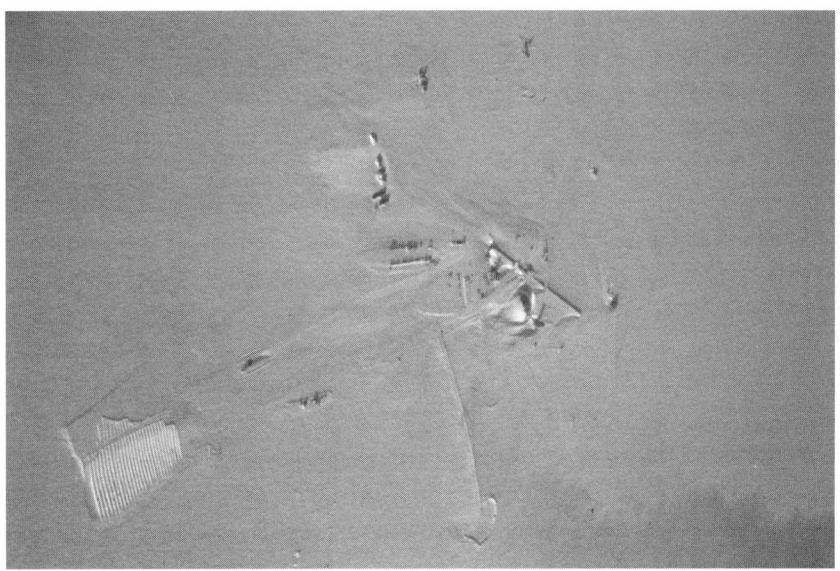

44. South Pole from air, January 1984.

45. Behrendt at South Pole,
December 1978.

# CHAPTER SEVEN

46. Astronomical observatory at South Pole, February 1995. Note box at right for recycled material.

and melting on the bottom of ice shelves. He wrote a number of papers and a book on glaciology back in the Scott days.[1]

*16 Feb. Thurs.* At 0445 George Toney woke us and told us to be ready to leave for Christchurch in fifteen minutes. It was snowing and visibility was near zero. We read our gravity meters [to make a tie from McMurdo to Christchurch] and the fourteen of us USARPs that were scheduled to go, piled into various vehicles and drove to the strip.

This was the sea ice strip, which was unusable in late summer in the 1990s.

It was 1030 when we took off in the Connie (R7V) with 68 passengers aboard, including Tom Laudon, Dick Wold, and me. Our plane crossed the coast of New Zealand and landed at 1915. The green fields with neat rows of trees with small villages scattered here and there looked most inviting in the late afternoon sunlight. It was quite a contrast to the bleak, stark continent of Antarctica. The air, pleasantly cool, but humid, smelled of earth and green growing things. There were even women.

The next morning I was wakened by a sweet young girl knocking at my door;

she brought me a cup of tea and a "biscuit" (cookie) to my bed. What a contrast to George Toney shaking me the previous morning in McMurdo. Christchurch now has hotels with private baths, unlike the Gainsborough, but sweet young girls no longer wake you with a cup of tea to sip in bed.

> Thus ends another season in Antarctica. We took a bit of battering around, and the program dragged out a bit longer than anticipated. But we got the job done and one can take a certain amount of satisfaction in that.

Actually, we got a tremendous amount accomplished. We made aeromagnetic measurements along 15,000 kilometers of widely spaced flight lines. Combined with Bentley's Sentinel Mountains Traverse (1957–58), these data first identified the vast extent of volcanic rock beneath the West Antarctic Ice Sheet (and the sharp boundary with the sedimentary rock province on the east). The two profiles measured between McMurdo and Hallett Station were the first to roughly define the very high amplitude Polar Three magnetic anomaly over the western Ross Sea.

Our airborne radar elevation and barometric altimeter measurements along the 14,000 kilometers of aeromagnetic profiles over the ice sheet from the Amundsen and Bellingshausen sea coasts to east of the Thiel Mountains and nearly to the South Pole resulted in the first map of the ice sheet elevation in this area. These results also showed the existence of the unnamed ice stream draining the East Antarctic Ice Sheet into the Filchner-Ronne Ice Shelf system.

The seismic soundings between the Hudson Mountains and Mt. Murphy demonstrated that there was no bedrock ridge above sea level and defined the drainage basin into the Pine Island Bay–Thwaites Glacier area north of the divide of the West Antarctic Ice Sheet. Geologists Laudon, Ford, and Aaron made the first reconnaissance of the volcanic rocks of the Hudson Mountains.

The extremely precise gravity ties we made between McMurdo and the South Pole, together with repeat measurements made over a ten-year period by others, showed a slight, but significant increase of gravity at the Pole. I published a short paper on this increase,[2] which created some controversy as to its explanation. ◆

# EIGHT

## Turbulent Transition

I spent a week or so waiting in Christchurch for a military flight to Sydney. To while away the time we enjoyed the company of the local women we met, took sightseeing tours, and wandered through the beautiful, green Botanic Gardens. The next Sunday, I traveled, with three others from the ice, by rental car over Arthur's Pass, crossing the New Zealand Alps to the west coast of South Island. This scenic road was unpaved in those days and it took us all day.

I flew uneventfully with Tom Laudon on a military plane to Sydney, Australia, where I spent a delightful 3–4-day weekend with friends from Wisconsin. They introduced me to a sweet graduate student. I immediately fell in love as we body surfed at Bondi Beach. Unfortunately I had to leave for Perth in three days and I never saw her again.

With my gravity meter, I flew across the vast Australian desert to the west coast. I flew all night from Perth to Johannesburg, South Africa, stopping for gravity measurements at Cocos and Mauritius Islands en route. This was the first gravity tie from Australia to Africa, and also the last tie between all of the continents, most or all of which had been made by our UW group.

I looked around Johannesburg a bit. Apartheid was total at that time and I saw few black people in the areas I visited. I flew all night to London via Salisbury, Rhodesia (now Harare, Zimbabwe), Nairobi, Khartoum, and Rome, making gravity measurements at the airports.

I arrived in London early on a Friday morning looking to spend some time with my old girlfriend from Madison, Sara, who was living and working there. We had a nice couple of days and saw Harold Pinter act in his new play *The Caretaker*. But she was living with an Englishman at the time, so I moved on.

I made a quick trip during the next week, tying gravity base stations together in Paris, Frankfurt, Hannover, Copenhagen, and Amsterdam. I had a somewhat sleepless night in Hannover, when the chronic but usually mild pain in my appendix increased. I decided it was time to head for the States.

A few years later, when I was a USGS geophysicist, I never would have dared, as a U.S. government employee, to make these very precise gravity ties with few visas or permission from the countries I passed through (many only in transit at the airports, i.e. without officially entering the country). Woollard was very casual in sending us graduate students all over the world making gravity ties. I suppose we were expendable. I and others from UW always managed to talk our ways out of the occasional scrapes we had with authorities in the various countries where we so nonchalantly made measurements. Although there was a geologic reason for tying gravity surveys together in a common worldwide system, the reason the U.S. Air Force was paying for this work was for correct navigation of intercontinental ballistic missiles.

A year later (1962) we all survived the Cuban missile crisis, and I (along with the rest of the world) came face-to-face with the realization that we had been within a few hours of nuclear war. This changed my perspective about these international gravity measurements.

I continued on to New York and Madison. The following weeks and months were very hectic and eventful. First, I dropped in on the head surgeon at UW Hospitals, who had treated my severely frostbitten toes in 1955, and told him I wanted my appendix removed. He said, "Oh and what makes you think you need this?" I explained and he poked around and agreed. A week or so later he took it out and I spent two nights in the hospital.

I then completed my Ph.D. thesis,[1] *Geophysical Studies in the Filchner Ice Shelf Area, of Antarctica* and defended it. I recall that Charlie Bentley gave me a hard time and George Woollard was easy. At any rate I passed and got a pay raise from $6500/year to $7500/year, which I thought grand.

I went on a weekend canoe trip on the Wolf River in northern Wisconsin and split some cartilage in my right knee doing a little scrambling on boulders before we put the boats in the water. I couldn't straighten my leg and therefore couldn't canoe. The water was extremely high and very cold. I met the group still on the water at a lunch stop. Immediately after lunch one canoe tipped and dumped the passengers, not wearing life preservers, into the fast-flowing stream.

Oscar Strickholm, an old mountaineering and Antarctic friend, clung desperately to a rock as long as he could hold out in the cold water. He disappeared beneath the turbulent rapids to the horror of all of the rest of us, who watched and tried to help. We searched until dark, but never found him. I recall hobbling on my injured leg along the banks for hours. Although I had experienced close calls during our traverse on the Filchner Ice Shelf in 1957–58[2] and as described in the previous chapters, this was my first experience with actual accidental death.

Two weeks later I went back in the hospital and had my cartilage removed and was on crutches for a week. I exercised my wasted leg for several months so I could go mountain climbing in British Columbia in August.

I was only 29, so fortunately I healed quickly and passed my Navy physical exam to return to Antarctica. Charlie Bentley asked me to lead the 1961–62 over-snow traverse into an unexplored area of southern Ellsworth Land northeast of the Sentinel Mountains and east of where his Ellsworth Highland Traverse had ended in February. I agreed and enthusiastically made preparations. I was scheduled to leave Madison on 7 October.

Another significant event in my life took place. I married Donna Ebben the evening of 6 October. We had been dating at first casually and then after my return in March, regularly. She participated in a few rapids canoe trips and the climbing trip in August. The Unitarian minister had impressed me at an outdoor memorial service for my drowned friend Oscar Strickholm, so we asked him to perform the service in the beautiful Frank Lloyd Wright church in Madison. We used passages from Gibran's *The Prophet*, such as breaking bread together, but eating from separate loaves. So our marriage went for 22 years.

Donna and I flew together to San Francisco on Saturday, 7 October to spend a four-day honeymoon before my military flight across the Pacific. Early on Wednesday morning I called Travis Air Force Base to check on my scheduled departure that night. I was shocked to discover that the plane had arrived from Washington, D.C. and would leave in one hour for Honolulu. I was more than an hour's drive away! I was dismayed and embarrassed; Donna was delighted. I immediately called George Toney at National Science Foundation in Washington and explained that I had missed my plane. He gave me a hard time and rescheduled me for a flight the following Wednesday, 18 October. He had to change schedules of others, because as traverse leader, I had a high priority. I did not tell him of my recent marriage. My friends in Madison thought it all a great joke and kidded me about it mercilessly.

The year 1961 was eventful in a larger sense. Kennedy had been inaugurated as president of the United States, and the fiasco of the Bay of Pigs invasion in Cuba occurred. The Berlin Wall went up, and some U.S. reserves were mobilized. The Cold War reached a new intensity. Antarctica looked better and better. ◆

47. Sastrugi formed by wind.

# NINE

# Angst at Old Byrd

I arrived at McMurdo on 24 Oct. at 0600 and spent a busy week getting the logistics organized for the Antarctic Peninsula Traverse.

*24–31 Oct.* It was –7°F at the strip. Lee W. Kreiling, our UW traverse mechanic, showed me around. He had wintered over getting our vehicles ready. The three black Tucker model #743 Sno-Cats seem to be in pretty good condition, with minor things to be done. They are quite nice inside. Each has two long shelves built into the form of desks. There are bunks suspended by chains built over these which fold against the bulkhead. The seismic gear is mounted and the big radio is just about in place.

We have named the Sno-Cats. *Barbara* is the cat Lee Kreiling will travel in; Perry Parks named the seismic cat *Tamare Riatia* after an old schooner that travels in and out of Tahiti; I called the lead cat, which I'll drive and sleep in, *Argo*. I guess that makes us Argonauts; we'll have to find the golden fleece.

Phil Smith, the NSF USARP representative, has the same position as George Toney the previous season. Smith, Krebs, the Commanding officer of VX6, Bob Farrington (OIC of VX6 at Byrd), and I had a planning session for the air support. We will need 72,000 pounds of materiel airlifted in six C-130 flights to Camp Minnesota in the Jones Mountains where Charlie Bentley's Ellsworth Highland Traverse ended last year. I've just about got everything located or accounted for now.[1]

Major Emby (USAF) talked to me about the three C-124 (Globemaster) air drops we need. He was surprised to find that the positions are 1600 nautical miles from McMurdo. They will have to fly about 7000 feet elevation to carry even 18,000 pounds that far.

I saw the doctor about a burn on my shin, the result of a minor accident, which had become infected.

Everyone down here had heard about my marriage. My old friend and former mentor, Ed Thiel, head of a University of Minnesota geophysical field group, was quite surprised.

Ed and I hung out one night in the officers club and talked over old times at Madison and Ellsworth Station. He was at this time an assistant professor in Minneapolis and I had not seen him since returning from Antarctica the previous season. On 30 Oct. Charles Swithinbank, Ed Thiel, and their party left in an R4D-8. They planned to investigate the glaciers entering the west edge of the Ross Ice Shelf. Although Ed was in the field with Charles Swithinbank's party, he would be flown into McMurdo to make a historic first flight with the UW airborne magnetometer from McMurdo to the Soviet Mirnyy Station soon. They then planned to continue on to Wilkes Station before returning to McMurdo.

I found out [Tuesday, 31 Oct.] that there was a C-130 flight scheduled for Byrd. I got a ride down to the strip and waited until 1900.

I had a few things to get ready at Byrd, but the main purpose there was a reconnaissance into the unexplored area to the east of the previous season's Ellsworth Highland Traverse. Perry Parks, Con Merrick, Lee Kreiling, and John Molholm (assistant glaciologist), soon to be joined by Pete Wasilewski, who was working at Byrd, would get the three Sno-Cats and everything else ready to load on the C-130 flights to Camp Minnesota.

Conrad G. Merrick was the USGS topographic engineer who would be our navigator and survey in accurate locations of any mountains we might encounter. Peter Wasilewski, U.S. Coast and Geodetic Survey, was a geophysicist assigned to make magnetic observations at the main stations we planned to put in. His work would compliment the magnetic profile we planned to measure along our traverse route.

*31 Oct. Tues.* I arrived at Byrd about 0400 on 31 October (Byrd time and date). Hiromu "Hiro" Shimizu[2] (the Japanese glaciologist who had just completed the winter at Byrd), Pete Wasilewski [who would return to McMurdo soon], Ken Moulton (NSF) and others were there to meet the plane. It was about –25°F, with little wind and quite pleasant. There are some more supporting beams in the tunnels, and the floor in the science building is being crushed by the weighted roof pushing down on the supporting beams there.

Hiro's English has improved a lot since last season when I first met him. Amusingly, he has learned many words [during the winter just ended] from the Seabees, which are their common usage, which won't go over so well when he engages in polite conversation in the States.

Charlie Bentley and the others on the Ellsworth Highland Traverse the previous season thought that Hiro needed preparation to spend the winter at Byrd with the Seabees, so they taught him a lot of profanity. He never learned another word for "waste basket" other than "shit can," one of the milder common terms. The colorful Seabee vocabulary, as spoken by many of the men, seemed to require some form of the word "fuck" to be used at least once a sentence, as in "It's six o'fucking clock."

*1 Nov. Wed.* Another of the clear sunny days that we have had continuously since I arrived in Antarctica. The USAF have been making about three airdrops a day here with C-124s. The drop zone is quite close to the Jamesway hut in which a lot of us sleep outside the tunnels on top [a few days later I moved down into the station], and some of the loads come pretty close. Most are composed of fuel in barrels, and only a so-called "ribbon" or stabilizing chute is used. Consequently the 1800-pound pallets come down almost in free fall. It isn't very relaxing to lie in bed in the canvas Jamesway and hear the roar of a C-124 a few hundred feet overhead, and then the "whomp, whomp" as the pallets hit the snow. Tonight we had a low overcast for a few hours and they were dropping through it with a man on the ground directing by radio.

Unfortunately the R4D-8 program here at Byrd looks discouragingly like last season. The R4D has radar trouble now and the P2V is down with hydraulic trouble. So far there have been two abortive flights to the eastern Horlicks [Thiel Mountains].

*2 Nov. Thurs.* Another clear day and the R4D-8 took two of the USGS team out to the eastern Horlick Mountains [Thiel Mountains].

I got a message from Perry Parks at McMurdo tonight telling me they plan to start C-130s to Camp Minnesota at 0800 on the 10th. Bob Farrington got a message ordering him to complete the recon for me so as to meet the C-130 schedule. Hiro and I will make the trip approximately over the planned traverse route. Upon returning to Byrd, we will then fly out to Camp Minnesota from Byrd in the R4D-8 with about 4000 pounds. This will be a recon for the C-130s, which will launch from McMurdo at the word from us. We will pick up one C-130 load and C-124 air drop of fuel and explosive at Sky-Hi [a summer field camp to be put in for VLF radio studies], and have additional resupply by R4D.

Eventually this is what happened, but there were many delays, which I describe here in a shortened form.

*4 Nov. Sat.* It was clear and cold (about −25°F) today and we launched the recon at 1130. It was very cold in the cabin as the heater wasn't working properly.

Our traverse and this flight were preparing to enter unexplored territory. The Antarctic Peninsula Traverse was planned to start at Camp Minnesota in the Jones Mountains on the coast of the Bellingshausen Sea and work through eastern Ellsworth Land and the southern Antarctic Peninsula for about 900 kilometers to the east. This was an essentially unexplored area in 1961.

Lincoln Ellsworth had made a flight from the Antarctic Peninsula in November 1935 and saw the northern end of the Sentinel Range (but not the highest peaks in Antarctica, which were obscured by clouds) and a few other peaks. Finn Ronne named the Sweeney and Lowell Thomas Mountains, and a few others, from trimetrigon photographs taken on a single flight from the southwest corner of the Weddell Sea bordering the eastern part of this area during the RARE, 1946–48. These features were not accurately located, and no one had been in the area since.

We headed for 74°S, 84°W and got there at 1550 after passing over some clouds. It was clear and we could see a mountain range off to the northwest about 60 miles.

This was a distance measured from radar. The only range this could possibly have been is the Jones Mountains, but these are about 120 miles (about 220 kilometers) from our calculated position.

We turned toward Mt. Combs, but after crossing over the coast line at 1606 and turning east we failed to see it. The snow surface was smooth and crevasse free as we came down until quite close to the sea. There was an ice shelf and then some open water. The area in general was covered with heavy pack ice. The plane crossed over the high ice front of the ice shelf at 1657. We could see some nunataks off to the east.

We ran into clouds about this time, which forced us above them. At 1712 the navigator, Tom Underwood, reported a nunatak on radar at 74°05'S, 80°15'W just a mile or two to our left.

This was probably Mt. Tuve, which we later accurately located at 73°47'S, 80°08'W. See the discussion of the recon flight on 12 November 1960 above.

I was in the cockpit in the left-hand seat all this time, but could see nothing through the clouds. The radar showed more nunataks in the distance to the east, but went out of commission before a bearing could be taken.

The plane turned east toward Mt. Vang in hopes of clearer weather but found none. We were flying near Mt. Rex and other reported nunataks but could see nothing. We were on top of the clouds and climbing to stay above them. About this time Bob Farrington in the right seat said jokingly "You take it" and left the cockpit. We were flying on the automatic pilot of course, but for a minute I was alone up there with no one around flying over unexplored Antarctica hidden in the clouds.

Chris Christoffersen, the copilot, moved into the right seat and took over. He has the annoying habit of falling asleep at the controls and was out for five minutes a couple of times. The plane captain came up and saw him thus and shook his head, remarking that he had better keep checking up here.

I assume Bob Farrington was napping in the seat on the port side just aft of the bulkhead behind me. As Christoffersen slept, we slowly descended towards the clouds not far below. I was watching the heading and altimeters and would have wakened Chris if anything was wrong.

Christoffersen finally did wake and we climbed to about 10,000 feet, or about 7000 feet above the hidden snow surface below.

Finally the clouds forced us up higher than was practical to fly, so we turned at 1810 and headed for the Sentinel Mountains. This was at 74°04'S, 75°30'W and about 875 nautical miles (about 1620 kilometers) from Byrd. At 1938 we broke out of the clouds and saw the spectacular 16,000-foot Sentinel Mountains ahead. To the right was a sort of escarpment running perpendicular to the range with low ice on the left. We flew through some low peaks with some crevasses associated with them and then headed north to check the terrain over which we will be driving in February. It looked good and at 2016 at 76°52'S, 86°30'W. We turned and headed for Byrd.

> About 2045 the gyrocompass went haywire. We flew back to Byrd by shooting sun lines and arrived at 2350. We had flown for 12 hours, 11 minutes.

During this flight the radar and gyrocompass had both quit.

> It was a somewhat discouraging day, as we flew about 1500 [nautical] miles (2775 kilometers) and only saw about 200 miles (370 kilometers) of our traverse route.

> *6 Nov. Tues.* Buddy Krebs and Ron Carlson [VX6 officers] came out from McMurdo for a conference this morning to coordinate the big airlift to Camp Minnesota on the 9th [10th at McMurdo]. Jim Weeks, the plane commander of R4D-8 #219 [the plane whose wing hit a rock in the Crary Mountains a year earlier, as described in chapter 1] is flying in today.
> After the conference, Bob Farrington flew Bill Long and his OSU party out to their camp in the central Horlick Mountains. After they returned in the evening, they flew rest of the USGS party (Art Ford and two others) out to their camp in the eastern Horlicks [Thiel Mountains]. They had plane trouble out there and didn't get in until breakfast time.

> *8 Nov. Wed.* This operation is rapidly snowballing. We now have planned or committed 7 C-130 flights (counting 1 flight for removal of the field party at the end of the season), 3 C-124 flights, and about 8 R4D-8 flights. Just about midnight someone found a serious defect in the tail ski of #853, which will take some time to fix. As #219 is still down, Bob had to radio a 24-hour postponement.

> *9 Nov. Thurs.* A message came in from Admiral Tyree to VX6 to suspend all operations in support of the traverse until further notice. Something is up at McMurdo.

Considering the detailed planning described above, this message was ominous.

> I heard this evening at late chow that the P2V, which had flown with Ed Thiel from McMurdo to Mirnyy [the main Soviet station], and then on to Wilkes, had crashed on takeoff from Wilkes. I'm quite concerned about Ed. It's a rather discouraging end to a gloomy day. I'm somewhat despondent.

I had an infection in my leg, which eventually healed, but spent most of this day confined to bed. I have not described the problem further in this book, but it was potentially serious and could have kept me off the traverse.

> *10 Nov. Fri.* Ken Moulton woke me at 0600 to tell me Ed had been killed. Phil Smith sent me the following message:
>> Priority 100626Z
>> From Rep USARP McMurdo
>> To: Byrd Sta
>> Info CNSFA, USARP Wash DC, Rep CNSFA Wash DC
>> Unclas Nr 33 Pass Behrendt
>> 1. Must regretfully inform you of death Ed Thiel in P2V crash Wilkes. A crash occurred in takeoff after fire producing smoke obscuring pilot vision. Five of nine killed.
>> 2. Evacuation of injured from Wilkes by C-130 planned. Will delay departure traverse several days.

> That plane must really have hit hard to kill so many. Ed is the first U.S. scientist who has been killed in Antarctica since the IGY began.

Apparently the runway was very rough at Wilkes. The official Navy investigation found that a bolt holding the internal fuel tank had sheared during the takeoff run, and the tank had ruptured. Aviation gas spilled along the fuselage and the JATO started a fire.

In 1996 the Australian Antarctic journal *Aurora* published a brief account of this crash by Bill Burch, the photographer at Wilkes on that day:

> "His teeth I remember most about him. An absolutely perfect set. . . . Six foot something, crew cut hair, big beaming smile, looked to be barely twenty. His mother must have been very proud of him!

> "I was helping him refuel the Neptune P2V aircraft on the plateau

above Wilkes Station from numerous 44 gallon drums. . . . I think he was an aircraft mechanic. He and his eight compatriots had just landed after a flight from Mirnyy, final stop McMurdo. . .

"I remember, too, feeling more than a little miffed when one of the first things he said . . . was 'That was one hell of a rough landing strip you guys have—nearly as bad as Mirnyy.' . . . there was not really a strip at Wilkes, just a slightly flatter area of plateau defined by survey pegs. . . .

"So eventually we were done and trundled back to the station to join the party. Lofty, our cook, had excelled in the pastry department. . . . And our visitors had brought with them some fresh meat and vegetables, . . . we 'pigged out.'

"Next morning: some of us who had not blown ourselves away at the party escorted the nine visitors back up to the aircraft to see them off. My toothy friend told me about the JATO bottles they carried and would use to boost the take-off. . . . As official photographer, I had charge of the 16mm camera on the base, which had a magnificent 200mm lens. So I lugged the heavy tripod out to the strip and on advice from the pilot gave myself a good advantage point to film the takeoff, especially the firing of the JATO.

"We said our farewells. . . .

"The cockpit crew certainly had the better of the accommodation. The rest were plopped around in little cramped jump seats, mainly sharing its belly with the long-range fuel tank.

"The engines started with a whine and the ungainly-looking bird waddled over the wind-blown snow waves like a pelican, wings outstretched, to the more or less flattened sastrugi called the Wilkes airstrip. . . . I had to commit to the long lens for the whole takeoff sequence and the JATO rockets just filled the view finder at the start of the roll. Everything was looking good.

"The engine pitch rose to a scream, making the propellers tear frantically into the still air, and a huge puff of snow billowed out as the plane began its roll. Right on cue, I saw the JATO rocket flames spit rearwards, seeming to paint the side of the plane in fire.

"Hey! hang on! It wasn't seeming at all. It WAS suddenly burning right into the tail.

"The plane was now well into the air—thrown there by the JATO's thrust.

"The sharp-edged JATO flame had vanished, no longer flaring from the bottle, yet there was fire all over the rear of the aircraft.

48. P2V crash at Wilkes Station 9 November, 1961. Thiel and four others died. (photo by Bill Burch)

"It turned into a steep left bank, and I could hear some frantic garbled shouts over the nearby Weasel's radio about fire, smoke, and not being able to see anything. I kept the camera rolling, but a nearby rise in the plateau screened us from the remaining drama.

"I am sure we all hoped in those few seconds that somehow the pilot had succeeded in any kind of safe return to the earth. But the black geyser of smoke above our snowy scene signalled immediately that he had not.

"The next few minutes will remain in my memory as one of those nightmare sequences. Imagine riding pillion on a D4 going flat out across sastrugi at about 10 kilometers per hour, trying desperately to cover perhaps a kilometer in case we could help. The Weasel beat us of course, and we came over the brow of the rise to see through the thick smoke three shadowy figures staggering to the Weasel, all with their hands over their faces.

"In fact four had escaped. The other five could not be seen or heard, and the heat from the burning wreck prevented us getting closer than about 20 meters to the fuselage, which was largely intact. The rest of the plane was scattered over a wide area.

"Apart from severe burns to exposed skin, those who got out were relatively lightly injured. It was agreed that the five others must have perished and our priority lay with getting the injured back to base as quickly as possible. Max and I were asked to stay and record the wreck site as well as we could, in case a blizzard wiped out vital evidence for any crash investigation. Locating the bodies for recovery was also part of the plan.

"In forty minutes or so, we had paced and photographed all we thought was relevant and now the centre of the burnt-out metal bird was cool enough to approach closely. Knowing where most of the crew had been sitting, it was obvious where they should be, and led by the faint sweet sickly smell of badly burned flesh, we found a jumbled mass of almost unrecognizable bodies—all but one.

"He was fixed in the remains of the exit doorway; his hands on what must have been the release levers. I knew who he had been.

"My friend of less than a day.

"The perfect teeth were still perfect—but black; and clenched horribly tight.

"I wondered what they would tell his mother."[3]

Ed Thiel must have been one of the "jumbled mass of almost unrecognizable bodies." He and the others were only identified from dental x-rays.

It's hard to realize that Ed is dead.

Ed and I had spent the summer of 1955 in the Uinta Mountains and I used the magnetic data I had collected for my MS thesis. I wrote the report in 1962, with Ed as coauthor. Its publication in 1963 helped get me my job at the USGS in 1964. All this and my thesis and publications on the Filchner Ice Shelf Traverse I owed to Ed, as I realized sadly.

All sorts of thoughts have been going through my mind today—too many to write down here. I wrote Ed's widow. Although we did not know it at the time, Pat was pregnant. Charlie Bentley and Ned Ostenso in Madison were notified first of Ed's death. Ned immediately went to Minneapolis and personally told Pat.

However, youth is resilient, and I had exciting work to do. We commenced a frantic effort to make up for lost time and get the traverse into the field.

*11 Nov. Sat.* Krebs, the VX6 commanding officer at McMurdo, called up for a voice conference with Bob Farrington and me tonight. The airlift to Camp Minnesota is scheduled to start tomorrow at 1630 local.

*12 Nov. Sun.* The Univ. of Minnesota lead group, consisting of John Anderson [the party leader and one of Cam Craddock's students] and two others took off tonight for the Sentinel Mountains. They crashed on landing in the rough sastrugi at the north end of the range about 1415. It was similar to the mishap in the Horlicks last year and with the same plane.

This was also the same plane in which we had hit the wing on a peak in the Crary Mountains that year as described in chapter 1.

No one was injured, but the skis collapsed, and the wings, engines, tail, and body are damaged. They probably won't be able to salvage it.

This wrecked plane and the location define the geologic formation in the Sentinel Range named the Crash Site Quartzite.

The crash meant we had to postpone again. Byrd made radio contact at 1445, with the downed plane. Although the weather here was poor with blowing snow, it improved by suppertime. Bob Farrington and his crew went out in #853 later in the evening, but when they reached the Sentinels, visibility was so poor they couldn't see the downed plane. As the radar is still out on #853, they couldn't use this, and not liking the unseen peaks around them, they returned to Byrd.

The people in #219 are, of course, very well equipped because they have all the Minnesota supplies, motor toboggans, etc., in addition to their own emergency gear.

I got a phone patch with Donna through a Chicago ham station tonight. It was poor quality, but a great morale booster nonetheless. Apparently everyone has heard about Ed's death, but we can't talk about the P2V or R4D-8 crashes over the ham radio.

*13 Nov. Mon.* Tonight #853 successfully evacuated the people from

#219. They decided to call it a strike (i.e., beyond repair).

*14 Nov. Tues.* The Camp Minnesota airlift was on again as of this morning. However, later in the morning, C-130 #321 landed at New Byrd with only three engines. It taxied over here and now awaits a prop change. C-130 #320 left McMurdo about suppertime for Byrd, but aborted with one engine out.

Because C-130 #318 is up in ChiChi with body repairs, only #319 is up [operational].[4] All of these aircraft problems will cause another postponement in the Camp Minnesota flights. [We needed three operational Hercs for our traverse deployment.]

*15 Nov. Wed.* [Because there was not insufficient] C-130 capability for the lift to Camp Minnesota, they will establish Sky-Hi. Our R4D will go to Sky-Hi with Floyd Johnson. The C-124s will make six drops there; viz. three for us and three for the station. This means a delay at least to the 19th for the traverse.

*16 Nov. Thurs.* Floyd Johnson flew out to Sky-Hi with Bob Farrington. Unfortunately the area was clobbered by clouds, and they couldn't land. A flight like that is really discouraging, as the area over most of the 600+ miles was clear.

Bob Farrington made Lt. Cdr. [lieutenant commander]. It couldn't happen to a nicer guy.

Dr. Cowan took over the station command from Dr. Walk several days ago. Walk was briefing him once when I was in the next room soaking my leg. Walk told Cowan to call the Navy men by their last names and the civilians by first names. Everyone should call him Dr. (rather than Lieutenant) including civilians, rather than a first name. I think he is a little embarrassed about this when it comes to me. [I have never had anyone call me "Dr."] He treats my leg and we play bridge together, etc. I call him "Doc," but he doesn't call me anything.

NSF tried to be very "correct" in using "Dr." in paperwork for all university scientists in Antarctica in those days—but not for USGS geologists who, incidentally, were all Ph.D.s. A few years later after I had joined USGS I realized how pompous the title seemed to "Survey" scientists. Every few years at a satirical show put on by the Geologic Division of the USGS an old song with new words to the tune of "Pretty Baby" was sung with a chorus: "Call me Doctor, call me Doctor." This was always aimed at some particular scientist who "hadn't gotten over his or her Ph.D. yet."

*17 Nov. Fri.* The C-130 that was down here at Byrd has been repaired and flown back to McMurdo. A C-130 landed today with a fire in one engine, had it repaired, and flew back to McMurdo.

*18 Nov. Sat.* We launched for either Sky-Hi or Camp Minnesota at 0235, and I promptly spread my sleeping bag on the deck and crawled in. Our radio lost contact with Byrd almost immediately due to ionosphere fluctuations. The weather was poor but we could see the snow surface under a broken overcast about 70 miles from Sky-Hi. The plane still had no radio contact, however, and rather than landing and hoping the comm would improve, we turned towards Camp Minnesota. The area was all socked in towards the Bellingshausen Sea, and we turned back to Byrd. I was in the cockpit at this time hoping to recon something or other.

About an hour out of Byrd we established radio contact, but it was too late to prevent the P2V from launching for SAR. Most of our flight back to Byrd was in clouds with occasional prop icing. We landed at Byrd at 1045. The people at Byrd had been upset about our lack of radio contact for six or seven hours.

I went to bed at noon and slept until supper. A message came in from McMurdo to launch again for Sky-Hi at 2100. Bob tried to get off but they found that the prop-feathering motors were not operating, and have not been all season. Bob wanted to fly anyway, but the navigator told me he wouldn't go. If an engine failed, we could lose a wing or crash without being able to feather the prop.

Bob Farrington fired the navigator, who had refused, from his crew. Bob admitted the prop feathering motors were defective, but felt that the urgency of the mission justified the flight. As they couldn't go without a navigator, the flight was also canceled. Now Bob has asked for a replacement from McMurdo.

This incident epitomizes the vast change in attitude from the U.S. Antarctic Program during the late 1950s and early 1960s and today. Now, safety is paramount, and the national need is not considered great enough a justification for risk. We all received 25 percent pay differential on the Ice and were deferred from the military draft to work in Antarctica. We were prepared to accept accidents and death for the sake of the program. Before I left McMurdo, I was asked to fill out a form regarding disposition of remains in case of accidental death. My request was for burial in Antarctica. I assume Ed Thiel had filled out a similar form; at any rate his remains were returned to Wausau, Wisconsin, his home town, for burial.

*19 Nov. Sun.* When I got up this morning, I found that they had discovered a malfunction in the tail ski assembly. Parts are needed and this will keep the plane down until Tuesday.

They appear to be in a real hurry now at McMurdo about getting the Sky-Hi and Camp Minnesota operation underway. I am in a hurry too.

*20 Nov. Mon.* The air crew worked on #853 all day and got it fixed tonight.

*21 Nov. Tues.* Jim Weeks flew up in #188 about 0100, so we now have two operational planes again. Bob Farrington launched in #853 for Sky-Hi with Floyd Johnson about 0400. Unfortunately (it seems that many things are unfortunate) they aborted as the clouds clobbering the Sky-Hi area were still there.

Sky-Hi was a misnomer, as it turned out. The planners who had picked the location thought it was at a relatively high altitude along the crest of the ice sheet over the spine of the subglacial mountains connecting the Antarctic Peninsula to the Sentinel Mountains. They were wrong, but we did not know this at the time. The elevation was only about 450 meters and circulation patterns over the Ronne Ice Shelf and the southern coast of the Weddell Sea resulted in very high snow accumulation and cloudy weather in the area.

The weather deteriorated all day, and when the plane got back about 1400 it was blowing about 30 knots here. The blowing snow made the landing difficult here and is causing much drifting.

*22 Nov. Wed.* Jim Weeks told me at 0100 they would try for Camp Minnesota in the morning.

The reason VX6 wanted flights to the north at this intense rate was for weather reconnaissance for the C-130 air operations planned. Ideally one plane would launch every 12 hours to track changing conditions in the area. Sky-Hi was planned about 1100 kilometers (700 nautical miles) from Byrd. There were no people anywhere in Antarctica closer than we at Byrd were at the time, although a few British, Argentine, and Chilean stations about 1500 kilometers to the north of the Sky-Hi-location were reporting their meteorological observations daily.

We took off in #188 at 1100.[5] I had only managed to get an hour or so of sleep last night so I spread my sleeping bag on the explosives cases and got about a four-hour nap. The heaters in the plane were broken and the temperature in the cabin was about +9°F, making it a fairly uncomfortable trip. The forecast was for bad weather near the coast and we ran into clouds after crossing the divide of the West Antarctic Ice Sheet north of Byrd. We were high enough above the clouds to get sun shots, but as the surface was obscured, we had no drift. Our course was towards the new range we discovered on the first recon. We didn't find the mountains and turned left towards the Jones Mountains and Camp Minnesota. Visibility was very low, but we could see some crevasses below and eventually, mountains.

When we got a close look at these approximately 4000-foot-high flat-topped, black, volcanic-appearing peaks, we could see more crevasses on the low north side. The mountains showed steep north-facing scarps and there were several isolated peaks. It was concluded at the time that these were the peaks of Thurston Island. The snow surface at the north side appeared about 2000 feet, whereas it should have been about sea level for Thurston Island.

The clouds became very thick and we headed for Byrd. We eventually flew a line of position from a point approximately abeam of Byrd and found we had been 135 miles from our calculated position when we finally located the station.

Again, as was not unusual in unexplored areas of Antarctica in these early years, we had been lost. I have included the confusing description above to illustrate this.

The plane landed at 2056 local. This makes five straight aborts into that area. We flew about 1300 miles today. There were no meals, so all I had all day was two pancakes for breakfast and numerous cups of hot coffee.

There were two sleeping bags and room to spread them out in the cabin, which saved the day for four of us—Hiro, and two others and myself.

Back at Byrd, the cook had some steak, mashed potatoes, and green beans ready for us when we came into the galley during the movie. It was greatly appreciated.

*23 Nov. Thurs. Thanksgiving* Big dinner and another abort to Sky-Hi. I slept until 1500. We will try for Camp Minnesota again in the morning. ◆

# TEN

# Into the Field

Finally, after nearly a month at Byrd and much pain and suffering, we were ready to go. While Hiro and I had made three flights into the area south and east of the Bellingshausen Sea coast, we still had no reconnaissance in the unexplored area east of the proposed Camp Sky-Hi. The five men at McMurdo had been chafing at the bit. All supplies there had long been ready to be flown to Camp Minnesota.

Hiro had constructed a beautiful, ingenious, folding, plywood privy, which was lashed on top of the cases of explosive in cabin of the R4D-8. On the basis of my experience on the Filchner Ice Shelf Traverse, I thought that this was an unnecessary luxury. On the basis of Hiro's previous season experience on the 5000–6000-feet-high (1500–1800 meters) ice sheet of Ellsworth Land, he deemed it a necessity.

*24 Nov. Fri.* I didn't go to bed last night. We flew out to Camp Minnesota today after passing through some clouds and landed uneventfully.

For the previous several months I had been mildly concerned about how we were going to drive our Sno-Cats several thousand feet up from Camp Minnesota on the north side of the Jones Mountains at the coast of the Bellingshausen Sea. Charlie Bentley had led the Ellsworth Highland Traverse Land Traverse down a steep, crevasse-free slope at the west end of the Jones Mountains. We had some concern as to whether we could pull our loads up the same slope. Besides, we intended to travel east and needed a safe, gentle route up onto the Palmer Land area of the West Antarctic Ice Sheet.

The arrangement I had with Bob Farrington was that we would fly to the Jones Mountains and make a reconnaissance to search for a good route. I was in the cockpit in the right-hand seat and Bob flew the plane from the left.

We made one wide turn around the east end of the range. Although we could see some crevasses through the partly cloudy weather, I thought there was a feasible route for the Sno-Cats. I took several pictures with a Polaroid camera. The 3-by-4-inch-prints would provide the only maps of these crevassed areas. Bob was anxious to get on with the program, so I said that things were OK. I felt we could do it.

Continuing our counterclockwise circle, we spotted the Camp Minnesota Jamesway hut, almost completely buried in the snow. The landing was uneventful and the snow was smooth and soft. We climbed out and immediately went to work.

There was a thin overcast, but sufficient snow definition for the C-130s to land safely. As there had been two Herc flights from McMurdo to the Jones Mountains in December 1960, VX6 was confident about easily landing on the snow here. Bob Farrington radioed to McMurdo to start the operation. Three C-130s launched about 15 minutes apart, bringing the Sno-Cats first.

We had a lot to get ready before the planes arrived. The Ellsworth Highland Traverse party had been concerned about the rapid snow accumulation at the Jamesway site, apparent by the previous February. When we landed, there was less than a foot of the arched hut visible above the snow surface. Bentley's party had parked their three Sno-Cats, sleds, wanigan, Rollitrailer, and a drill rig on a "blue ice" area closer to the mountains. This obviously wind-blown site seemed likely to remain snow-free until we arrived.

Oh how true! We walked over to the vehicles about half a mile away and found the Sno-Cats partly on pedestals of wind-packed snow. The winter gales had scoured snow from beneath the tracks. Paint was blasted off the exposed surfaces on the windward sides as if by sand. Several of the white stake side panels of the one-ton sleds and one of these small sleds were blown away. All we found of the wanigan, which formerly had stood about eight feet above the surface, was the orange runner assembly and frame of the former 2–1/2 ton sled on which it had been built at Ellsworth Station in 1958. The heavy walls and roof constructed from Clement hut panels had blown completely away. All cooking equipment, stoves, first-aid kit, and other items that had been stored in the wanigan were gone with the wind as well. I sent a message to McMurdo reporting this, and requesting an entire set of stoves, pots, dishes, and other necessities be sent out. Someone there really hustled to get this done; the first C-130s were already in the air en route.

The three Sno-Cats were filled inside with drifted snow. Fortunately, everything bolted into the vehicles was there. The massive Rollitrailer, with its four 500-gallon fuel tires, although almost completely drifted over, was otherwise unaffected.

One of the air crew and I quickly dug into the snow-filled vehicles so we could get into the driver's seats on the left-hand side. While digging, we broke a

49. Sno-Cat unloading from C-130 at Camp Minnesota.

hose in one vehicle, so we could get only two started. The batteries had been left fully charged the previous February and disconnected. We connected the cables and the gasoline engines started easily. The temperature was a little below freezing, much warmer than at Byrd because we were close to sea level (560 meters elevation at the Camp Minnesota hut).

I recall standing at the tiny galley in the R4D-8 frying some ham and eating a sandwich while we waited. I was famished, as this was the first food I had eaten since we left Byrd.

The first three C-130s, with Perry Parks, Lee Kreiling and Pete Wasilewski, landed uneventfully and we backloaded two old Sno-Cats and the drill rig, which we planned not to use.

The clutch on one of the Sno-Cats was inoperable, but I managed to get it shifted by "double clutching" (varying the engine speed and meshing the gears that way). When the Hercules C-130s landed there was so much engine noise we could not communicate with the loadmaster. When someone backed a new Sno-Cat off, I just drove the old one with the damaged clutch in. I stopped by switching the engine off, leaving the vehicle in gear, but we later heard they had great difficulty getting that Sno-Cat out of the plane at McMurdo.

*25 Nov. Sat.* I didn't get to sleep until 0300.

My journal doesn't even say where I slept, but I probably threw my sleeping bag into the new Sno-Cat *Argo*, which had just been unloaded.

Up about 1000. Three more C-130s arrived in quick succession with Con Merrick, John Molholm, fuel, food, etc.

Etc. included scientific equipment and explosives. When the Hercs with the Sno-Cats landed, the planes parked and we backed the Sno-Cats out carefully. However, for these last three landings, the pilots just opened the tail ramp and the crew pushed the drummed fuel and everything else out while the planes taxied at high speed. I was really angry at seeing the sensitive seismic equipment and explosives dumped over a line about 100 feet behind one plane that barely slowed at all for that particular landing. Fortunately there was no explosion and nothing was damaged.

It occurs to me as I write this in 2003 that they may have been angry at me about the Sno-Cat with the damaged clutch that had had to be removed before these flights could be loaded and launched from McMurdo.

Bob Farrington left after noon in the R4D-8, which had stayed during the six C-130 landings for radio communication and weather reporting to McMurdo. After weeks of delay, this operation went off without a hitch about 30 hours from the time we took off from Byrd.

Brief lunch in *Barbara*. We will probably eat and cook in this Cat.

It was good to have our crew together and on our own after a month in Antarctica preparing and waiting.

One tire on the Rollitrailer was flat, but Lee and I pumped it up. I filled this tire with 9.5 drums of diesel fuel.

The Rollitrailer had a flat bed about 20 feet long, suspended between the four huge, 5-foot-high, 3-foot-wide, 500-gallon, tires. We proceeded to fill the tires at Camp Minnesota with the drummed fuel just delivered. The Sno-Cats had air compressors, so we used an air pressure pump, which made the job easy compared with the hand pumps we had used on the Filchner Ice Shelf Traverse in 1957.[1]

The Rollitrailer was an improvement over 55-gallon drums loaded on sleds for carrying fuel on the oversnow traverses. However, the new Sno-Cats we had just unloaded were not quite powerful enough to pull this heavy vehicle without damage.

Unlike the older gasoline engine Sno-Cats, our three new ones had diesel engines for better reliability. We started the engines by firing an ether cartridge mounted on the dashboard directly into the engine. This provided several cycles of power and heat, sufficient to ignite the diesel fuel.

> Perry worked on radios, but can't find the power cable for the ANG/RC 19 [radio]. So he built one. As he had no plugs, he wired directly into the chassis of the radio.

Perry Parks, Hiro Shimizu, and John Molholm were on the Ellsworth Highland Traverse the previous year and had a good knowledge of where equipment from the previous season might be. Perry had been the seismological assistant and electronics expert on that traverse, and would be so on this one. His technical experience proved invaluable to me as a chief geophysicist as well as party leader. This was his third traverse and he spent one winter at Byrd (1960).

John Molholm was Hiro's assistant glaciologist and had been so the previous season. He had also been assistant to Richard Cameron, glaciologist, during the 1957 IGY winter at Wilkes Station.

> We have been cooking and eating in the Jamesway and sleeping in the Cats. Steak for dinner [from Craddock's leftover year-old food] about 2230. We switched to Central Standard Time, or two hours ahead of Byrd. This will make our radio sked at 2130. Weather warm and sunny (about +20° to +30°F).

We were a little south of 73°S at Camp Minnesota, so although the sun was always above the horizon, there was a marked difference between noon and midnight.

> *26 Nov. Sun.* I was wide awake at 0400 due to the heat. It was cold when I went to bed, but warmed up a lot.

Unlike the old orange Sno-Cats, our new #743 models were painted black, which absorbed heat well and kept the insides quite warm throughout the summer. Heaters were rarely used. Lee Kreiling had made canvas flaps, which hung down over the front grill. Inside we would open the 6-inch by 2-foot-wide horizontal hinged door to the engine covering and let the heat warm the vehicle. On the warmest days, we would roll up the canvas covers on the grill to avoid overheating the engines.

> I got up at 0700 and helped Con Merrick cook breakfast. Everyone worked at getting ready. Con and I filled the three remaining tires of the Rollitrailer. We used 41 drums [55 gallons each] of diesel fuel, including filling the Sno-Cats. We still have four drums.

I wore leather mittens with wool inserts and the diesel fuel soaked the leather and splashed our black cargo pants and parkas. Working around Sno-Cats is certainly different from using sled dogs or snowmobiles. We were always ripping clothes on the heavy vehicles and sleds. Fuel was always leaving traces on our clothes and we smelled more like garage mechanics or big-rig drivers than traditional Antarctic explorers.

I always wore my black "many pockets" wind pants, held up by suspenders. These suspenders attached to the sides only, so one could easily drop one's pants when defecating in a driving wind. On top I usually wore a heavy knit sweater, which I had bought in White Horse, Yukon in 1959. Over this while outside in wind or cold I wore a Gerry pullover anorak. As mentioned earlier, the orange zipper parkas furnished in these seasons ripped easily on the vehicles. Beneath my outer clothes I wore two-piece waffle-weave long underwear, and under that briefs, which I changed only once or twice during the next three months. There was no opportunity to wash anything or to change my outer clothes.

The others wore either personal clothes or the USARP orange issue parkas. Hiro had his own yellow windbreaker anorak, and Perry and John had a lot of their own clothes.

I also wore a belt and because of the need for mittens when working outside, carried a big Army field knife (in a sheath). I used the knife to cut wire, blasting cord, food, to open cans, and to dig holes for geophones in hard-packed snow. I broke the very tip off this knife prying something open and felt a real regret. I still have this knife, although I only carry a tiny Swiss Army knife now.

> We ate lunch at 1400 and dinner at 2200. Perry got the ANGRC/19 on the air at 2130 and I sent my first sitrep [situation report].

50. Jones Mountains as viewed from Camp Minnesota. Sno-Cat in distance. Note geologic unconformity between 12-million-year-old, black volcanic rocks (basalts) overlying a flat erosion surface above pink granite 200 million years old.

Perry or I operated the AN/GRC 19 125-watt transceiver we used to communicate by voice across Antarctica. This was mounted in *Barbara*, on the left side just aft of the small radio. I would write out a situation report daily, giving our position and other information, including weather. One of us would read this out to the Byrd Station operator and write down any incoming messages.

I also sent a message to Phil Smith asking for a first-aid kit.

What a contrast to the extremely elaborate medical supplies we carried on the Filchner Ice Shelf Traverse.[2] We traveled for the next several weeks with essentially no first-aid supplies.

Con and I got our faces sunburned today although it clouded up for several hours. It is really quite beautiful here when the sun is shining as the mountains rise up several thousand feet just a mile from camp.

The 1500-meter-high (5000-foot) Jones Mountains, as viewed from the north side, display a spectacular geologic unconformity between 12-million-year-old, black volcanic rocks (basalts) overlying a flat erosion surface above pink granite 200 million years old. Campbell Craddock and his Minnesota party (see above) had reported glacial striae the previous season on this erosion surface where it was overlain by the volcanic rock just above the unconformity, which indicated that the Antarctic Ice Sheet was present more than 12 million years ago.

Pete Wasilewski's inexperience got him into quite an adventure one of these nights, but I did not find out about it at the time. He wanted a geologic sample, and while everyone else was sleeping, started up the mountain. Pete took the mattock used for digging snow pits as a substitute for an ice ax. He intended to climb up the steep snow to the edge of the rock face, but his boots slipped and he came tumbling down. He tried to stop himself with the mattock, but having no training in ice ax self-arrest techniques, he lost his grip and the mattock. He was not injured, but had to "fess up" when Hiro could not find the mattock just before we left the area.

Although Pete, Lee Kreiling, and Con Merrick had no experience in Antarctica or mountaineering before this season, the other four of us had years of Antarctic field experience behind us. Lee Kreiling, Perry Parks, Hiro Shimizu, John Molholm, and I had all wintered over at various Antarctic stations. John, Hiro, Perry, and I had been on several traverses each. Hiro, John, and I also had a lot of mountaineering experience, and Con Merrick was an experienced topographic engineer in the United States.

I was the only person who had experience in operating Sno-Cats in crevassed areas (on the Filchner Ice Shelf Traverse of 1957–58).[3] The previous oversnow traverses out of Byrd, in which the others had participated, were all essentially in crevasse-free areas of the West Antarctic Ice Sheet. We hoped the Antarctic Peninsula Traverse that we were about to start would be the same.

Since the mid-1960s, a very good field safety program has been run by NSF at McMurdo, providing at least rudimentary instruction in crevasse rescue and other snow emergency techniques for all personnel who might find themselves in survival situations. I have taken this 36-hour course in Antarctica a couple of times (as recently as 1990) and relearned a few things I had forgotten. Camping out, building snow shelters, and so forth prevents panic and gives people new to Antarctica confidence that they can survive in these conditions.

I was pulling the Rolli today with *Barbara* when the forward differential on the Sno-Cat went out. I hope this doesn't happen too often. Lee replaced the differential, and all vehicles are up now.

51. Shimizu barefoot in snow, just before entering hut at Camp Minnesota.

The loss of one of the small one-ton sleds during the winter at Camp Minnesota required that we load about half a ton of explosives on the flat bed of the Rollitrailer, which added a significant additional load.

All of our new Sno-Cats had A-frames and winches on the front so we could lift the side of a vehicle to repair it, or lift something out of a crevasse.

We still have Sno-Cat *Hootmon* from last year as they didn't bring a loading ramp for the second three C-130 flights. We saved 250 gallons of mogas [automotive gasoline] from the Rolli when we emptied it to make room for diesel fuel. We hope to drive *Hootmon* to Sky-Hi. It will have to operate on white gas also, of which we have about 200 gallons.

*27 Nov. Mon.* Clear and sunny all day. We hurried to get ready so we can leave tomorrow.

The three Sno-Cats were each equipped with a military 7.5-watt Angry 9 [AN/GRC9] radio with limited range. In the era of vacuum tubes, these olive-green, heavy, "small" Army radios were about 2 feet high, 1.5 feet wide, and 7 inches deep. They were strapped into a rack that bolted to the wall just behind the driver. We could listen to a small speaker or as was normally the case because of vehicle noise, on headphones. The radio was always on while the Sno-Cats were being driven. A microphone on an elastic-coiled wire hung on a hook. A whip antenna mounted on the roof worked well between vehicles.

With three Sno-Cats constantly using radios, we needed names for them. In contrast, on the Filchner Ice Shelf Traverse with only two vehicles (numbers 1 and 2), no radio identifiers were necessary when communicating between vehicles.

I mounted the magnetic tank compasses, taken from the old Sno-Cats, and helped keep everything going. Con and Lee dug out the old runner assembly for the wanigan that blew away, and built a new sled, which is now loaded with fuel in drums.

I fried steak for dinner. It is quite cozy in the Jamesway even if it is buried.

I took a picture of Hiro just outside the entrance to the Jamesway, barefoot in the snow and holding his boots, one in each hand. He took them off just before climbing down the snow steps and entering the hut in traditional Japanese fashion.

*28 Nov. Tues.* Overcast all day. We finished up about all of the preparations. Perry completed checking out the radios, and then we fiddled with the magnetometers until past midnight.

Counting the weight of the seismic batteries, the entire seismic equipment weighed about 1500 pounds, which was primarily because of the vacuum tubes. Therefore we had to carry the gear in a Sno-Cat that only got about one mile per gallon. For safety we needed three Sno-Cats. Thus, the vacuum tube dictated the logistics of the oversnow traverse program.

Hiro and I went over the maps about a week earlier at Byrd and worked out a route for the first part of the traverse prior to reaching Sky-Hi.

From Camp Minnesota to 74°S, 90° (an ice-movement stake area left the previous season by the Ellsworth Highland Traverse, [EHT]). Then we will head to 76°58.5'S, 81°41'W (EHT mile #972), to a radar-reported nunatak at about 74°8'S, 80°15'W, thence to Sky-Hi [which has not been established yet].

The only maps we had were the rather crude air navigation charts used by the Navy. These were quite small scale (about 1:2,100,000) and were useful primarily as plotting charts. Only a few nunataks were shown in the area we were going to, based on the flight by Ellsworth flight in 1935 and the two Ronne flights in 1947 over George IV Sound and the Orville Escarpment south of the front of the Ronne Ice Shelf. All of the poorly located mountains were only seen to the side from distances of greater than 100 kilometers.

> *29 Nov. Wed.* All ready to go in the morning, but the weather clouded up on us. We waited.

I wanted good visibility because I was concerned about getting past the crevasses at the east end of the Jones Mountains, which we had seen from the air. The snow surface to the south of the 1500-meter-high Jones Mountains rises to about 1700 meters (5500 feet), or about 200 meters higher than the highest peaks. We needed to climb up an east-west-trending ridge to about 1200 meters.

> People slept a lot today, as we have all been working about 18 hours/day since we got here. It became nearly a whiteout. I went to bed about 1900 and slept until the next morning. ◆

# ELEVEN

# Camp Minnesota to Sky-Hi

**30 Nov. Thurs.**

*It was clearing this morning, so we took off. By the time we finally got going it was 1100. I figure we were moving about 100,000 pounds when started.*

We flew two American flags. I got a 48-star flag from Phil Smith before leaving McMurdo. Although Alaska and Hawaii had just been admitted as states, there were no 50-star flags available in Antarctica. Lee had mounted an aluminum pole for the flag on *Argo* just behind the driver's door, and we carried it across unexplored Antarctica. We did not make any claims, however; the Antarctic Treaty had just entered into force and no claims were now allowed. John Molholm put up a higher pole on *Barbara* and flew a bigger flag.

*Hootmon* broke a U-joint and one of the magnetometer cables was damaged. Even after these were repaired, it took several hours to get shaken down.

We towed the sensing heads of the two magnetometers on nonmagnetic fiberglass "half" akios about 40 feet behind the sleds or Rollitrailer to avoid the magnetic effects of the vehicles.

Hiro and I went first in *Argo,* accompanied by John and Con in *Barbara.* The others followed four miles and about one hour behind in *Tamare Riatia* and *Hootmon,* so we could get double occupation of magnetic and altimeter stations. I pulled the ice-core box (a 6-foot by 4-foot, by about 10-foot-long refrigerator on a sled) and the 2–1/2-ton sled full of drums. *Barbara* had the three small sleds, which needed some fixing quite soon and thus caused us another delay. Perry and Pete in

*Tamare* pulled the wanigan sled, and Lee pulled the Rollitrailer with *Hootmon*. The Rolli hitch broke and a few more things went wrong, which we fixed.

The Sno-Cats headed east from Camp Minnesota along the front of the Jones Mountains. We dropped about 300 feet and then pulled up again. Although I could see some crevasses to our right, we never came close to any. By mile #24 we were climbing up around the east end of the range.

The first 10–15 miles I drove very gingerly, using the Polaroid photographs we had taken from the plane during our reconnaissance prior to our landing as a map. We continued south until mile #40 and camped.

Mile #40, 73°34'S, 93°09'W.

Con Merrick,[1] a USGS topographic engineer, was our navigator. Using a theodolite and U.S. National Bureau of Standards radio station WWV to check his chronometer regularly, he was shooting stars to obtain positions at our overnight stops accurate to about ±200 meters (about 600 feet). He had an astronomical almanac, which allowed him to precompute the time a particular star would come into the field of view of his (telescopic) theodolite. He would note the time to about 0.01 seconds using a stopwatch. Stars are quite observable even in daylight, if one knows exactly where to look with a telescope. Using star shots from a theodolite on a tripod was quite a bit more accurate than using a sextant in a moving, sideways drifting, unstable plane, to measure the elevation of the sun above the horizon at these high polar latitudes.

Merrick would also determine true north astronomically and therefore magnetic north using a precise magnetic compass. We could then correct for magnetic declination for the tank compass I steered by in *Argo*. The IGY traverses originally were supplied with fragile, expensive gyrocompasses, mainly because of the generally false impression that magnetic compasses do not work in Antarctica. Despite this myth to the contrary (particularly among pilots), magnetic compasses work very well in Antarctica except very close to the south magnetic pole, more than 2000 miles away from our traverse. The mistaken impression comes from the very high magnetic declination due to the geometric effect of the convergence of longitude at the poles. For example, if one were to walk around the geographic south pole (the location of South Pole Station) holding a magnetic compass, the needle would obviously point in the same direction all of the time, but the magnetic declination would have changed 360°.

By 1960 we had changed to Army surplus magnetic tank compasses. These worked very well and were rugged enough not to be damaged by the rough ride of the vehicle.

*1 Dec. Fri.* We got going about noon. Clear and sunny as we drove over rolling terrain to the southeast. Lee had much trouble with *Hootmon* over-heating and eventually Perry pulled the Rollitrailer with *Tamare Riatia*.

We were settling into a routine. Lee, our regular breakfast cook as well as mechanic, would rise first, heat water, wash his hands, and start making breakfast. I was second up and got to wash my hands in the still-warm water Lee had used. Each successive man had dirtier and colder water to wash in, until the later ones just stayed dirty. Clean, however, was a relative term. All the water, of course, had to be melted on a two-burner Coleman stove that burned white gas.

I woke Perry just prior to our departure so he could read the magnetometer and four altimeters in *Tamare Riatia* at the same time we read the second magnetometer and another set of four altimeters in *Argo*. The others never needed to get up and start readying themselves as long as I was in camp, as we would take about an hour to arrive at the next four-mile station, which gave them plenty of time.

Con Merrick would take a number of sun and star shots throughout the period we were camped to obtain an accurate position. When mountains and nunataks were visible, Con had a very busy schedule surveying these as well. At this time, however, there was only the featureless snow horizon to see.

We roared out of camp at a speed usually between three and five miles per hour. The noise of the engine and the clatter of the tracks drowned out any conversation. The driver, wearing headphones connected to the Angry 9 radio mounted on the wall immediately behind him, was in constant radio contact with *Tamare Riatia* and *Barbara*. There was no radio in *Hootmon*. There was always a bit of high frequency noise from the speaker behind the driver, and occasionally a call from Perry: "*Argo*, this is *Tamare Riatia*." The driver would turn and grab the mike from its hook on the radio behind. "*Tamare Riatia*, this is *Argo*." The message, which could only be clearly understood over the noise in the vehicle by the driver wearing headphones, would usually be an indication of some minor or major trouble with the vehicles or sleds.

At an even four miles, *Argo* would stop and mark a station with a small red flag. Hiro or I would call Perry and let him know we were there. Then, simultaneously with Perry at the previous flag four miles back, we would read four pairs of surveying altimeters and the two magnetometers. In this way we were able to

52. *Argo* pulling Rollitrailer. Magnetometer sensor is towed behind.

correct for changes in air pressure and the magnetic field during the past hour.

Pete Wasilewski routinely read the second proton magnetometer at intervals throughout the period we were camped, and made other magnetic observations. We used his averages as the absolute value at that station. Perry also read the large LaCoste Romberg gravity meter every four miles, using a tripod dropped through a hole in the floor of *Tamare Riatia*.

At these four-mile stations, the driver of *Argo* at the time would read the altimeters and magnetometer, while another (Hiro or I) used a sling psychrometer to measure the temperature accurately (to about one degree) in the shade to correct the altimeter measurements. This involved swinging the instrument so that the bulb end of the thermometer moved rapidly through the air. Even in the shade, there was so much background solar radiation that the temperature would rise almost immediately.

I usually drove at the beginning of the day and Hiro the second half. When not driving I was likely to pull off my rubber thermal boots and crawl into my sleeping bag for a nap (or read) for an hour or less. The Sno-Cat would lurch and bounce over the rough sastrugi, as each of the four separately articulated pontoons climbed and dropped abruptly. I was glad that the slight sag in my canvas bunk acted as a basket to hold me in place. Every hour, I would abruptly awake when the vehicle stopped, pull my boots on, and stagger sleepily out to

53. View behind Rollitrailer. The trail is straight despite wobbles.

measure the temperature. Then I would get back into the bunk to sleep or read for another four miles.

We split the distance traveled each day (usually 32 miles as measured on the odometer),[2] and the driver would follow the compass course determined by Con Merrick in advance using the magnetic tank compass. The driver was extremely busy. The magnetic compass floated in a fluid and bounced around, varying plus or minus 5 or 10 degrees either side of our projected course. Nonetheless it worked. Standing on the roof of a stopped Sno-Cat and sighting back along the track I could see large curves marking our weaving, but these averaged to a straight line. Although the three new Sno-Cats each had a compass, usually the other vehicles just followed *Argo's* tracks.

At 0.5-mile intervals, the driver would switch on the Varian proton magnetometer and read the vibrating reed indicator, interpolating to the nearest five units,[3] and record the result, as well as the mileage, in a data book. He would also read one of the altimeters to one meter or so precision and record that. The driver also had to be on the lookout for any crevasses, or mountains that might suddenly appear in the distance or through the fog and clouds. At the 4-mile stations the driver would carefully read each of the four altimeters.

Perry and Pete thought our routine in *Argo* was too hectic for them, so one drove and the other recorded the same observations we made in *Argo*. They also traded off, about halfway through a day's drive. However, they never got to rest during the day, and were much more fatigued by the time we got to camp and started our seismic and glaciology work.

We are flying two flags on *Argo* now. Just before we started today, Hiro broke out a Japanese flag and asked if he could put it up. I agreed and he attached it from the same mast below the American flag. We stopped at mile #80 with the last Sno-Cats arriving at 0230.

Mile #80, 73°48'S, 91°25'W

We were retracing part of the Ellsworth Highland Traverse of the previous year as we worked our way to the southeast, so we did not make any seismic or glaciology stations for the first several days.

*2 Dec. Sat.* We got going again after a breakfast of spam at 1415. I pulled the Rolli. At mile #84 we ran into very hard sastrugi, up to a meter high. While starting here, I broke the chain connected to the Rollitrailer. The trailer rolled back over the magnetometer sled, crushing the sled. We retied the chain, pulled the Rolli off the sled, and I punched the sensing head back through the bottom. It worked fine.

The big sastrugi made it a very grueling ride. Twice Hiro was knocked out of his bunk onto the deck as I was driving. Perry lost some barrels off his sled and had to go back for them, which delayed us about four hours. It began to cloud up late in the day and there were patches of ground fog.

*3 Dec. Sun.* We finally all arrived at mile #112 at 0545. Our dead reckoning showed we should be at the movement stake area set by Charlie Bentley last February. John saw one of the stakes about half a mile ahead, which cheered Con and me. Perhaps we will find our way around here after all. We got to bed about 0730 after a steak dinner.

Unlike on the Filchner Ice Shelf Traverse where I did most of the cooking,[4] I cooked only occasionally on the Antarctic Peninsula Traverse. Lee usually made breakfast and the others took turns at dinners. We snacked during the driving.

I got up about 1400 and puttered around the Sno-Cat. It was cloudy with occasional breaks to let the sun through. Lee got up about 1445. I told

54. View of vehicles in ground blizzard.

him Hiro and I were going out to look for flags at the measurement stakes, and we would be back in time for breakfast.

We drove to the one nearest camp and then out a mile or so. I finally saw two more, but the visibility became obscured. We decided to go back for breakfast, but couldn't see the Sno-Cats. I drove back on our tracks.

By the time breakfast in *Hootmon* was finished, the wind had come up and there was much blowing snow. The storm steadily built up all day and was blowing about 30 knots by 2100. Lee welded the broken tow bar for the Rolli in spite of the bad weather. We ate dehydrated steak and rice, which I cooked. Everyone went to bed about 0100 to wait the storm out.

Mile 112, 73°56'S, 90°01'W.

*4 Dec. Mon.* It stormed all day with increasing wind and more snow-fall, causing heavy drifting. We slept or read in our own cats most of the day. By 2100 most of us were up and congregating in *Hootmon* for supper.

I sat with my back to the rear door, which I had carefully sealed with crumpled toilet paper to keep the wind and drifting snow out. Just as the last missed gap was blocked and we felt no more snow blowing in, someone opened the door from the outside to come in and all of my work blew away in an instant.

55. Parks in front of Sno-Cat.

The poor individual who entered was surprised at the hostile looks and loud complaints that greeted him.

This storm made me appreciate the luxury of the plywood privy Hiro had built—a standard toilet seat nailed to a wood frame that stood on the snow inside the privy and which in turn was situated over a dug or drilled hole. The protection from the driving wind and snow was highly valued by the traverse party.

> *5 Dec. Tues.* Continuing storm all day. There was still much drifting snow and no visibility. Much new snow has fallen.

Generally there is very little snow accumulation in Antarctica and storms just blow the surface snow around. However, we were near the coast of the Bellingshausen Sea in one of the areas of highest snow accumulation on the continent, north of the divide of the West Antarctic Ice Sheet.

> We have made no radio contact since mile #32. Probably the magnetic storm [we have been experiencing] was associated with a communications blackout.

> *6 Dec. Wed.* The storm seemed to be letting up today, but towards

56. Digging out after storm. Kreilings repair shop at left; ice core refrigerator at right.

evening the weather got worse. We still have no radio contact.

*7 Dec. Thurs.* Hiro came into *Hootmon* for a drink about 0200 and I wished him "Happy Pearl Harbor Day!" We reminisced about the events 20 years ago. It seems strange to be here on the 20th anniversary of World War II beginning with a Japanese person in a Sno-Cat flying the U.S. and Japanese flags. Times change.

The storm blew harder than ever, and the pressure dropped an amount equivalent to 160 meters elevation change.

We almost had a radio contact tonight when Byrd answered our call once and then faded out.

*8 Dec. Fri.* It started to clear this morning so we dug out and started moving.

Digging out was easier said than done, because the snow had drifted tight around all our equipment and covered anything that had been left flat instead of vertical. Fortunately we did not lose anything, but the bed of the Rollitrailer was completely filled. This work took several hours. We had been stopped by the storm for five days.

I felt we had lost too much time in the storm, so we didn't survey the movement stakes. Visibility was quite limited. The soft snow made pulling the Rolli quite difficult, and we drove in second gear at about 3–4 miles per hour.

We had a good radio contact tonight and Perry got our traffic out and received several messages for us. They are sending a one ton sled to Sky-Hi [toward which we were heading] for us and want to know our ETA [estimated time of arrival] there for scheduling a C-130 flight.

We had not had any radio contact since we left Camp Minnesota and arrived at Mile #32, so our sitreps had not been sent out. USARP had become concerned about us and had informed Charlie Bentley in Madison. He in turn informed Donna, my wife, and told her that they were planning to send out a search and rescue (SAR) flight in a few days if radio contact were not made. As we were 144 miles out of Camp Minnesota at the end of this day, it would have been difficult for an aircraft to have found us even with radar.

It cleared through the day and was 0°F when we stopped at mile #144 about 2200. Hiro and I started fueling and finished soon after the others came. *Hootmon* and *Barbara* both stayed in the rear today with *Tamare Riatia* so Lee could get some relief driving.

We continued this way through the rest of the traverse, later with Con riding in *Argo* so we had three in the forward vehicle for safety, in case we encountered crevasses.

Mile 144, 74°06'S, 88°37'W.

*9 Dec. Sat.* I bounded out at 0820, and got Hiro up. We ate breakfast in a hurry, read the instruments, and pulled out about 0915.

It was clear and cold with a building wind all day. We broke a magnetometer cable, but replaced it satisfactorily.

There are many hills and valleys around, which are hard pulling with the Rollitrailer. We got stuck about 1930 in soft snow, but got out after much jockeying back and forth. We stopped about 2145 at mile 192 having driven 48 miles. Tomorrow we will leave the route of the Ellsworth Highland Traverse and proceed toward the Bryan Coast of the Bellingshausen Sea, which we flew toward on our recon flight on 5 November.

Some are not too happy to be pushing as hard as this, but we have to make up for lost time somehow.

Each Sno-Cat burned about one gallon per mile of fuel so on this day we needed to pump about 48 gallons into each vehicle. This was accomplished by connecting hoses to a fuel tire on the Rollitrailer and connecting an air compressor to the tire being drained. This operation went relatively rapidly but was always a messy job.

There were always other chores such as cooking, rearranging the equipment on the sleds, and melting snow for water. As our days progressed, our camp routine became quite efficient.

The three new Sno-Cats had a bunk bed on each side, with a 4-inch-thick foam pads for a mattress. Each of us had a double Army mummy-type sleeping bag consisting of 40 percent down and 60 percent feathers enclosed in a strong cotton fabric. The outer bag had a nylon lining so the inner bag could slide easily. These were too heavy for backpacking but excellent for our needs.

The seismic equipment was mounted on the shelf on the left side of *Tamare Riatia,* so there was no room above for a bunk. Perry slept on the floor, and Pete on the bunk on the right side. John Molholm, Lee Kreiling, and Con Merrick shared space in *Barbara.*

Mile 192, 74°15'S, 86°21'W.

*10 Dec. Sun.* We got going about 1000, but the Rollitrailer got stuck in soft snow about 3.5 miles out of camp. I tried several ways, but finally had to call back for help. It took *Hootmon* and *Argo* both to pull the Rolli out of the soft snow [using a cable between the vehicles]. We tried to go again, but got stuck a couple more times. Finally we traded loads with *Hootmon* so the Rolli could follow a broken trail. With *Argo* and *Barbara* in front this worked quite well.

When the Sno-Cats made tracks in soft snow, there was mixing of deeper (colder at this time of year) snow with the surface snow. The temperature difference caused a hardening after an hour or so. Because the other Sno-Cats traveled an hour behind *Argo* the track was quite hard and the Rollitrailer pulled more easily. Immediately after it passed, the Rollitrailer tracks would be quite soft to walk in, but an hour later seemed as hard as pavement. This "sintering" phenomenon was used in making runways for wheeled aircraft on the snow surface with some success, particularly by the Soviet Antarctic expeditions.

> After 16 miles (to mile 200) we turned east northeast off the Ellsworth Highland Traverse trail and descended over 100 meters before stopping at mile 224.

We would now be entering unexplored territory.

> I started to lay out the seismic spread and found that we had lost a reel of cable off the Rolli. Fortunately, we have a spare. Next we found that one of the seismic batteries had low voltage so we couldn't shoot tonight. Therefore we will have to spend tomorrow here, which is welcome news to everyone but me.
>
> A few days ago when I nearly forgot to place a small flag at one of our four-mile stations, Hiro got out his felt tip marking pen and drew a flag in the corner of the windshield and wrote *vergissmeinnicht* under it. I smile each time I look at it—and I don't forget the flags.

Mile 224, 74°14'S, 84°46'W.

> *11 Dec. Mon.* Everyone slept quite late today. I laid out the other cable before breakfast.

The procedure we used was essentially the same as described in chapter 3 for the previous year's airborne traverse. However, on the oversnow traverses we used a 24-channel system and two 330-meter-long cables with 12 geophones each usually laid out in an L-shaped array with the Sno-Cat at the apex. I would normally lay out each of the 330-meter-long cables and connect the geophones, while the other two Sno-Cats were driving the last four miles. I would also usually drill the shot hole. When Perry arrived, he would warm up the photographic solutions on a Coleman stove and operate the instruments in *Tamare Riatia*, while I fired several shots. I would come into *Tamare Riatia* and examine the record after it was photographically developed for each shot and decide whether and how to shoot and record the next shot. Perry and I would then each pick up one of the seismic cables and the 12 geophones connected to it. Perry would also wash the records in water and hang them on a wire (left from a fired blasting cap) inside *Tamare Riatia*.

We had to change a battery with *Hootmon*. This took some time to fix and when we were ready to shoot, the tuning fork in the camera started to burn up. Finally this was fixed and we fired a shot, but I didn't get the camera running in time. The next shot misfired. The cap went off in the primer but didn't detonate it. This can be dangerous; I hope it doesn't happen again. Finally we got a shot off and recorded a strong reflection with a multiple. It looks like the ice is only 1 kilometer thick here, which makes rock about +100 meters or about 200 meters higher than EHT mile #1044. We shot a couple of shots and rolled up the spread. I tried to make the radio sked, but couldn't reach Byrd. It was 2200 when we ate supper.

Perry worked after supper on a few more bugs in the seismic gear, while I plotted up some of our elevation, magnetic and ice thickness results.

I kept a continuous profile for the whole traverse of preliminary results. This profile, plotted every day, was quite interesting and exciting, as well as scientifically important. We were not only exploring unknown geographic terrain, but the changes in the surface and bedrock elevation combined with the magnetic anomalies gave us a three-dimensional picture of the apparently flat featureless snow surface. The surface slope changed so gradually that everything looked the same as we drove along. Yet, throughout the traverse, we were encountering several kilometers of change in surface elevation and bedrock configuration.

*12 Dec. Tues.* We got off at 0815 today and drove 32 miles to mile 256 uneventfully about 1600. The sky was mostly overcast, but cleared slowly as a strong wind built up. I laid out a spread and drilled a 4-meter hole by the time the other cats got here. Hiro and John dug their first 4-meter pit and worked quite late after that. After supper, about 1800, we shot several times, including two air blasts [shots fired in the air using a charge suspended from a pole]. The rock is now somewhat below sea level. We were all packed up by radio time at 2130. I wish every day could go as smoothly as this.

The 35-knot wind kept the cats quite cold, even though the air temperature was up to +5°F at 2300.

These black Sno-Cats absorb a lot of heat from the sun. When the wind blows, drifting snow sticks to the warm lee side when the sun is shining on it and melts. The melt water runs down the side and forms icicles, which project out away from the side as the wind directs. I broke off quite an amount of ice this way to use for making water in *Tamare Riatia* tonight. [Apparently I wasn't worried about any paint contamination in our drinking water.]

Mile 256, 74°13'S, 83°15'W.

*13 Dec. Wed.* We got going early and left camp at 0800. The wind was blowing stronger and increased all day getting up to 40 knots by evening. *Argo* arrived at mile 262, where we got a call from Perry. He and the others hadn't started yet. We waited and then got a call saying that *Hootmon* had broken a differential. We had only one spare, and I didn't want to use it on *Hootmon*. Lee thought he could fix it to run only on the front tracks and pull a light load. Later Perry called and said that the transmission was also damaged and that Lee would put it permanently in one gear. Later he called and said that they had broken an oil line in getting at the transmission.

I drove *Argo* back to mile 260 to wait as snow was drifting our tracks over and I was afraid that the others would not be able to follow. Perry called again and said that they planned to start soon because everything was apparently fixed. He called later and said that they had apparently put the transmission in the wrong gear, and *Hootmon* wouldn't move. They had also rebroken the oil line, the cable on *Barbara*'s winch, and the sensing head on their magnetometer. The latter broke as they pulled away, and the little sled with the magnetometer sensing head had drifted in.

I decided to abandon *Hootmon*, as it was 1930. I drove *Argo* back, and we camped at mile 256. The wind was terrific, but I found my way along the old tracks without too much difficulty. There were five-foot drifts around camp, and the pit was completely filled. Snow static was so bad I could hardly hear anything on the radio.

Snow static resulted from snow blowing against the antenna. We could produce a half-inch spark from the static charge built up in this way across a gap created by disconnecting the antenna.

It was a pretty tough day for the crew back at 256.

In addition to the failed repairs, they had to move sleds around and disconnect and reconnect them, all in the driving wind.

We ate our last meal in *Hootmon* tonight. I wish we could have gotten it to Sky-Hi.

*14 Dec. Thurs.* Lee overslept and we didn't pull out until 1020. The wind was still blowing 35 knots and it was very unpleasant outside, as it never got above +4°F all day. We managed to follow the old tracks fairly well for the first 6 miles. Perry had a hard time reading the gravity meter due to the wind and his cat could only pull the Rolli in 2nd gear, so progress was quite slow.

If we had been using Snowmobiles or dogs in this weather we would not have been able to travel at all. Forward visibility was very limited when the wind blew above 20–30 knots because of drifting snow but I had only to follow the compass blindly and read the instruments inside the cab. Of course this assumed there were no crevasses. Perry also read the gravity meter inside *Tamare Riatia*. Probably the limiting factor was the trailing vehicles' ability to follow our tracks one hour behind as the wind drifted them over.

The snow static got so bad by mile 284 that we couldn't use our receiver and had to wait until the other cats came up before we proceeded. It was 2313 when we pulled into mile 288 and I started to lay out the seismic spread. There was so much blowing snow I couldn't see the Sno-Cat from the end of the line. The sastrugi were so hard that I had to chop holes with my ice ax to put in a bamboo pole or plant a geophone.

There was no danger of my getting lost in the driving snow because I could follow the cable back to *Argo*.

Mile 288, 74°11'S, 81°41'W.

*15 Dec. Fri.* It was about 0200 when the other cats had arrived and we got two shots off, recording a good reflection in spite of the wind. [We electronically filtered out the high frequency wind noise.] The rock is

57. Behrendt warming up inside Sno-Cat during storm.

much the same level as yesterday. Hiro cooked supper in *Argo* and we ate there. It was 0400 before we got to bed.

John woke us at 1130 for breakfast in *Barbara*. It was still blowing 30 knots and becoming overcast. There was no surface visibility in the direction we wanted to head, so I decided to wait for the weather to clear. We spent this day working at various tasks. Lee repaired a couple of heaters and I calculated the ice thickness at the previous station and plotted the elevation and magnetics.

In general the rock is fluctuating near sea level and the snow surface is around 900 meters.

We had steak in *Argo* after the radio sked. I cooked.

16 Dec. Sun. The weather cleared about 1400 although the wind was blowing a gale. I woke everyone so we could get going. It was miserable digging drifts away. Perry tried to pull the Rolli out and broke the rear differential and universal joint in *Tamare Riatia*. A piece of gear came flying out the rear cover, tearing a hole about three inches long. Lee swore mightily and set to work fixing it, while the rest of us dragged out canvas to make a wind screen around the area. We got the rest of the sleds

out using the two cats and a cable.

Pete dug all the snow away from the front of the Rolli so it could be pulled forward when *Tamare Riatia* got fixed. Meanwhile the rest of us hooked up *Barbara* and *Argo* and pulled the Rolli out backwards. Pete was quite disappointed. He must not have been too tired though, because later in the day I saw him chinning himself on *Argo*'s A-frame.

The wind and blowing snow plastered our beards, eyebrows, eyelashes, and sunglasses with ice. We had dinner in *Argo* about 2200 and Lee finished up shortly.

*17 Dec. Sun.* It was about 0200 when we finally got ready to move out. The wind was blowing 35 knots with gusts of 40, and the snow static completely knocked out the receivers. Con, Hiro, and I drove out about 0.8 miles, but lost radio contact. As we are approaching a mountain sighted on radar on our recon flight, there may be crevasses. Consequently I don't feel safe without radio contact or visibility. We didn't see the other Sno-Cats until we were within 100 feet as we returned.

At this point I decided that pushing so hard in a storm was counter-productive. We only damaged equipment and wasted everyone's energy and time. We all went over to Barbara and drank some whisky before going to bed after what was a tiring and fruitless day.

---

The wind was down to 20 knots and there was no snow static when I got everyone out at noon. We got moving at 1355, but had very slow going due to heavy sastrugi. Our magnetometer cables and sleds needed continual attention, as the rough surface damaged them. The small one-ton sleds started breaking, which caused much delay to the second party. The tow bar of the Rollitrailer broke about 2100 when we had come about nine miles. *Barbara* had to come forward with a cable, and we used that. This broke and had to be repaired.

Meanwhile we had come into sight of a nunatak about 1620 and changed our course 35° and headed toward it.

The nunatak is Mt. Tuve; Con Merrick's final USGS surveyed position is 73°47'S, 80°08'W. Ronne indicated a peak on a map[5] at 74°00'S, 85°00 W about 160 kilometers to the southwest of Mt. Tuve, which he reported from a flight in

1947. He named this peak Mt. Tuve, but we could find no peak in that area on our recon flight on 12 November.

> We descended and could see water sky and possibly the sea about 30° to the left [of our route].

We could see what later was named Eltanin Bay at the coast of the Bellingshausen Sea.

> *18 Dec. Mon.* We reached mile 300 exactly at midnight. As we approached the mountain about 20 to 30 miles ahead we could see dark rock outcrops along the left-hand skyline of the snow cone of the peak. By mile 308, which we reached at 0425, we had dropped 250 meters from mile 288 and could no longer see the peak. I decided to change course 75° right and climb up a bit.

At this point we were about 18 miles (25 kilometers) from the coast.

> The peak we are approaching is one of two mapped by radar on our recon flight. There is another south of this one which we haven't seen yet.
>
> We waited at mile 308 and at 0540 heard from *Tamare Riatia* that the wanigan sled had lost a runner and would need several hours to repair. We established radio skeds at 0830, 1200, 1500, and 1600 progressively. We ate some soup and canned macaroni and got some sleep. Con is traveling with us now and slept on the floor in an extra sleeping bag of mine. The other crew took a runner from the 2–1/2-ton sled and rebuilt the wanigan sled with it. They stopped for chow, but when I talked with Perry 30 minutes ago (1600) they wanted to keep on going. The weather has improved and the wind is quite low so I'm for going on if they aren't too tired. They have been up for 28 hours now.

There was no point in our going back to help them because they had enough people for the job (four) and it would have been a waste of time (and fuel).

---

> When they were ready, we started about 1640 and continued downhill for a while, before starting up [on the same course]. We climbed steadily over

rough sastrugi until we stopped at mile 320 about 2050. The others didn't get in until 2345. By this time I had the complete spread out and Con drilled a 4-meter hole. We had clam chowder with rice before going to bed.

Mile 320, 74°03'S, 80°30'W.

*19 Dec. Tues.* It was overcast this morning when we got up. The wind was picking up and some snow fell. We shot our reflection and prepared for an additional seismic experiment but the weather worsened until visibility was reduced to 100 yards or so. Lee welded the tongue back on the Rollitrailer.

We changed to +5 time (Eastern Standard Time in U.S.) at 2300.

In trying to reach Byrd tonight, I raised the P2V flying in and gave our sitrep to them. They passed a message to us from Byrd giving the location of Sky-Hi as 75°18'S, 78°00'W. These coordinates sound too nice and even. I suspect they are a plane navigator's position and could be in error several miles. That's about 100 statute miles from here.

*20 Dec. Sun.* We got up to do seismic work and found a clear sky and 40 knots of wind from the south. As the wind yesterday was from the northeast our whole camp layout is not the best and drift is happening fast. The wind increased a bit and was gusting over 50 knots. Maximum visibility was about 70 feet, which is less than the spacing between the farthest vehicles. The gusts nearly blew me over walking across camp. This miserable wind is destroying my traverse!

*21 Dec. Thurs. Midsummer's Day.* It stormed all day and we slept in. I had a voice conference with Ken Moulton at Byrd tonight. They will send the R4D-8 out to Sky-Hi for our recon of the proposed traverse route to the northeast. Moulton doesn't want to send the two differentials if we can do without them as they are in short supply. I told him we need them anyway.

*22 Dec. Fri.* I got up about 1800 today, when the wind began to die down. I rousted out the rest and dug out a drifted seismic cable while John and Con were getting breakfast. One reel for the seismic cable was missing in the high drifts around *Tamare Riatia*. Perry and I probed and dug while the others got the rest of the stuff ready. It was clearing and the wind was down to 25–30 knots.

*23 Dec. Sat.* We must have dug tons of snow before we finally gave up on the lost [empty] reel about 0400 and ate dinner. [The seismic cable was hand coiled.] We were really tired at this point and all took a drink of Canadian Club mixed into fruit punch.

This energized us, so we got going. This is the only time we drank any alcohol before driving.

Two other nunataks came into view about 40° to the right of the one [Mt. Tuve] we have been watching for several days. Unfortunately clouds closed in on these before we had obtained compass bearings.

About 0600 Hiro, Con, and I drove out on a course for Sky-Hi. It had cleared and the wind was only 20 knots—the best weather in some time. We climbed as we headed southeast, until we reached 1200 meters at mile 352. The Rolli tongue broke at the weld and we rehitched with the cable. The others had trouble with loads falling off their sleds too.

While driving along about 0700 I heard Sky-Hi. I called them and Steve Barnes answered that he heard me loud and clear. I had a long chat with Floyd Johnson. They wanted to know where we were, and I got their position.[6] They have three nunataks in sight, including Mt. Rex, 27 miles north-northeast. The station lies in a north-south valley. The area looks good to the north and there are crevasses 15 miles to the east. Their elevation is about 450 meters, which is quite a bit lower than the (approx.) 1200 meters elevation here.

Their ham set is working well and a Wisconsin ham has been calling Sky-Hi asking about us. They have 100 gallons of water melted for us and a shower. We exchanged Christmas greetings and made a sked for tonight.

When we pulled into mile 352 at 1700 the sky was still clear, but by the time the others arrived snow was blowing at about 30 knots and the sky was obscured. I had both spreads laid out and the hole drilled when Perry pulled in. He was as tired as I've ever seen him and very disappointed that I planned to shoot tonight. He didn't even eat our steak supper, but went right to bed when we had finished about 2100. I reeled up one spread and left the other until morning.

I had been up for 27 hours, but had probably napped while Hiro was driving.

Mile 352, 74°22'S, 79°27'W.

*24 Dec. Sun.* It stormed all day with winds up in the 30 knot range. It was overcast, making a whiteout, which caused us to stumble over the drifts around camp. It is not nearly as unpleasant as the last storm and the drifts are quite soft due to the lower wind. We have parked everything for minimum drifting, which seems to be working out.

That is, we parked the vehicles and sleds broadside to the wind and away from each other so the lee side of one did not become the windward side of the other. Of course, the drifts built up on the lee sides of everything. The previous storm in which the wind had changed direction after half a day really gave us terrible drifts. The only positive thing I can say about snow drifts is that although hard to chop into, a shovel full of dry hard snow weighs a lot less than a shovel full of sand or dirt!

I got up about 1700 and went in to *Barbara.* No one else was up, but when I made up some clam chowder, John and Con rolled out to eat some. We all sat around and talked. I made contact with Byrd tonight and received Christmas greetings from Phil Smith at McMurdo and Allen F. Waterman, Director of NSF.

Perry got up about 2200 after sleeping about 26 hours and complained that his hands were numb. They show no signs of frostbite and appear normal. I hope it is nothing serious.

*25 Dec. Mon. Christmas* We ate dinner in *Argo* after the radio sked. It certainly doesn't seem like Christmas, in spite of all the snow. I went to bed about 0700. . . .

So went my fifth Christmas in Antarctica. I never even thought to mention what we ate for our Christmas dinner. This was the fourth storm since leaving Camp Minnesota and the delays were discouraging.

. . . I got up at 1800 and could see the other Sno-Cats, so I knew the weather was improving. By 1900 it was definitely breaking up, so I woke everyone and we ate rice and spam for breakfast. Con took a sunshot and we got going about 2100. We had about 80 miles to go to Sky-Hi and I figured to do it with one stop at 40 miles.

*26 Dec. Tues.* We soon ran into a fog limiting visibility to about 100 feet. We descended all the time and observed numerous gravity and magnetic anomalies.

The gravity anomalies resulted primarily from the irregular rock topography beneath the thin (0.4–1 kilometer) ice along this part of our route. The magnetic anomalies were caused by highly magnetic rock[7] at a shallow depth beneath the bedrock surface.

There was some concern expressed over possible crevasses. I didn't think there were any, but I watched the surface slope as shown by the altimeters for signs of a sudden steepening.

About 0600 at mile 381.7 we broke the front differential in *Argo*. The soft snow surface had been making pulling difficult and we had been in second gear all the while. The still air didn't cool the engine sufficiently and we had the hood open inside the Sno-Cat for additional cooling. It got so hot inside that we had the doors open. When we finally broke down I decided to put in a seismic station while Lee fixed the Sno-Cat. It was about +15°F and very pleasant.

It always seemed to be the Sno-Cat pulling the heavy Rollitrailer that broke the differentials.

We got going again in about five hours. The reflection showed the ice to be about 900 meters thick, which brings bedrock below sea level at this place.

*Argo* continued on until mile 404, arriving about 1710. I laid out the spread and drilled a hole by the time the rest came. We shot before dinner and found the ice is about 1.7 kilometers thick. The surface elevation is only about 400 meters, which places the rock over a kilometer below sea level. This is extremely interesting.

There is now known to be a deep trough between the Ellsworth Mountains and the southern Antarctic Peninsula. This sounding was the first evidence that the geology, structure, and topography of the Ellsworth Mountains is not continuous with the Antarctic Peninsula, as had been the conventional wisdom before this traverse.

Mile 404, 74°56'S, 78°00'W.

*27 Dec. Wed.* We got started about 0830 and drove for Sky-Hi with clearing overcast. *Tamare Riatia* broke down with a pontoon bearing out. As we waited about mile 414, nunataks began appearing out of the clouds. Our course seemed to be running somewhat parallel to an escarpment or rising snow surface off to the left. The nunataks [one was Mt. Peterson, named but mislocated by Ronne] project out of this, and Mt. Rex[8] is probably the southernmost of three small peaks.

We spotted Sky-Hi from about 12 miles out and arrived about 2020. It was sunny, warm and everyone came out to meet us. We had a large bag of mail waiting there, which was most welcome.

I luxuriated in my first hot "shower" since leaving Byrd Station in late November. I stood inside the warm Jamesway hut in a small plastic dish pan just big enough for my size 12 feet. Using a one-gallon tin can with holes punched in the bottom, I scooped from a bucket of water warmed on a space heater. Holding the can over my head with one hand and soap in the other, I managed to get fairly wet. After scrubbing as well as possible, I rinsed with a second can of hot water. This primitive shower felt wonderful at the time. It was my last bath until the end of the traverse in February.

There are seven people here besides us: Floyd Johnson (in charge), Pat Caywood, Gordon Angus, Chuck Neuner, Neil Brice, Jim Bunham, and Steve Barnes. The latter three will leave on a C-130, which will shortly come out with avgas, JATO, and stuff for us. They have three Jamesways, many and sundry antennas, cables, magnetometers, etc. scattered around the area. They also have some crevasses in sight to the east.

The Sky-Hi ham radio, KC4AAE, is working the best of any in Antarctica, and several of our fellows got phone patches.

This group of radio researchers was also the most electronically competent party in Antarctica that season. Because Sky-Hi was approximately at a magnetic conjugate point on the earth from Fort Churchill in the Canadian Arctic, simultaneous measurements at these two observatories proved valuable. A few years later, Eights Station was established at the site of Camp Sky-Hi and operated for several years. Subsequently, Siple Station was built about 200 kilometers to the west-southwest for similar radio studies and operated for some years until closed in the 1980s. ◆

# TWELVE

# Exploring the
# Southern Antarctic Peninsula

**W**e had been waiting for a reconnaissance flight into the unknown area to the east of Sky-Hi.

After supper on 28 December R4D-8 853, with Bob Farrington et al., flew in from Byrd with a lot of stuff and mail for us.

There were some letters from Donna and I was able to get a phone patch to her after I had read them. I told her we were about to make a recon flight into unexplored territory to our northeast and would give her a call in a few hours [which I later did].

We off-loaded the plane, put on fuel [which had been flown from McMurdo 1600 nautical miles away] and took off about 2145 with Perry, Hiro, Lee, Con, a National Geographic photographer, and me. A ground fog came in about the time we took off, and we had trouble seeing the terrain toward Mt. Rex. It looked good to the left of the route we were flying. We went up slope steeply, and turned around the left end of the peak and headed for Mt. Vang.

We were flying over unexplored territory, but Carl Ecklund and Finn Ronne had noted Mt. Vang (about 400 kilometers north-northeast of Sky-Hi) on their dog sled trek south along George IV Sound from East Base far to the north in 1939–41 with the U.S. Antarctic Service Expedition. Ronne had again seen and named this peak Mt. Vang on his 1947 flight south from East Base. We were approaching Mt. Vang from the opposite direction and hoped to find it so we could tie our work to that from the north.

All along we saw many nunataks and rolling topography.

Our oversnow traverse into the area would mark the first time that people navigated on the surface, allowing us to determine locations accurately. From the cockpit, I shot Kodachrome 25 film with a 35mm Alpa camera and used a Polaroid camera. I noted every picture in a data book by time taken. In the main cabin Perry and Hiro shot Polaroid pictures to the right and left and noted times in their data books. We planned to use the Polaroid pictures taken from the air as an approximate map. These photos would give us the advantage of knowing the relative positions accurately as we approached the peaks and possible crevassed areas.

> The plane crossed an escarpment that continued parallel to us on the right. There was no mountain at the location shown on the air naviga-tion chart for Mt. Vang, but we saw a few small nunataks around.
>
> We made a right turn, to the southeast, and flew over a high snow dome to the Latady Range [photographed by the RARE]. I could see mountains to the right and left for over 200 miles. We turned to parallel the escarpment and headed for a new range, not mapped, which I named the Thiel Mountains. This is only about 70 miles from Sky-Hi.

This proposed name was not accepted because the range formerly called the Eastern Horlick Mountains, several hundred miles to the south, would be named the Thiel Mountains. This is appropriate because Ed Thiel had taken his airborne field party into that range and collected geologic samples in the 1958–59 season. The range for which we were heading may have been photographed by the RARE, but is not shown on the map in Ronne's geographic report.[1] A few years later the range was named the Behrendt Mountains because I led the Antarctic Peninsula Traverse. However, throughout the next weeks, we referred to it as the Thiel Mountains.

> Here we turned left (south) and dropped down on what appeared to be an ice shelf at an elevation of about 0–200 meters.

> I was making barometric elevation and radar height above the surface obser-vation using the aircraft instruments in the cockpit, as I had done the previous season (1960–61).

> The area was crevassed and there was no good way down for the traverse.

We turned and flew back to Sky-Hi, which was completely clobbered [by an undercast of clouds]. The pilot made a perfect landing. [He did this by flying at a constant rate of descent and keeping the altitude properly adjusted and his eye on the radar altimeter.] It was so foggy we could not see the snow surface when we finally touched down.

Neil Brice[2] and others came out to the sound of the airplane engines and guided us in to Sky-Hi camp.

*29 Dec. Fri.* It was about 0200 when we got back inside.

I got to bed about 0400 . . . and was awakened at noon by the National Geographic Society photographer, who wanted to take our picture. He brought Hiro a cup of tea and me a cup of coffee in our Sno-Cat. We got up and everyone else got out. We posed for a few pictures and then Bob Farrington and the rest took off in the R4D-8. They will bring us more fuel near [our easternmost point].

Hiro, Perry, and I spent the rest of the day going over our notes and the Polaroid pictures. It will be difficult for us to follow the plane route; we will have to run more south [to avoid crevasses].

A C-130 came in from McMurdo about 0100 with a load of fuel and other supplies for us. Phil Smith came in to see me for twenty minutes. We discussed the future route and he was all prepared, I'm sure, to give me a big sales talk to terminate at Sky-Hi. From what we had seen yesterday, I had reached that decision myself.

Two days earlier Perry and I had started a several-day seismic experiment[3] about a mile out of Sky-Hi. Our reflection showed ice 2140 meters thick, or about 1800 meters below sea level. Starting this morning and continuing with the help of several others we completed the work an hour after midnight.

*31 Dec. Sun.* I was up at 0800 and we worked all day getting ready to leave. Perry and I juggled all of the sleds around, unloaded 3000 pounds of explosive off the Rolli to other sleds to lighten the load, and an additional ton of drifted snow.

No wonder we had been breaking differentials.

*1 Jan. 1962, New Year's Day, Mon.* Perry fired off seven 1-pound primers in the air at the stroke of midnight to celebrate the new year.

I got to bed about 0500 and up about 1130. Pete and I fueled the Rolli with drums of diesel brought in by the C-130 flight, and found that we can now drive in third gear. We don't want to break any more differentials on the towing vehicle. The explosive is all on another new sled [which had just been delivered].

Perry and I helped John and Hiro hand core the last four meters of a 21-meter-deep hole tonight with the SIPRE auger.

Because we had to pull the string of 1-meter-long rods three times for each meter cored to remove snow and firn cuttings, this was quite an operation. Hiro and John had been digging pits and taking 9-meter cores at a number of our stations. They measured the 9-meter temperatures to an accuracy of about $\pm$ 0.1°C as an approximation of the mean annual temperature. Were someone to remeasure these temperatures today, an estimate of climate warming in the area could be obtained.

We carried the firn and ice cores in a refrigerator sled as we proceeded. These would be used for glaciology studies and to look for micrometeorites that had fallen on the surface and been buried. Even though the air temperatures were always below freezing, the object was to keep the cores from recrystallizing by getting too close to the melting temperature.

Lee had been making repairs and carrying out routine maintenance on all of the Sno-Cats and sleds. Con had been determining a very accurate position of Sky-Hi and shooting in positions of Mt. Rex and the other peaks we could see.

The weather has been about 20°F with about 20-knot winds and is quite pleasant.

*2 Jan. Tues.* Con and Pete built the shell of a mess wanigan using plywood; it will be quite comfortable, I think.

They put dark canvas on the outside to warm it and keep out the wind. We had a small table we could all crowd around. All of our mess equipment, current food supplies, and a stove were carried inside.

On the outside of the wanigan we had a small wood crate in which we stored the bread we would use next. When we were delayed so long getting out of McMurdo in November, all of the many fresh-baked loaves had totally dried out in the sun waiting on pallets for shipment to Camp Minnesota. By the time we

58. Wasilewski resting at Camp Sky-Hi. Akio behind chair.

were underway and wanted to eat it, the bread was like cardboard. At first, we could only use it for French toast using powdered eggs. However, we discovered that the blowing snow over the partly open food box on one of the sleds had allowed enough snow below the melting temperature to blow past the bread and freshen it. Now that we had the wanigan, we systematically freshened three or four loaves for several days in a partly open-sided crate on the side of the wanigan by letting snow blow through it. The water vapor sublimating off the snow moistened the bread while keeping it frozen. When we wanted such a loaf, we just thawed it inside the wanigan.

> *3 Jan. Wed.* The traverse party left Sky-Hi about 0830. It was overcast with poor visibility all day. We drove back to our seismic station and then headed 10° left (north) of Mt. Rex to avoid the crevasses along the direct route.
>
> We approached Mt. Rex and the three lesser peaks to the left, finally stopping at 2031, 32 miles from our seismic station near Sky-Hi. The slope became too steep for the Rolli in the soft snow. I laid our the seismic spread and started drilling a hole when the wind, which had been about 20 knots, picked up. It was a strong 45 knots when we tried to shoot a reflection. We didn't get any, and stopped for a steak dinner in the new wanigan. The exhaust in *Barbara* is broken and fumes really

come into the cat badly when it is rolling.

This could have been dangerous. Carbon monoxide has poisoned a number of people in Antarctica and killed at least three (Indian geologists who died in their sleep in a tent in the early 1990s). However, Lee repaired the problem as he routinely did many similar vehicle difficulties.

I had a hard time with the radio tonight and didn't contact anyone.

Mile #464, 74°57'S, 76°00'W

*4 Jan. Thurs.* It was socked in all day until about 1600 when the wind dropped. Perry and I shot about a dozen times[4] until we finally got a reflection indicating ice about half a kilometer thick. We worked after dinner until around midnight.

*5 Jan. Fri.* It cleared and we made up a geology party of Hiro, Perry, and me on one rope and John and Pete on another. I led the route up toward an outcrop on Mt. Rex about a kilometer away. We crossed a few small bridged crevasses and a fairly large *bergschrund* before we descended into a moat and reached rock.[5] There are very few lichens around and although we saw no melt water, we did see refrozen patches of same.

Next we went north across the pass to a small summit on the ridge of the nearest left-hand peak, a beautiful pointed snow summit. We climbed up the steep snow and some ice using crampons until we reached a little saddle next to rock. From there it was an easy scramble to the top of the little peak. The rock here is essentially the same as on Mt. Rex, but with larger phenocrysts, up to an inch across. It was clear, warm, and sunny and a real pleasure to be on rock.

We discussed the feasibility of driving through the pass. Perry and Hiro didn't think we could pull up the slope because of the soft snow. We got back to camp about 0600.

Perry and I took in the seismic line and we had dinner again about 0830.

Perry, John, and I sat around talking climbing before going to bed. I wanted to move on because the weather is good, but the others were more interested in a bit of sleep. We were all tired after our climbing trip.

We had all been up more than 24 hours.

We got up about 1730. It was foggy and we couldn't see the mountains at all. It lifted a little and we hitched the Rolli to *Tamare Riatia* (without its sleds) and *Argo*, using a cable between the two Sno-Cats, which drove in parallel, and started through the pass about 2030.

We kept in constant radio communication and managed to keep the Rollitrailer on course without letting one Sno-Cat get ahead of the other. We headed into the saddle to the left of Mt. Rex. Everything went fine, and we climbed about 100 meters in the first mile through soft snow. *Tamare Riatia* went back for its load of sleds while we waited. We started out finally on a course about east-northeast.

*6 Jan. Sat.* There was a several hour delay at one point while Lee tightened the clutch in *Argo*, which was slipping. We continued on until we reached mile #496, about 1600. The ice is very thin here also, about 400 meters. I got to bed about 2030.

Mile 496, 74°52'S, 74°28'W.

*7 Jan. Sun.* We got started about 0830. It was overcast, but we could see three nunataks ahead. The two to the left were somewhat steep, but we drove to the top of the third. It consisted of broken-up sandstone. There were many fossils, including brachiopods.

As I stepped out of the Sno-Cat and reached down and picked up a 180 million-year-old belemnite, I realized mine were the first eyes that had ever seen these fossils even though they may have been exposed here next to the ice for thousands of years.

A couple of years later Tom Laudon and I published a paper in *Science* reporting some worm fossils collected here as Cretaceous in age from a USGS identification. This age was incorrect, as a few years later Graham Stevens identified (correctly) the belemnites we collected as Jurassic in age. These were the first fossils collected in this part of Antarctica.

We found one igneous erratic also [which had been deposited by the ice]. It cleared while we were here, but later clouded up again. We built a cairn and left a note in a seismic paper can.[6]

Although we called them "Johnson Nunataks," some wiser soul later officially named these nunataks "Lyon Nunataks." Johnson Spur in the Ellsworth Mountains was named after Floyd.

It is ironic that even though we left cairns with our suggested names in them, the U.S.-Advisory Committee on Antarctic Names (US-ACAN) gave them different names and assigned the names we proposed to different features. We used the names we proposed in various geological and geophysical scientific publications, which added to the confusion. Obviously the US-ACAN never checked to see what names were currently being used in the published scientific literature. In recent years, various field parties have revisited the peaks we sampled on the Antarctic Peninsula Traverse, found our cairns, and contacted me regarding the names they found there.

Mile #516, 75°00'S, 73°58'W

505 Johnson [Lyon] Nunataks 74°52 S, 74°02'W

We made a zig to the south for 10 miles and then continued on course to the east to avoid the possible crevasses we saw on the recon flight. *Argo* stopped at mile #528 at 2039.

Mile #528, 74°59'S, 73°22'W

*8 Jan. Mon.* Perry and I were up at 0700 and began shooting. We tried a variety of shots and finally recorded a very shallow reflection at about 80-meter depth shooting 10 feet of primacord 30 meter offset from the spread with 2-meter spacing of the jugs. This is quite different from the usual [1-pound] Nitromon primer at the center of the spread with 30-meter geophone intervals. It took 20 shots and all day to develop this technique, which probably will not be applicable at the next station.

There was an art to seismic reflection ice sounding as well as science. Nowadays, with digital recording of the seismic data, a geophysicist can partly process the data right after shooting to obtain the optimum result. However, field technique is still a significant variable in trying to acquire good data.

Since about 1966 scientists have been making radar ice soundings more or less routinely from the air and on the surface of ice over three kilometers thick. This new technique ended the oversnow traverse program as carried out from the IGY to 1966. Of course, because radar waves cannot penetrate seawater because of its high electrical conductivity, the seismic reflection method is still the only way to measure depth to bedrock beneath the vast Antarctic ice shelves that float on the seas overlying the continental shelves.

This was a day station for the glaciologists. Hiro and John did not dig a pit at every seismic station, because snow accumulation, mean annual temperature, and other parameters of the snow do not vary that rapidly in the smooth flat areas of Antarctica we were traversing. On the Antarctic Peninsula Traverse, the accumulation varied more than on any of the other oversnow traverses from about 50 g/cm² close to the Bellingshausen Sea to less than 20 g/cm² farther inland. The snow pits we put in were quite adequately spaced, and we covered much more distance by traveling almost every day, weather permitting.

It was very warm (about 25–30°F) with little wind and occasional breaks in the usual overcast we see almost continuously in this area. During one clear period I could count 15 nunataks. Con Merrick is busy surveying these in and we are naming the ones we visit at the time.

We were primarily a geophysical-glaciological party, with geology only a secondary objective. Therefore, although it was frustrating, we could not spend much time traveling to the nunataks that were so close at hand. Because none had ever been visited or sampled, the geologist nature in all of us made us want to go to each one.

*9 Jan. Tues.* We had breakfast at 0630 and went back to bed as the wind was up, with blowing snow. It was very warm and not unpleasant out, but I didn't like to drive up to nunataks and possible crevasses with no visibility.

By noon things had improved and we started out. Visibility dropped and at mile 536 *Argo* bogged down on a steep hill we could not see due to fog. I contoured the slope and we ran completely on instruments, with Con holding the altimeter in his lap and me steering by the compass.

Finally things improved a bit and I drove up to a nunatak at mile #538, which we named after Steve Barnes [Cheeks Nunatak].

In approaching the rock, I pushed on harder than I should have, and finally couldn't pull the slope. As we have no brakes, the Rolli pulled us back down the hill, jackknifed, and stopped with the Sno-Cat against the tow bar. Other than crushing a box for fueling apparatus, there was no damage.

This small peak, about 100 meters above the snow surface, was an easy scramble to the summit. We built a cairn, left a note, surveyed, studied geology,[7] collected lichen, read gravity, magnetism, altitude, and decided to camp here tonight.

Mile 538, 75°00'S, 72°53'W.

*10 Jan. Wed.* We got off to an early start, after breakfast at 0600. I detoured south a few miles to avoid some crevasses we saw from the peak, and continued east. We could see the Thiel Mountains [Merrick and Behrendt Mountains], which appear to be divided into two groups of peaks, close to the right. The party stopped at small outcrop in the eastern Thiels [Merrick Mountains] for a couple of hours of geology. The rock was zoned vertically or steeply into 10- to 50-foot-wide bands of varying igneous lithology.[8]

The weather was cloudy as usual and visibility was poor. We continued north-northeast from this outcrop at the northwest end of the group, through fog and overcast. We climbed through a pass between a snow-covered peak and a bare one, but couldn't take time to stop.

I'm sure this last remark would make a geologist cringe. Here we were in unexplored Antarctica where no one had ever set foot and we had to hurry on (at four miles an hour). I imagine that the first men on the moon felt something similar, surrounded by rocks but able to collect only a few.

We stopped at 1730 close to a group of three large peaks, which looked like they were composed of sedimentary rock. The visibility was up and down and we could occasionally see crevasses between us and the peaks. I laid out the spread and drilled a 3-meter hole while the others were driving in. We shot and recorded a reflection indicating a quite shallow depth. The gravity meter measurement suggested quite thick ice so we shot some more and found that we had blown out the bottom of a crevasse snow bridge 4–5 meters thick. The record showed noise of falling snow, which looked like a reflection.

We had been parked on the snow bridge and firing explosive. If we had used a bigger charge, all of us might have dropped into the crevasse.

We gave up and went to bed about midnight. No radio contact tonight.

Lee in particular and everyone in general aren't too happy about our crevasse situation. We have been speculating whether the hitch on the

Rollitrailer would break before it pulled *Argo* into a crevasse if it fell.

We ran out of the small trail flags that we leave behind at the 4-mile stations for the following cats. Hiro started using other things to mark the stations. At mile #568 he left a nude pinup (from a Japanese magazine) supported by two small bamboo stakes. It's now up on the wall of *Tamare Riatia*.

Mile #572, 74°50'S, 71°43'W

*11 Jan. Thurs.* Perry's birthday today. We got started this morning at 0930.

I recall (but didn't record it in my journal) that I had words with Con that morning. He, as usual, walked off with his theodolite to shoot angles on the peaks. Because of the crevasses, I was worried for his safety and spoke sharply to him about this. He didn't argue, but was obviously unconcerned. He had not had any previous experience with crevasses, despite his great amount of field work.

It was overcast as usual, but with fairly good visibility. We backtracked a mile out of the crevasses, turned right for three miles, then right again for four miles, 120° right for five miles, and got to a small peak in the group we were near last night. We named these Sky-Hi Nunataks.

This is the only name we proposed that actually was accepted by the US-ACAN.

Con and I climbed up the ridge, and just as we got to a small summit about 90 meters above the Sno-Cat the weather socked in and we could only see about 100 feet. The rock was a porphyritic igneous type [arkose and dacite]. Con went back down the ridge while I was making some geologic observations.

Although we were geophysicists and glaciologists, we measured dip and strike with Brunton compasses, and took Polaroid photos, which we taped into the data books and annotated. We always collected a great abundance of rock samples when we stopped at nunataks.

I followed soon and retraced my ice-ax holes in the snow back to *Argo*.

We ate some toast while we waited for the others. Fortunately when it was clear, we had seen good surface in the direction we wanted to go, so we struck out through the fog as soon as *Tamare Riatia* and *Barbara* arrived. We came out of the fog soon and started climbing a featureless snow surface.

We arrived at #604 about 2000 and found ourselves about 1700 meters, 200 meters higher than Byrd. The ice is 800 meters thick.

In this area, we were crossing rugged, mountainous subglacial topography along the buried crest of the southernmost extension of the Antarctic Peninsula. Even though the ice was relatively thick, we were recording reflections from separate mountain peaks off to each side of us.

Mile 604, 74°38'S, 71°03'W.

*12 Jan. Fri.* It cleared during the night and the temperature dropped. We shot a wide-angle seismic [experiment] today. Perry went out by himself and fired shots up to 4.8 kilometers. The Tellurometer worked OK, although we had to operate standing on the roofs of *Argo* and *Tamare Riatia*.

The Tellurometer was an electronic distance measuring instrument with which we could obtain accuracies of a few centimeters at several kilometers between a pair of instruments; this was far better than anything available during the IGY.

We had a quick steak supper about 2030 and then worked until 2300. There is getting to be quite a difference between night and day temperatures. The sun will start setting in a few weeks.

*13 Jan. Sat.* We got off at 0800 and drove uneventfully for 32 miles. I wish I could say that every day. At mile #624.5 we dropped down a relatively steep escarpment trending at right angles to our course. I doubt if we could climb back up with one cat pulling the Rolli in this soft snow. We dropped 300 meters today. The ice is 2100 meters thick here or about 700 meters below sea level. The snow is very soft and about knee-deep. Even Perry used skis to bring in the spread. Normally he prefers to walk.

I got quite casual about shooting explosives, as I was reminded on one occasion. When the reflection quality was high, we could get away with a two-meter (six-foot) open hole (one with no snow filling to help contain the charge). I was kneeling at the blaster as usual, and was nearly looking down the open hole when

I fired. I was rudely reminded that this really was one pound of high explosive when I was nearly deafened by the explosion as loose snow and acrid fumes blew up almost in my face. I decided I needed to pay more attention in the future. In the course of these two seasons, I fired several hundred of these small charges.

Pete made meat bar hoosh tonight; it was very good.

Meat bars, essentially pemmican, consisted of cooked, dried, generic meat with about 50 percent added fat and some mild seasoning and came sealed in aluminum foil. Generally, meat bars were used by geologic field parties in Antarctica in the 1950s and '60s to make a stew or "hoosh," but we used them mainly as a lunch or snack, warmed on the engine from inside the Sno-Cat as we drove, or cold. I rather enjoyed them, perhaps because my body craved fat as we worked in those low temperatures. At McMurdo in January 2003, I saw a meat bar in a display case of ancient Antarctic artifacts next to the mess hall.

Mile #636, 74°16'S, 70°10'W

*14 Jan. Sun.* We got off to a good early start today under clear sky, but had to stop at mile 661 while Lee replaced a differential on *Tamare Riatia.*

The procedure involved using *Argo* disconnected from the sleds and driven perpendicular to the damaged vehicle. Operating the winch from inside, I lifted the frame of the other vehicle using the A-frame on *Argo,* which had the winch cable running over a pulley. In this case, John Molholm had driven *Barbara* up in the tracks of *Tamare Riatia* while pulling five or six of the small sleds. While we were carrying out this operation, the throw-out bearing in *Argo* went out and I could not raise or lower *Tamare Riatia. Barbara* could not back up because of the sleds, so we were trapped with three immobile Sno-Cats. Fortunately, after a few minutes of struggling, I managed to shift gears for the winch and lower *Tamare Riatia.*

We could see two nunataks to the northwest on the escarpment we crossed yesterday. We could see a nunatak with a black cliff face along this. This is probably Mt. Vang, or at least the closest rock to Mt. Vang shown on the map. It clouded up as we drove along, descending about 240 meters to 668. We stopped there at 1830 and made tracks with the Rolli for the other vehicles to park in, which gives them an easier time starting in the soft snow in the morning. The rock is about 200 meters

59. Sno-Cats *Barbara* (left), *Argo*, (lower flag), *Tamare Riatia* (right).

below sea level, or shallower than at mile 636.

There has been a slight undercurrent of ill will among a few. Pete and Lee sometimes resent me and I get a little fed up with them. Tonight after the radio sked I went into the wanigan. They were inside having a drink so I joined them. We talked on for an hour about magnetics, mechanics, and sundry subjects. It was an enjoyable break, and has convinced me that alcohol in moderation is a good thing to help relax tension in a field party like this.

Unlike wintering over at Ellsworth with Finn Ronne,[9] we had all the liquor that anyone wanted on this traverse. It was never abused.

Mile 668, 73°54'S, 69°26'W.

*15 Jan. Mon.* It was sunny with clouds until late afternoon. Our battery died at 684, which delayed us an hour and a half while Lee repaired the charger. The surface continued as it has for the past 200 miles flat, soft, and no sastrugi. [This is a very high snow accumulation area.] We descended to 1000 meters by station 700 at about 1800. We got a good reflection on the first shot from rock about 200 meters below sea level.

We were descending toward sea level, into George VI Sound, although

60. Shimizu sketching.

the contact with the floating ice was still about 50 kilometers to the north. The escarpment continued off to the right. I decided to turn to the south at this point.

I had a good contact with Sky-Hi tonight. Tomorrow is a day station.

Unlike the Filchner Ice Shelf Traverse, we usually shot our reflection at night after our arrival at the station and moved on the following day. This was the only way we could make up for all of the time we had lost in November before we got into the field, and December because of the storms. Of course, we took some risk traveling with poor visibility "on instruments," but I figured that the objectives justified our pushing hard. Perhaps this schedule and driving in the fog or blowing snow engendered the discontent mentioned above.

Mile 700, 73°32'S, 68°40'W.

*16 Jan. Tues.* It was foggy and snowing all day. This is the first free time I've had since we left Sky-Hi. I much prefer it this way than the way we had it in December.

*17 Jan. Wed.* We turned south. It was whiteout and snowing all day.

We took a course to avoid an obviously bad part of the escarpment we had seen previously and went 32 miles to mile 732 with almost total lack of visibility. I could only see about 60 meters [the spacing of two geophones] as I laid out the seismic spread about 1800. A good reflection showed about 1200 meters ice thickness. As we climbed about 550 meters today, it means the rock rose about the same amount.

Mile 732, 73°43'S, 67°17'W.

*18 Jan. Thurs.* It was pea soup out when we started this morning.

I drove using only the compass and altimeters for guidance during these many hours of zero visibility. Con Merrick had determined the magnetic heading we would take for the day and I steered on this heading, hoping that there were no crevasses and that the snow surface was not too steep.

We climbed steeply for eight miles up to 1600 meters elevation, where I was sure we were up the escarpment. We then turned toward the Latady Mountains and continued rising all day. The weather improved and we stopped so Con could get a sunshot—the first in three days.

We were at about 2150 meters elevation when we stopped at mile 764, and the ice was about 1000 meters thick. We could see a nunatak and some disturbed ice directly ahead, and another nunatak to the left about 100°. It was below 0°F tonight.

Mile 764, 74°04'S, 66°36'W.

*19 Jan. Fri.* It was pretty foggy when we started, so I changed course to the right to avoid the peak. We passed it about a mile abeam at about mile 770 and turned more right. We climbed for about 12 miles to an elevation of about 2350 meters and then gradually descended.

This was about the highest we got on the entire traverse. We were crossing the ice divide of the southern end of the Antarctic Peninsula in Palmer Land.

The snow surface changed abruptly from 9–12 inches of powder to a smooth crust at the top of the hill. We drove in third gear all afternoon. We reached mile 796 about 1600 and laid out the 660-meter-long refraction spread by supper. A reflection showed about 1200-meter-thick ice here. We are about 2200 meters elevation.

I could only get our position through to Sky-Hi tonight.

We planned to be resupplied at that point, where we intended to spend several days carrying out a major seismic refraction experiment. The weather was stormy for most of the next nine days as we tried to work there.

Mile 796, 74°27'S, 67°08'W.

*22 Jan. Mon.* Storm continued. Two R4D-8s are at Byrd waiting to fly to Sky-Hi when this weather breaks.

*23 Jan. Tues.* By evening it cleared but the wind stayed up to 25–30 knots. I called Sky-Hi at 2300 and got R4D-8 853, who asked our weather. I gave it (the temperature was –3°F) and asked their position. They were a half an hour from us. Everyone got outside to watch for them and about 10 minutes later they flew over.

*24 Jan. Wed.* The plane landed, we thought, somewhere downwind of us. The blowing snow obscured vision beyond 500 feet, and they were lost. Perry loaded the our big radio on 1500 hertz (the frequency of a homing beacon) and they managed to approach us with their radio direction finder. Eventually the plane saw us, using radar, and came in. We off loaded 9 drums of diesel, mail, and two seismic reels and some small stuff. The other R4D-8, 188, came over soon and landed out south of the seismic line. They taxied until they found our flags, and we had them cross over there. We offloaded the plane about 200 yards out from camp. I thanked the pilot, and they quickly took off, as weather was going down at Sky-Hi. [I gave him a couple of bottles of whisky for the crews. We had plenty and it was not as available at Byrd.] Both planes were airborne about 0230.

Mile 796 is about 1800 miles (2900 kilometers) from McMurdo. The fuel had to be flown from McMurdo to Byrd to fuel the R4D-8 to get to Sky-Hi. The R4D-8 then refueled at Sky-Hi with fuel flown there so they could fly a load (9 drums or 475 gallons) of fuel to us at our farthest point at Mile #796. The fuel at Sky-Hi had been airdropped by a C-124 and landed there by C-130s. I calculated from this convoluted description that it took 7 gallons of avgas to bring 1 gallon of diesel fuel to us at this location.

> We all ate dinner about 0300 and read mail while the wind whistled outside. I went to bed about 0400. I got up at 1700 and it was still blowing strong. Hiro left the door of the wanigan open and a lot of snow drifted in. I received the following message from the navigator of 99853 (R4D-8 #853):
>
> > Small crevasse area 75°30'S between 72°30'W and 73°30'W. Rest clear as far as could see to Sky-Hi.

I pondered this message for the next several days. I sent a message to Byrd requesting more information as to whether the crevasses were close to or out from the Thiel [Behrendt] Mountains we knew to be near that location.

> *25 Jan. Thurs.* The weather was fairly calm this morning, so we packed 1000 pounds of Pelletol explosive into *Argo* and Con and Perry drove out 20 kilometers and loaded up 500 pounds.

"Loading up" consisted of hand-drilling a 15-meter-deep hole, firing a small charge to "spring" the hole, and redrilling into the water-filled spherical cavity at the bottom. The 500 pounds of Pelletol (nitroglycerine dynamite in small pellet form) were then poured into the hole surrounding a several-pound Nitromon charge with a blasting cap inserted into the primer. A shot wire from the cap was fixed at the snow surface until we were ready to fire.

> The wind picked up, but I decided to shoot anyway.[10]

Perry fired the charge at a safe distance. A charge this size blew a huge crater at the snow surface even though it was buried 15 meters. We were always very careful to keep the two wire leads to the blasting cap twisted together until just before we fired so that a stray radio-induced current would not accidentally detonate the charge.

> The weather worsened and Perry and Pete came in with difficulty along the line of flags.

> *26 Jan. Fri.* Blowing hard all day until evening. Perry and Con drove out 15 kilometers and loaded 400 pounds. The wind had dropped, so we fired at 2250 and got a good record.

*27 Jan. Sat.* They continued in to 10 kilometers and fired a 100-pound shot. The wind was nearly calm and the sun was breaking through the clouds.

We had a steak dinner after I had finished digging up the 24 geophones buried about two feet deep along the spread.

As I came in I saw three skuas examining a geophone—preparatory to eating it I suppose. They waited until I was about 20 feet away before flying off. This is the first bird life we have seen since we left Camp Minnesota.

We were about 220 kilometers from the nearest source of food for the birds at the Ronne Entrance to George IV Sound.

We went to bed about 0730 and had breakfast at 1600. It was still clear and sunny but a strong wind had come up from the northeast. Perry and I took off at 1845 in *Tamare Riatia,* pulling the Rollitrailer and dragging one seismic cable.

We shot vertical reflections at the locations where we had fired the large charges. Although we were towing the seismic cable, we still had to plant the geophones and attach them to the cable, drill a 3–4-meter hole, shoot, and pick up the 12 geophones from the single 330-meter spread at each station.

A bank of clouds moved in from the northeast about 2045, the wind picked up, and it began to snow. Meanwhile back at mile 796 the others had been digging out and preparing to follow us. This storm hit them just as they were about to leave. They followed our trail with difficulty to where we were waiting. After a few hours sitting around, we got a break in the weather and moved out.

*28 Jan. Sun.* We fired reflections at 7.5 and 10 kilometers when the weather hit us again. I went to bed about 0600 to wait it out. By 1700 it was breaking, so Perry and I gulped down some chow and started out again dragging our cable. We were shooting at 12.5 and 15 kilometers when visibility got so bad we couldn't see the flags. The others left kilometer 10 at this point, nearly midnight.

*29 Jan. Mon.* After driving around in circles for a while (quite a trick with a 1000-foot cable dragging behind), we headed on a compass heading hoping to find the shot points at 17.5 and 20 kilometers, which we hit dead on. I'd have hit the crater left by the 500-pound shot at 20 kilometers if it hadn't been for the flag, which I spotted at the rim. While we shot our last reflection, the others came. Hiro, Con, and I ate some warmed-up meat bar hoosh and pulled out about 0400.

It cleared and we drove 32 miles uneventfully over dropping and very rolling terrain, arriving at mile 840 about 1100. We spotted a nunatak in the distance a bit left of our course. The temperature was +11°F and dead calm. This is the second sunny day (if it lasts; it's now 1340) since we left Sky-Hi. It's very pleasant out and we had the doors open on *Tamare Riatia* while we shot our reflections. The ice is about 450 meters thick and the surface elevation is about 1700 meters.

I went to bed about 1400. I was pretty tired, as I realized while carrying out the cable for the fifth seismic station of "today."

Mile 840, 74°58'S, 68°11'W

About 2230 I got up to make the radio sked. I stayed up and worked on data until Lee came in about—

*30 Jan. Tues.*—0230 to make breakfast. We were all set to go about 0330, by which time it had clouded over again. I started out and found we had no power. Lee replaced the fuel filter. He started it up to check it out and ran over the driver's seat, which he had taken out, with the Rollitrailer, and crushed it. He replaced it with *Barbara's* passenger seat after I had made a few uncomplimentary remarks. Then the radio didn't work and it was 0600 by the time we got that fixed.

It was clearing again. We saw some nunataks about a mile or two ahead after we had climbed a ridge. We stopped at the next station to survey them, but ground fog moved in and clobbered them. We turned 20° left to intersect them and proceeded. By the next 4-mile station we could see the nunataks again. We named them the Shimizu [Anderson] Nunataks, there are about seven in all, and drove up to the nearest. We parked near the outcrop and climbed about 30–50 meters to the top.

The rock is mainly metasedimentary (graywacke and basic dikes dipping to the west about 30°) and showing glacial striations at the summit; ice was at least this much higher at one time. Hiro got quite a thrill over us naming these after him.

We also built a small cairn on the summit and left a note with our names and the date. At Hiro's request we also left a small Japanese flag, a cigarette pack, and Navy matches. In 1984–85 a USGS party led by Peter Rowley visited this nunatak and returned the contents to me, including the note, which I have. Although I appreciated the thought, I would have preferred that the material was left in the cairn. I mailed the flag and cigarettes to Hiro.

Of course, the ACAN did not keep this name, but called the peak Anderson Nunatak and named Shimizu Ice Stream in the Horlick Mountains,[11] about 1500 kilometers away, after Hiro, even though the cairn and several geologic publications report Shimizu Nunatak at this location. Hiro Shimizu was never near the Horlick Mountains, but the ice stream is certainly a larger feature than this small nunatak.

We had a splendid view from the summit of this peak and saw that these nunataks are outliers of a larger range, probably the Sweeney Mountains, running east-west a few miles away.

Finn Ronne obtained oblique pictures of these and other mountains in the area from the air in 1947 as part of the trimetrigon photography program of the RARE. The mapped location shown is about 150 kilometers in error to the southeast.[12]

We took off on a bearing to the north-northwest and dropped down, contouring a ridge north of us. About 2.5 miles further on, our magnetometer gave trouble [which I fixed with some difficulty]. We could see some crevasses in the ridge crest on our right, which seemed to cut across our route ahead. As visibility was very poor, I turned back and returned to the other Sno-Cats at the nunatak.

We then turned left on a northwest course for four miles and again changed course more to the west [see map 8]. At mile 864, our aft differential broke. I laid out the seismic spread and drilled a hole while the others came up. Lee found that the forward differential was just about shot also. As we had only one spare left, this was serious. Lee stayed up all night and worked on them. He replaced the ring gear in the forward unit with a gear from one of our previous broken differentials.

The ice is about one kilometer thick here and the elevation is about 1550 meters. It cleared to the south about 2200, allowing the sun to shine behind the peaks of the Sweeney Mountains a few miles away, giving us a beautiful view.

A tough day.

Mile 864, 75°01'S, 68°52'W.

*31 Jan. Wed.* Up and breakfast at 0700. We drove southwest all day and 8 miles out collected rocks at a small nunatak (arkose wacke and black shale). The weather was beautiful as we worked our way around the west end of the Sweeney Mountains. Passing through a gap between peaks and mountains, we descended for several miles and then climbed again along side another group of peaks. It looked for a while like I might have led us into a *cul de sac*. However, from a small nunatak at mile 892, we could see a way down the escarpment we were on, by a rather steep, but straight forward slope. We collected rocks here (dacite), similar to Mt. Rex, and then descended the slope without incident. John Molholm and Pete Wasilewski collected rocks on a nunatak on the opposite side of this pass, and found andesite and dacite.

We continued on until 2200, when we stopped at mile 908, where we shot a reflection showing ice about 500 meters thick. We have left the main group of the Sweeneys behind, although we can still see peaks in all directions. I think we can see the Sky-Hi Nunataks and another prominent peaks to the northwest. The Thiel [Behrendt] Mountains are to the right of our course ahead to the southwest.

This was the most productive day of the traverse so far. I hope our rear end [differential] holds out. I am thinking of jettisoning 500 gallons of fuel (about two tons) to prevent another rear end going in *Argo*. I hate to do this considering it took seven gallons of avgas to get each gallon of diesel fuel to us at 796.

As I tried to fall asleep, I recalled the message sent from the plane regarding the crevasses near the south end of the Thiel [Behrendt] Mountains. I finally dropped off thinking that I would worry about this in three days when we got near the area.

Mile 908, 75°16'S, 70°50'W.

*1 Feb. Thurs.* We put in a wide-angle seismic station today. The weather was partly cloudy. I told Lee we had to dump 500 gallons of fuel. He didn't like the idea (nor did I) and said he would try to rebuild a differential. He spent most of the day with a torch burning the shaft out of a bearing from a broken rear end. He finally rebuilt one that he says will work. I hope we don't have to use it.

We had burned out six differentials, including the one in the old Sno-Cat that we did not repair and abandoned.

*Barbara* has a cracked frame. Lee tried to weld it, but the welder engine wouldn't work. I hope it holds the Sno-Cat together until we get to Sky-Hi.

Again as I tried to fall asleep, I was concerned about the crevasses reported ahead. However, I knew we had one more day of travel before we reached the area.

*2 Feb. Fri.* It was clear this morning and we got a good look at the mountains to the right and left as we drove to the southwest. We could see that ranges on the right are the two groups of the Thiel [Merrick and Behrendt] Mountains. In the distance we saw Barnes [Cheeks] Nunatak.

As we approached the West Thiels [Behrendt Mountains], we collected metasedimentary rocks (conglomerate and arkosic wacke) from a small nunatak.[13] As we proceeded towards a prominent peak at the south end, the ice thickened to 2 kilometers and we appeared to be approaching the trough. We stopped at 940 and measured 1930 meters of ice or 1100 meters below sea level. The weather clouded over and it started snowing so we couldn't see the mountains a short distance to the right.

That night I thought of the possible crevasses ahead the following day. We had never received an answer to my question about the proximity of the crevasses to the mountains.

Mile 940, 75°27'S, 72°02'W.

*3 Feb. Sat.* Clear and sunny when we started and we got lots of pictures of the beautiful West Thiel [Behrendt] Mountains, some of the prettiest so far. I planned to cut around the south end in close, taking a calculated guess that the reported crevasses were farther out.

But at 6.2 miles I felt a sudden lurch and a sinking feeling as we came to an abrupt stop. I knew immediately what had happened. Carefully, we peered out of the Sno-Cat to see what our situation was.

The Sno-Cat pulled mostly out of the crevasse we had broken into when the rear pontoons went in, but the front tires of the Rolli were canted sideways.

61. Behrendt Mountains with *Argo* (right) and *Barbara* (left) in foreground.

From inside the vehicle, however, we could not immediately fathom what our situation was. All we could see was that the fuel tires were dangling over a black void. We were concerned that any sudden movement by us inside would pull the *Argo* back and down into the crevasse.

I called the others on the radio:

"*Tamare Riatia, Tamare Riatia,* this is *Argo*."

"Roger *Argo*, this is *Tamare Riatia*," came back Perry's calm (and calming) southern drawl.

"We have broken into a crevasse about two miles ahead of you. We are all right, but we need help. Leave your loads and drive up carefully, exactly in our tracks. We are going to check our situation out and will keep you informed."

I imagine that this terse statement alarmed them, but we in *Argo* had other things on our minds at this moment.

Hiro, Con, and I gingerly exited *Argo* with our ice axes. I stood on the Sno-Cat pontoon and probed carefully. It seemed safe so I stepped down. The others followed and we roped up immediately. We kept nylon climbing ropes hanging on the head lights of each Sno-Cat, just for this purpose. Fortunately Hiro and I knew how to quickly tie bowlines around our waists, and we showed Con how to tie into the middle of the rope.[14]

We probed carefully around with our ice axes and partially defined the

62. Merrick surveying nunatak.

crevasse we had broken into. As usual with bridged crevasses, we could not see very far down into the darkness, but it appeared deep with vertical walls, and five or six feet wide where we had broken through. The Sno-Cat appeared stable and not likely to be pulled backward into the hole.

While belayed, we probed around the area further outlining the crevasse and searching for any other others. The heavy tires of the Rollitrailer made a pretty good crevasse detector—except for the fact that they were behind our Sno-Cat.

Meanwhile, two miles back, the other Sno-Cats disconnected from their loads and cautiously approached us in *Argo's* tracks.

They found a small crevasse a bit back on our trail that we had barely broken open in passing.

After their arrival, I was guiding Lee as he cautiously backed *Barbara* around, while trying to straddle our tracks in the snow. Suddenly he broke into another crevasse. Only the rear pontoons were hanging in and he drove it right out under my direction. Only after he got out and was able to see the hole he had broken into did he understand how perilous his position had been. But he suspected!

After disconnecting the Rolli, I swung *Argo* ahead, and backed over the

63. *Argo* with Rollitrailer broken into crevasse.

crevasse that we had broken into, crossing a narrow area we had probed out.

Although the sun was brightly shining beneath a blue sky, and every feature of the snow was clearly defined, we could see no evidence of these thinly bridged crevasses apparently surrounding us, including the ones we had broken into.

After much finagling, we hitched *Barbara* and *Argo* to the back of the front tires with cables, that the others had brought from the sleds they had left behind, and intentionally jackknifed the Rollitrailer out backwards. We hitched *Argo* to the Rolli and turned warily around.

We backtracked over the old trail, opening one more small crevasse, to the previous 4-mile station. I then headed *Argo* southeast, away from the mountains for 8 miles at a right angle to our previous course, before resuming the old course. After 8 more miles, we turned about west and drove on to 976 where we camped [see map 8].

On our second seismic shot (a one-pound primer) in a drilled hole we triggered an audible collapse of some sort, probably a crevasse or hoarfrost layer. The collapse gave the appearance of another shot on the seismic record. Our next shot (five pounds of Nitromon) produced a different sound and a different effect on the record. We got a reflection anyway, from about 2 kilometers deep. We are at approximately 400

64. Rollitrailer broken into crevasse. Merrick (standing) and Shimizu at right of *Argo*.

meters elevation here. The weather closed in but we got an occasional glimpse of peaks to the right of our course.

We were apparently still in crevasses.

Mile 976, 75°34'S, 73°37'W.

*4 Feb. Sun.* We drove 32 miles to mile 1008 uneventfully today under an overcast. The front spreading bar on the wanigan broke and delayed us for some time repairing it. The ice is only about 1300 meters thick and the surface is about 400 meters.

We had come down about two kilometers (or about 6000 feet) from the highest snow surface 230 miles behind us. We were descending towards the Ronne Ice Shelf, although we were on thick grounded ice here.

Hiro drew a sketch on the wanigan ceiling of our crevasse incident.

Hiro, an accomplished artist and cartoonist, produced an exaggerated caricature of a crevasse yawning almost as wide as the Sno-Cat and Rollitrailer combined. The front pontoons hold on the edge while one rear pontoon scratches futilely like a dog to keep from being pulled back into the crevasse. The rear tires of the Rollitrailer are just on the other edge of the crevasse and several stick figures can be seen valiantly struggling to keep the vehicles from dropping to their doom. Meanwhile, one figure stands on the roof of the Sno-Cat with a camera photographing the scene. This was probably supposed to be me.

Operations were going so smoothly (relatively) that I proposed making a dogleg toward the north end of the Sentinel range for 100 miles and two or three days' more travel before heading for Sky-Hi. Everyone very strenuously objected, and argued that next year's traverse could do it. I gave in and agreed on the most direct route to Sky-Hi. However, by the following season, the plans were changed and the Sno-Cats were flown by C-130 to an area several hundred miles southeast of the Ellsworth Mountains. No seismic or glaciological data have ever been collected in that area I wanted to survey.

Mile 1008, 75°22'S, 74°54'W.

*5 Feb. Mon.* We drove all day towards Sky-Hi under overcast sky. At mile 1028 we stopped and put in a reflection station. The ice is about 2 kilometers thick. Further on a U-joint broke on *Argo* delaying us another hour.

Mile 1028, 75°18'S, 76°54'W.

The weather started to go down by 1048, and we could see no sign of Sky-Hi, supposedly four miles away. Con discovered he had been using the wrong declination for the magnetic compass and we had been driving 5° to the right of where we thought and had been for about 20 miles.

Con had, of course, measured the magnetic declination when we had been at Sky-Hi previously.

We made a sharp left turn. I talked to Floyd Johnson at Sky-Hi and he said they would drive out a bit and look for us. Con and I were on the roof. [There was an overhead hatch for easy access.] I was talking on the radio to *Tamare Riatia,* when we finally spotted the Jamesway through the falling snow, which was beginning to blow. It was about 2200 when we pulled up at 1052.7. Floyd saw us driving in and came in too. It was getting quite dark and *Barbara* used her headlights by the time she got in about 2330.

65. Behrendt near end of traverse. 4 February 1962.

This is the only time it ever got dark enough for headlights.

We all enjoyed a good steak dinner after the termination of our traverse. There was a message saying they would pick us up on the 10th. We could have stayed out a couple more days.

*6 Feb. Tues.* It was blowing 30 knots when I roused out everyone at 0730. I figured they would launch a C-130 soon as they know we are here. It was miserable outside and we confined our work for the most part to cleaning, packing, and inventorying inside the cats. It got worse all day and by night it was blowing 40 knots. Several of us moved into the Jamesway hut tonight.

*7 Feb. Wed.* The wind was down and visibility improved all day. We got a message that we were to be ready and send hourly weather.

*8 Feb. Thurs.* I got five hours' sleep before a C-130 came about 0900. We had *Barbara* and *Tamare Riatia* down to meet it with sleds. The ice-core refrigerator (weight 4000 pounds full) went in first.

We took off about 1030 (they had shut down the engines because it was quite warm) using JATO [36 bottles—the maximum I ever experienced] and all three miles of runway.

We landed at New Byrd after two hours to refuel and eat dinner. It was –10°F at Byrd. [Hiro left us for some work he had to finish.] We took off again with JATO and arrived at McMurdo about lunch time—

*9 Feb. Fri.*—at 1100. We landed on the Ross Ice Shelf runway [now known as Williams Field] on skis as the sea ice has gone mostly out. I met all the other field party members and we swapped yarns. After dinner I discussed the traverse with Phil Smith. The NSF Public Information Officer interviewed me about our scientific results for a press release on the traverse.

Seismic reflection soundings on the Antarctic Peninsula Traverse demonstrated that there is no subglacial topographic ridge connecting the Sentinel Mountains and the southern Antarctic Peninsula, even allowing for isostatic rebound after ice removal. Answering this question was one of the primary objectives of the Antarctic Peninsula Traverse. Our geological reconnaissance showed that there was a great age contrast between the Jurassic rocks of the southern Antarctic Peninsula (about 180 million years old) contrasted with the Lower Paleozoic and Precambrian rocks (older than 500 million years) observed and collected by the University of Minnesota geologists in the Sentinel Mountains this same season. Our traverse magnetic data found many high amplitude anomalies over the ice sheet associated with exposed Jurassic volcanic rocks in contrast to the very smooth magnetic field we measured with the previous year's aeromagnetic flights over the ice sheet adjacent to the thick sedimentary rock sequences of the Ellsworth and Sentinel Mountains areas. There were many other geophysical and glaciological findings documented in the papers in the bibliography.

Smith and I discussed arrangements for data,[15] rock samples, ice cores, people, etc. Perry will wait for some more seismic experiments near McMurdo. The rest of us will leave tomorrow on a C-130 for ChiChi.

[I took my first shower since arriving at Sky-Hi in late December and put on clean clothes.] There was a party tonight in the new USARP lounge. I left about midnight.

Thus ended my fourth trip to Antarctica. We flew uneventfully to New Zealand. I shaved my beard and spent a few days enjoying summer. As always, green foliage and the smells of earth and flowers in Christchurch were a delightful contrast to Antarctica. I spent one pleasant evening at an outdoor buffet at someone's home, where I chatted with Admiral Tyree. It was strange to see all of us just off the ice in coat and tie or dress white uniforms in contrast to the heavy and dirty clothes we had worn for the previous several months. I wandered along the beaches and swam in the (relatively) warm Pacific. Eager to get home, I returned to Madison as soon as a military flight was available.

During the previous six years I had spent half my time in the field. I had managed to experience ten summers and only two winters (one in Antarctica) during this period, and I was ready for a change of pace. ◆

# THIRTEEN

# Afterword

I returned to my new marriage and two more years at the UW Geophysical and Polar Research Center. I concentrated on interpreting the data resulting from the two Antarctic seasons described in this book. I published 15 papers on this research as well as results of my earlier Antarctic trips, including my Ph.D. thesis on the Filchner Ice Shelf Traverse (1956–58). I also wrote a paper on work done with Ed Thiel (he was the co-author) in the Uinta Mountains in 1955; the data had been languishing as a result of Thiel's several trips to Antarctica.

My first research proposal to the National Science Foundation was funded in 1963 and allowed me to send two men to Antarctica to collect widely spaced aeromagnetic profiles across the entire length of the Transantarctic Mountains from Cape Hallett to the Pensacola Mountains bordering the Filchner Ice Shelf. These UW electrical engineering students, Per Gjelsvik and Richard Wanous, used two new magnetometer systems, designed by Dick Wold. They acquired digital data using available R4D-8s and P2Vs in the same way Ed Thiel had started in 1958, and as I continued as described here. Wanous operated out of Byrd, and Gjelsvik flew from McMurdo.

These undergraduate students acquired 48,000 kilometers of magnetic and snow surface elevation data, an amazing amount considering the limitations of that period. They had various aircraft incidents, but no catastrophes. Gjelsvik managed to obtain extremely long profiles over the Transantarctic Mountains as far as a few hundred kilometers south of the Scott Glacier because the Navy air crew he flew with carried drummed aviation gasoline inside the R4D-8 plane cabin and pumped it into the auxiliary cabin tank by hand. A spark would have demolished the plane and all inside.

Wanous, flying out of Byrd Station, obtained profiles across the Filchner Ice shelf and Pensacola Mountains. One of these flights was the first to show very high-amplitude magnetic anomalies over the Dufek Intrusion exposed in the

Dufek Massif and Forrestal Ranges of the Pensacola Mountains.

Because the data were all collected digitally, I quickly worked up the results in Madison with the help of a staff of student mathematicians and technicians at the Geophysical and Polar Research Center. In a paper published in *Science* in May 1964,[1] I summarized these results and those of all of the aeromagnetic surveys in Antarctica since 1958.

In the meantime, Charlie Bentley, now in charge of the UW Geophysical and Polar Research Center (Woollard had moved to Honolulu to start the Hawaii Institute of Geophysics), had made it very apparent that if I wished to remain in Madison in my research associate position at UW, I had to plan on regular trips to Antarctica. I decided to look elsewhere for work, because by 1963, Donna was pregnant, and the death of Ed Thiel had sobered us all.

I moved on to other research. Other Antarctic geophysicists of my age had similar experiences. As we matured into our early thirties, married, and became fathers, we gradually dropped out of Antarctic field work and went on to other activities.

In April 1964, I joined the U.S. Geological Survey in Denver and six weeks later my son Kurt was born. I started geophysical projects in Grand Teton National Park and the mountains of northern Colorado.

Almost immediately I was persuaded to take over a planned Antarctic geophysical project in the Pensacola Mountains in 1965 working with USGS geologists Art Ford and Dwight Schmidt. I recruited a geophysical team to carry out a 10 kilometer-spaced aeromagnetic survey, make seismic reflection ice thickness measurements and a gravity survey throughout the area, using U.S. Army UH1-B (Huey) helicopters.

The USARP geophysical program in Antarctica changed. From about 1966, when the oversnow traverse program ended, until about 1978, Charles Bentley and his students at UW were among the few who provided any continuity to the U.S. geophysical program on the Antarctic continent.

My second son Marc was born in 1967 and a year later we all moved to Monrovia, Liberia, in West Africa, where I was the geophysicist on a USGS geological mapping project. We had contracted a 400,000-kilometer, 800-meter-spaced aeromagnetic survey flown over a flat rain-forested terrain with very sparse rock exposures. Not too different from Antarctica (geophysically speaking). I made a gravity survey of the country along the few roads and navigable rivers, where precise elevations were available. There were no crevasses, but I encountered crocodiles and malarial mosquitoes.

At this time I also got back into marine geophysics, participating in two geophysical surveys of the Liberian continental margin. My family enjoyed the idyllic tropical life in Monrovia and upcountry with me during my gravity surveys. I even continued my Antarctic research, writing a paper on bottom melting of the Filchner Ice Shelf in steamy Monrovia.

Although malaria was endemic, only a few of the families (not mine) in the 10-person USGS team ever suffered minor attacks. We were paid a 25 percent hazard bonus to work in Liberia, as we had been in Antarctica. Although we treated any risks lightly, probably the hazards were more real than we realized. However, my two sons were spared the common winter childhood illnesses they had suffered in America.

I returned to Denver in 1970 and interpreted my Liberian and Antarctic data. I regularly traveled to Liberia over the next few years and participated in a USGS marine survey of the continental margin there.

In 1972 we moved to Woods Hole on Cape Cod, where I took over the administration of the USGS Marine Geology office at the Woods Hole Oceanographic Institution. Among other activities, we acquired marine multi-channel seismic reflection surveys of the U.S. Atlantic continental margin and an aeromagnetic survey of the same area. The objective was to provide the geologic framework relative to its petroleum resource potential. In 1973 world oil prices tripled and the USGS went heavily into research on energy resources and environmental hazards related to their possible development.

Also in 1973, in Antarctica, the U.S. research ship *Glomar Challenger* drilled a hole in the Ross Sea continental shelf and reported the presence of hydrocarbons. Although this result was later determined to be only biogenic hydrocarbon (similar to swamp gas) generated in shallow sediments beneath the sea floor, the Antarctic Treaty nations were "galvanized to action."[2]

I was asked to advise on Antarctica's petroleum and mineral potential to the USGS team preparing a classified (and later published) estimate of these undiscovered resources.

I completed my tour in Woods Hole and returned to Denver in 1977. I was asked to become USGS program coordinator for the Charleston (and eastern U.S.) Earthquake hazard program. I continued in this capacity for about seven years.

However, my Antarctic activities were resuming. I was immediately asked to go to London as a delegate and scientific advisor to the U.S. Delegation to the 9th Antarctic Treaty Consultative Meeting in 1977, the first to consider petroleum and mineral resources in Antarctica. The USGS Director asked me to coordinate Antarctic activities for the USGS. I continued participation in 21 additional Antarctic Treaty meetings in various parts of the world over the next 18 years. Within about 15 years more than 135,000 kilometers of marine seismic reflection profiles of the type used for petroleum exploration in other parts of the world were acquired over the Antarctic continental shelf by about a dozen countries. The membership in the Antarctic Treaty doubled because of the interest in Antarctic petroleum resources.

There was interest in offshore oil in Antarctica by the petroleum industry because of the 1973 tripled prices, which led to the negotiation of the Convention on the Regulation of Antarctic Mineral Resource Activities (CRAMRA) in the 1980s. During these negotiations, environmental groups such as Greenpeace and the Antarctic and Southern Ocean Coalition agitated about the danger to the fragile Antarctic ecosystem that mining and petroleum resource development would bring. However, throughout this period, the international mining industry was not at all interested in Antarctica. Most metal mines, except for gold, have been closed in the U.S. because of low prices. CRAMRA was adopted by consensus of the Antarctic Treaty in 1988 but never was ratified. CRAMRA was essentially rewritten (with the claimant nation accommodation removed) into the Environmental Protocol to the Antarctic Treaty, which includes a prohibition against future oil and mineral activities, except for scientific research. This Protocol was adopted by consensus in 1991 and entered into force in 1998 after ratification by the 25 Antarctic Treaty Consultative Parties.

By 1991 the price of oil was so low that the petroleum industry did not try to block the Environmental Protocol. I published a number of papers on this subject along with other colleagues, which may have helped persuade industry and government that there are no economic petroleum and mineral resources in Antarctica.

Since the signing of the Environmental Protocol in 1991, the level of marine deep multichannel seismic surveying almost ceased until 2000. The scientific data obtained during the frenzy of the approximate 1977–1990 period have been released into archives and are now available to all interested researchers.

However, as this is written in 2004, the price of oil is climbing again. I believe that within the next one or two decades interest in petroleum development in Antarctica will arise again, despite the fact that the oil shale in Colorado, for example, would cost about half as much investment capital (per first barrel) to develop as Antarctic petroleum.[3] The Antarctic petroleum and minerals issue cannot be reconsidered until 50 years after the Environmental Protocol is in force, but treaties have been brittle in the past, so concern is necessary in the future.

In November 1978 I returned to Antarctica to work with David Drewry of Scott Polar Research Institute of U.K. Using an American C-130 (now called LC-130), we flew a combined radar ice thickness measuring system and a magnetometer over large areas of West Antarctica and the Dufek layered intrusion in the Dufek Massif and Forrestal ranges of the Pensacola Mountains. Although both of these systems had been flown extensively in Antarctica, this was the first aircraft equipped to acquire coincident data. When crossing magnetic rocks such as volcanic structures or intrusions like the Dufek, the combined data allowed quite accurate modeling of the geologic bodies causing high-amplitude magnetic anomalies observed over the featureless ice sheet. However, as this type of aircraft was designed to operate efficiently at high altitude and with fuel available only at McMurdo or South Pole, the amount of data collected as low as 15 meters over the snow surface was extremely limited.

In January 1984 I returned to Antarctica to participate in a marine geophysical cruise in the Ross Sea based out of McMurdo. On the USGS ship *S. P. Lee* we collected marine multichannel seismic reflection and many other types of geophysical and geological data.

When I returned to the U.S. in 1984, my wife and I split up. My constant travel to Antarctica and elsewhere had put too much strain on the marriage. Unfortunately this has happened to a number of my friends as well. Since women became active in the U.S. program about 1968, they, as well as men, have frequently found their marriages and relationships over by the time they got home.

I returned again to Antarctica in November 1984 to work with a German aeromagnetic survey party operating from a remote field camp at the edge of the Ross Sea. U.S. LC-130s delivered fuel to the site and two small twin engine Dornier 228 aircraft flew an extensive survey over the western Ross Sea and northern Victoria Land at a 4.4-kilometer line spacing. In October 1960 I had flown two profiles between McMurdo and Hallett Station as described in the beginning of this book. The 1984–85 survey provided regional coverage of the same area.

In 1988 I again participated with Germans and Americans in a large offset seismic survey in the Ross Sea in a Norwegian ship *Polar Queen* chartered by the Germans.

By 1990 colleagues and I from the USGS and Ohio State University had organized a combined aeromagnetic, radar-ice-sounding, and laser altimeter-equipped Twin Otter aircraft to make measurements in a detailed survey over the West Antarctic Ice Sheet in the same area I covered in 1960–61 described above. Later we were joined by investigators from Columbia University and the U.S. Naval Oceanographic office so that aerogravity was also included in the first test season of 1990–91.

During this same season I was involved with a German-U.S. aeromagnetic survey over the northern Ross Ice Shelf. We used two Dornier 228 ski aircraft and operated out of McMurdo.

During the next eight years the U.S. aerogeophysical program over the West Antarctic Ice Sheet was quite successful. Robin Bell (Lamont Doherty Earth Observatory, of Columbia University), Donald Blankenship (University of Texas Institute of Geophysics), Carol Finn, and I (USGS) were actively involved as principal investigators. I participated in Antarctica for one-month visits as part of this program in 1992 and 1995. In 1993 we reported an active subglacial volcano beneath the ice sheet and in subsequent years hundreds of aeromagnetic anomalies interpreted to be subglacial volcanic centers at the base of the ice sheet.

In 1995 the USGS decided not to support my Antarctic research any longer and I was forced to retire. I felt this ironic considering that an Antarctic research project was one of the early assignments given me by the USGS.

I shortly took a position as a Fellow of the Institute of Arctic and Alpine Research (INSTAAR) at the University of Colorado in Boulder, where I continue to this day. I work on the aerogeophysical surveys in Antarctica with financial support from the National Science Foundation and the USGS. My most recent trip to Antarctica was a Ross Sea geophysical cruise in December 2002–January 2003, which ended at McMurdo. ◆

# Epilogue

*"Writing can take you places*

*you only understand*

*after you've written something."*

—Dan Chaon, National Public Radio, 20 January, 2002

*"Writing is not the survival of the fittest*

*but survival of the survivors."*

—*The Dante Club*, Matthew Pearl

Undirected, curiosity-driven, Antarctic research in the 1990s and early twenty-first century is much safer than forty years ago. The Antarctic air squadron VX6 had an accident rate eight times that of U.S. Naval aviation in other parts of the world at that time. Of the ten or so of us who went to "the Ice" regularly from the University of Wisconsin, two were killed in aircraft accidents, along with several tens of Navy men. Then the program was more directed and driven partly by Cold War priorities. Antarctic research is now a privilege rather than an obligation, as it was then, and little more than 20 percent of the proposals are funded by the National Science Foundation.

In contrast to the earlier era described here, only six people have died in field research in Antarctica since 1970,[1] three of these in one helicopter crash in 1992. Some think that Antarctic research may be *too* safe, that sometimes research objectives are thwarted because of inordinate safety concerns. In the early 1990s one field party of experienced glaciologists working in a crevassed area at the border of an ice stream draining the West Antarctic Ice Sheet was denied access from their field camp into the study area by an inexperienced safety officer, and they returned to the U.S. without even starting the research project. Fortunately, common sense has removed such barriers to science.

On the other hand, perhaps as students we took risks that may not have been justifiable working on our own and our professors' research. I have described here many dangerous incidents, as well as five deaths, all to carry out science on the coldest continent.

In 2001 *The Chronicle of Higher Education* published a scathing article,[2] *Research at What Cost?* attacking a noted glaciologist and Ohio State University for errors resulting in the death of a graduate student in 1997. The university won a lawsuit, but the article argued that the glaciologist and Ohio State bore major responsibility in the death.

Scientific field research in remote parts of the world is inherently hazardous and accidents will happen. Even such a staid and venerable field research organization as the U.S. Geological Survey has a long record of deaths, though infrequent, in the field. When, if ever, do the ends justify the means? It is one thing if mature individual researchers, professional technicians, aviators, and others take risks with full awareness of the hazards. But it is quite another thing if relatively naive graduate students and new Ph.D.s looking for adventure, such as my colleagues and I in the 1956–1962 period, are sent into harm's way, without knowing specifically what they will face, by ambitious senior researchers pursuing their personal scientific objectives, even though these may be of vital national and international importance.

I have worked both sides of this street in the past 50 years. Field science has always been risky since before Darwin set out on the *Beagle* and likely will continue to be. I am one of those willing to take these risks, but I have lost a number of friends and colleagues to research in Antarctica and elsewhere. I am not so sure I could recommend this path to others. I think it is essential that graduate students and other young assistants be well informed of the risks they *will* be taking. Then they can decide whether the data are worth it. ◆

# Maps

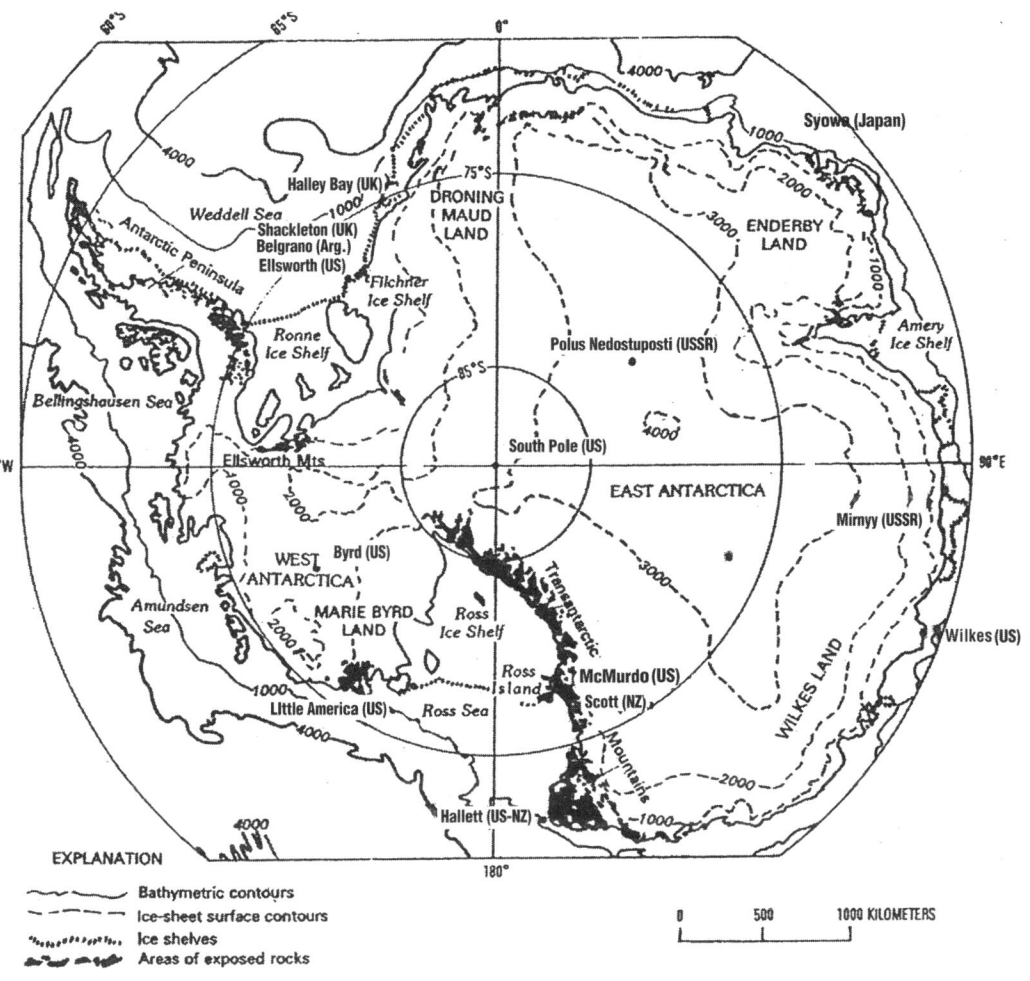

MAP 1. United States and selected other 1957 stations and bases on modern map of Antarctica. All place names are accepted by U.S. Board of Geographic Names. Elevations in meters. (From USGS.)

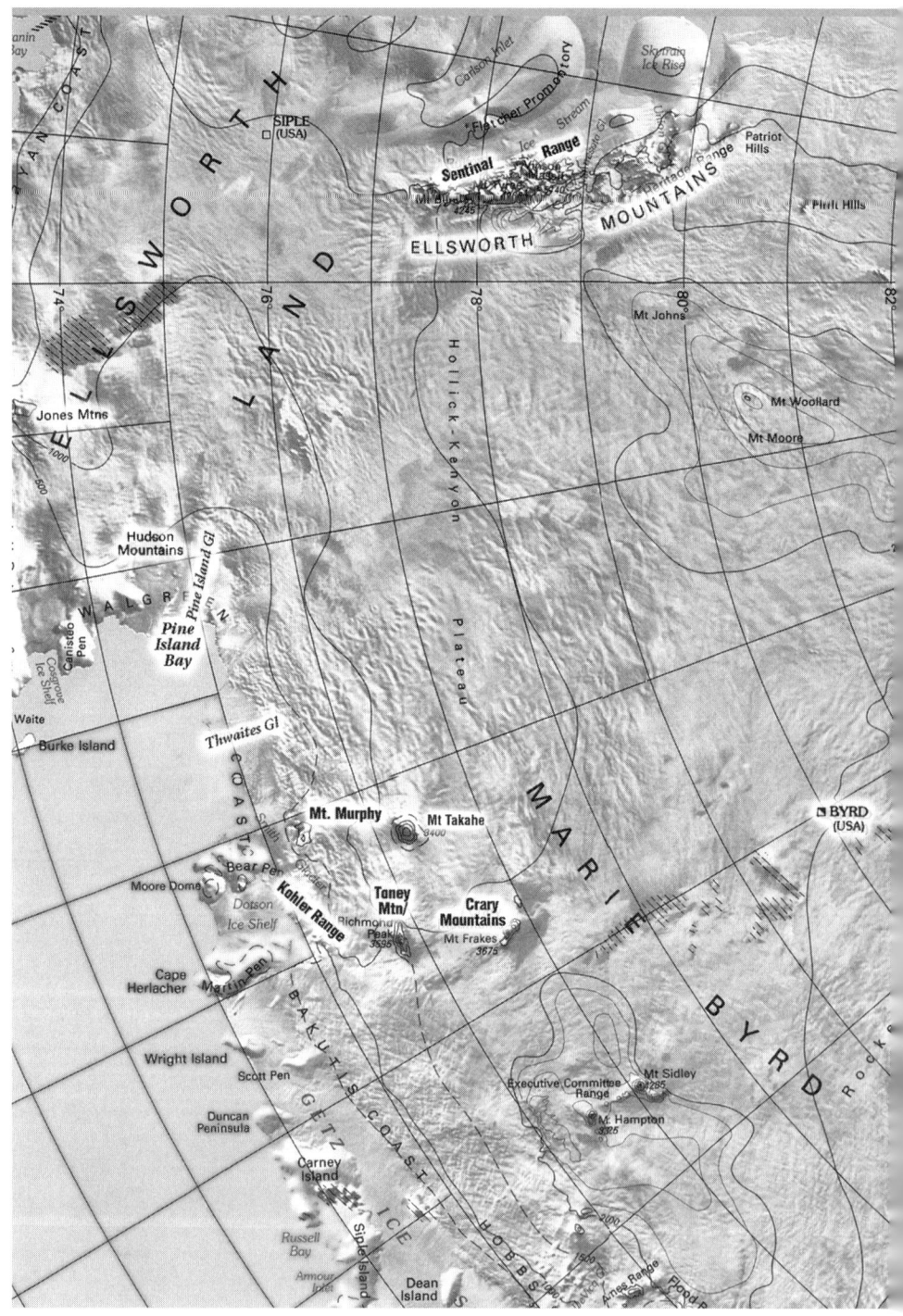

Manin Bay

ANAN COAST

E L L S W O R T H

SIPLE
□ (USA)

Carlson Inlet

Fletcher Promontory

Skytrain Ice Rise

Ice Stream

Sentinal    Range

Mt Wade
4285

Heritage Range

Patriot Hills

ELLSWORTH    MOUNTAINS

Pirrit Hills

L A N D

74°

76°

78°

80°

82°

Mt Johns

Mt Woollard

Mt Moore

Jones Mtns

1000

500

Hollick-Kenyon

Hudson
Mountains

Pine Island Gl

W A L G R

Pine
Island
Bay

Cosgrove
Ice Shelf

Canisteo
Pen

Waite

Burke Island

Thwaites Gl

COAST

Plateau

Mt. Murphy

Mt Takahe
3400

M A R I E

BYRD
(USA)

Bear Pen

Moore Dome

Kohler Range

Toney
Mtn

Crary
Mountains

Dotson
Ice Shelf

Richmond
Peak
3595

Mt Frakes
3675

Cape
Herlacher

Martin Pen

Wright Island

Scott Pen

B A K U T I S   C O A S T

Duncan
Peninsula

Carney
Island

Russell
Bay

Armour
Inlet

Siple Island

Dean
Island

G E T Z    I C E

H O B B S

B Y R D

Executive Committee
Range

Mt Sidley
4285

Mt Hampton
3325

Ames Range

Flood R

Rocke

1500

2100

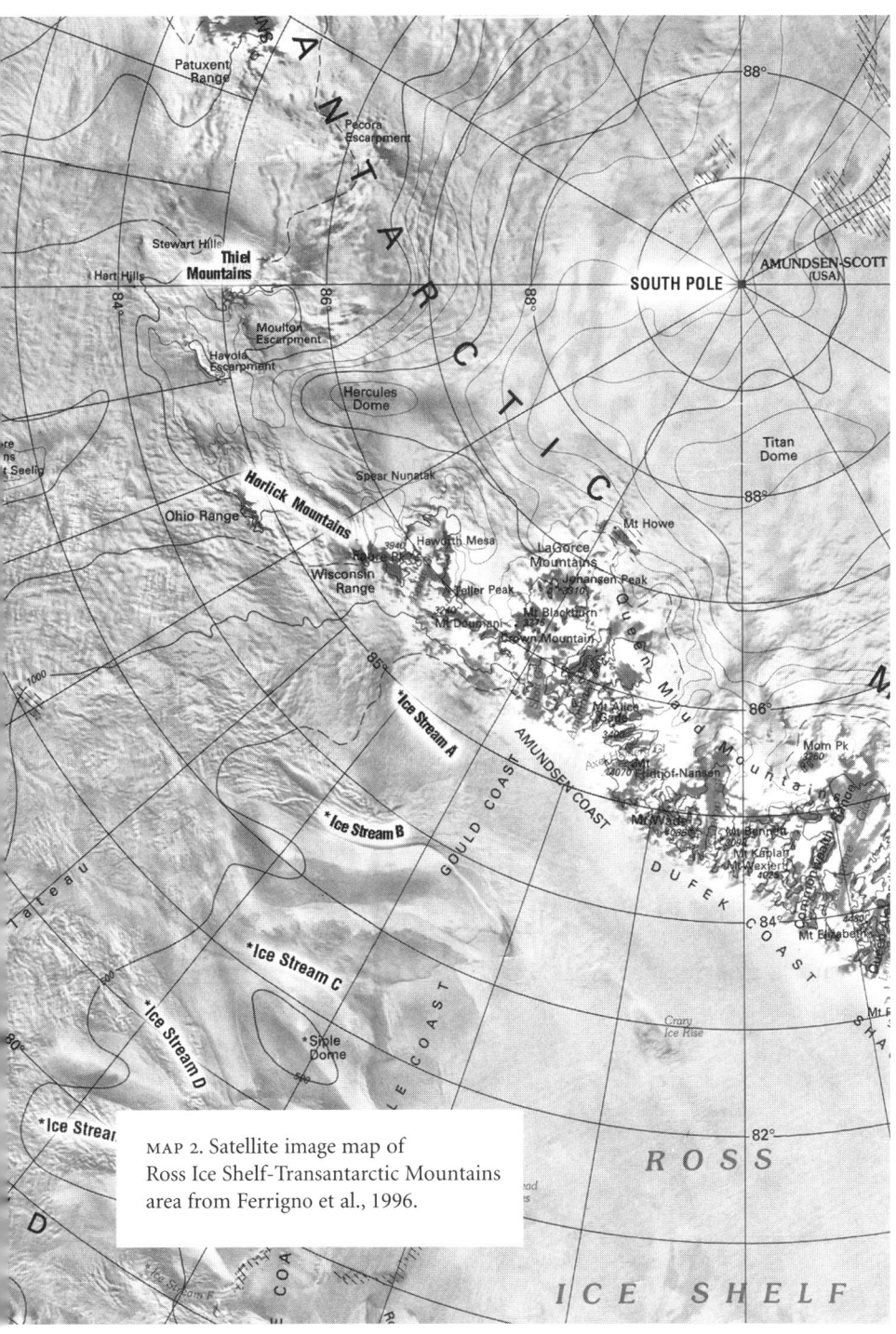

MAP 2. Satellite image map of
Ross Ice Shelf-Transantarctic Mountains
area from Ferrigno et al., 1996.

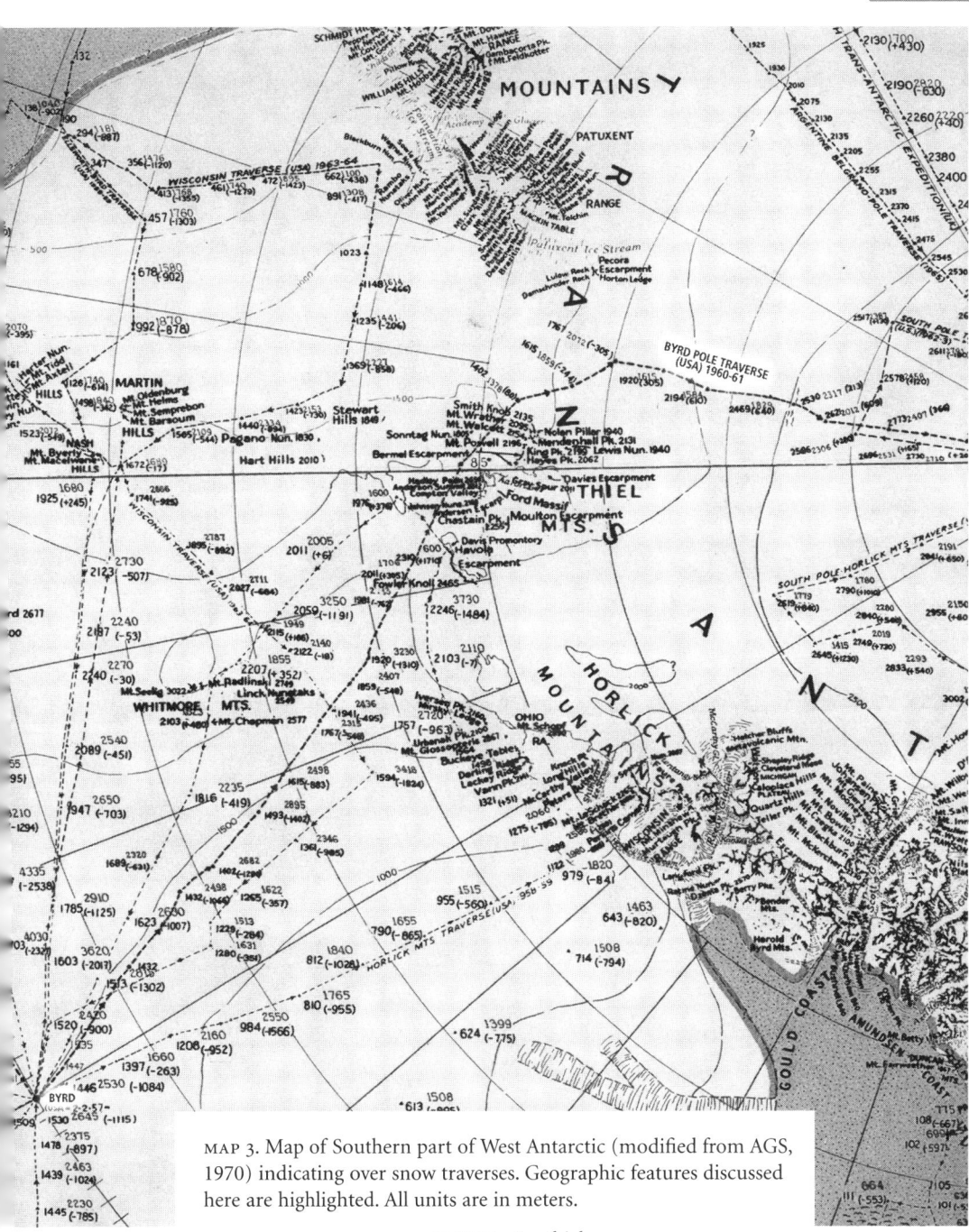

<small>MAP 3.</small> Map of Southern part of West Antarctic (modified from AGS, 1970) indicating over snow traverses. Geographic features discussed here are highlighted. All units are in meters.

KEY: Ice surface elevation   •875 1580 (-700)    Ice thickness<br>Elevation of subice rock surface

**Maps**

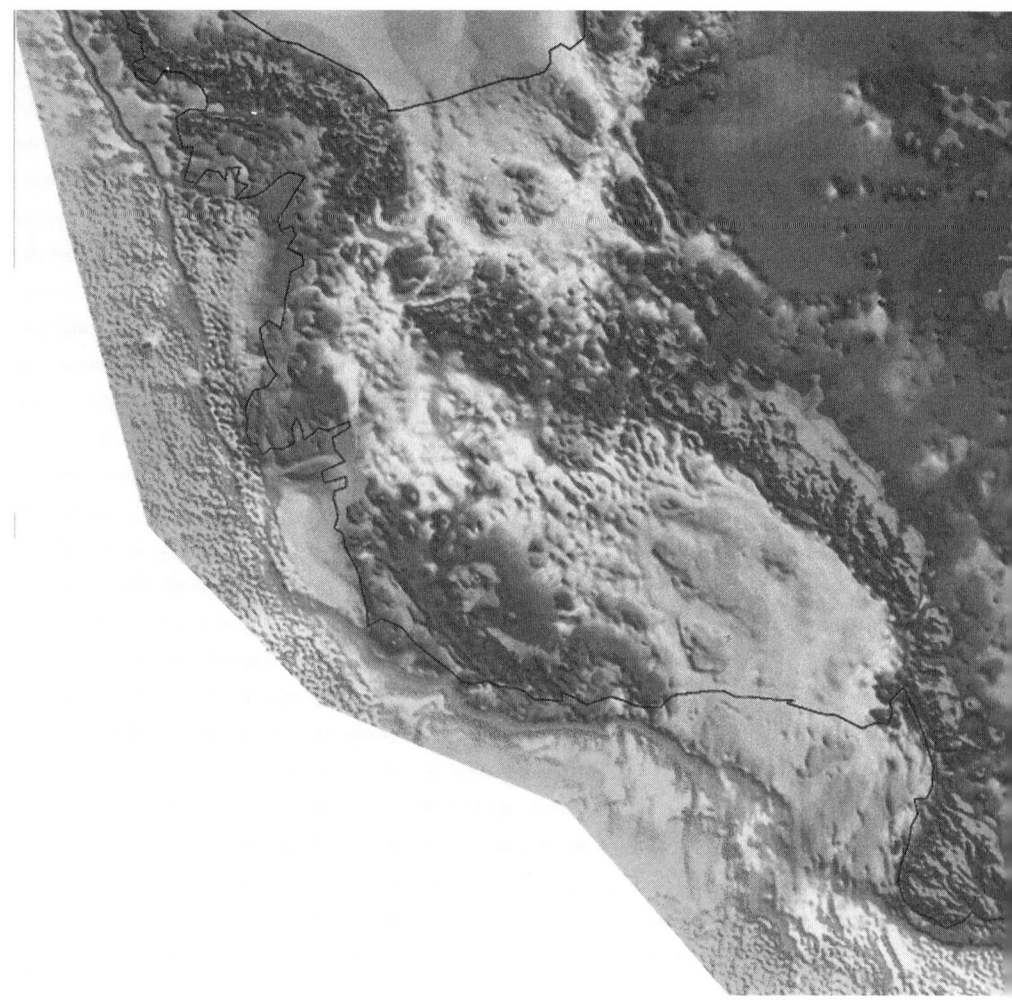

MAP 4. Shaded relief map of bed of part of Antarctic Ice Sheet. Compare depths in meters in Maps 3 and 7. Modified from Lythe and Vaughan et al., 2000.

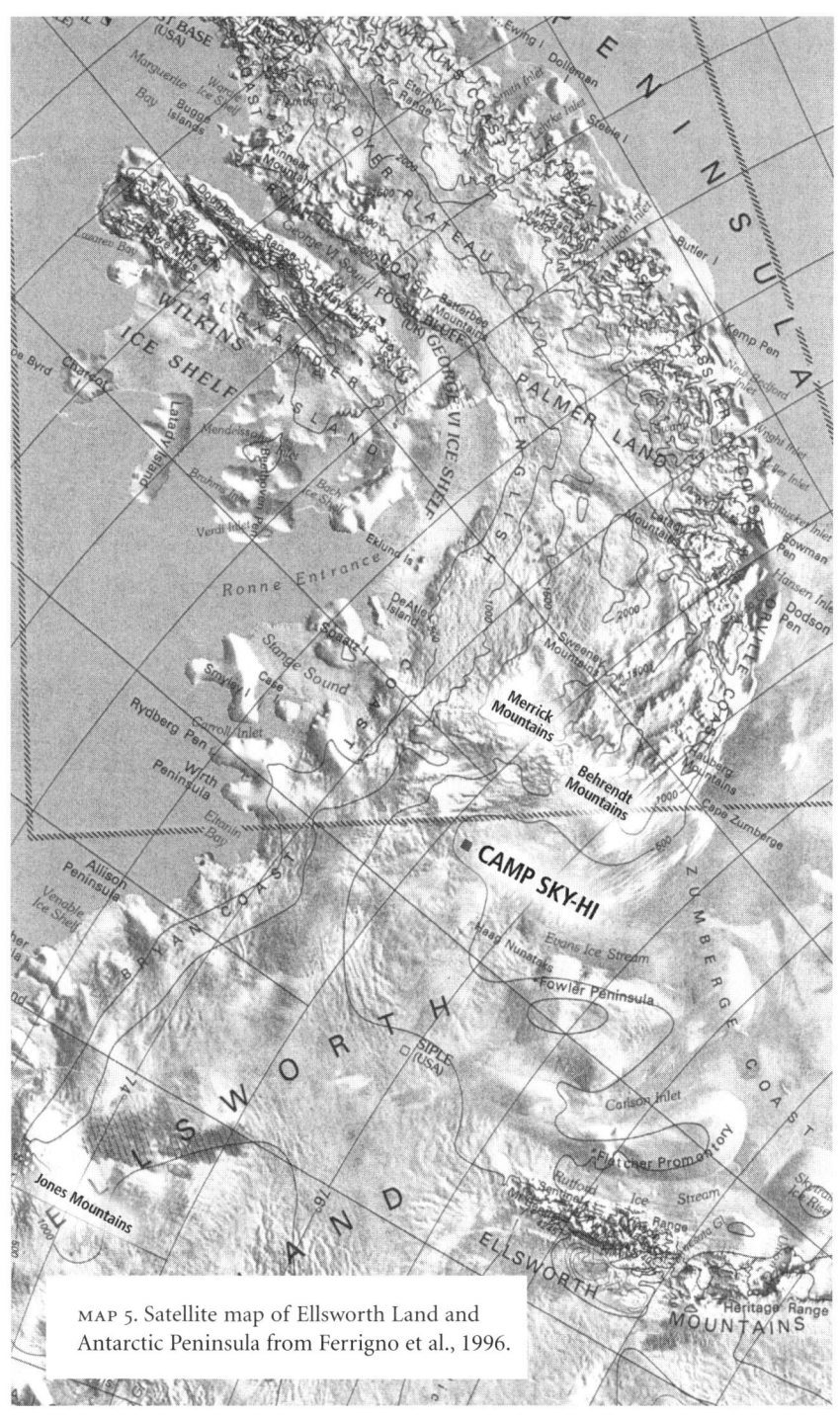

MAP 5. Satellite map of Ellsworth Land and Antarctic Peninsula from Ferrigno et al., 1996.

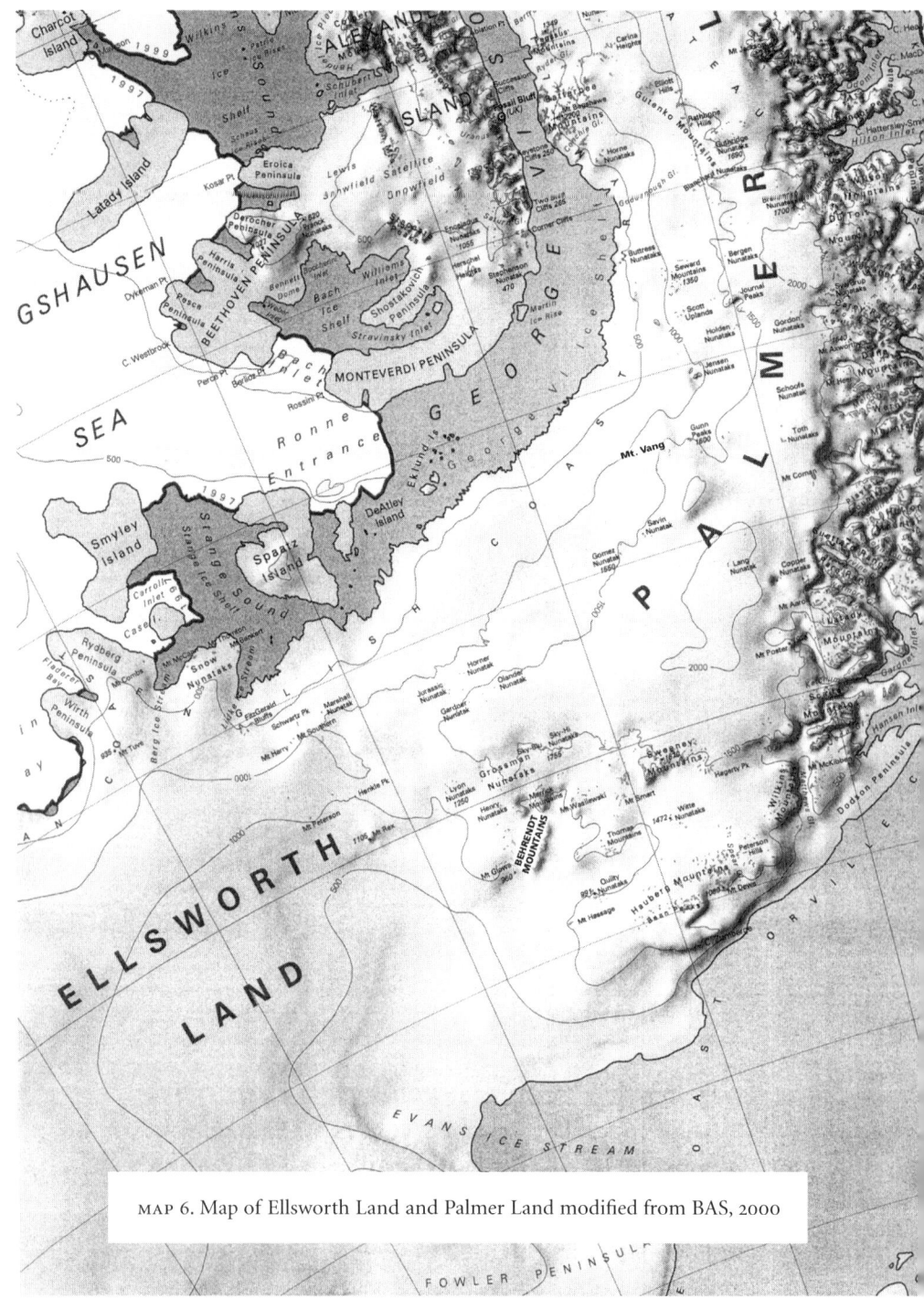

MAP 6. Map of Ellsworth Land and Palmer Land modified from BAS, 2000

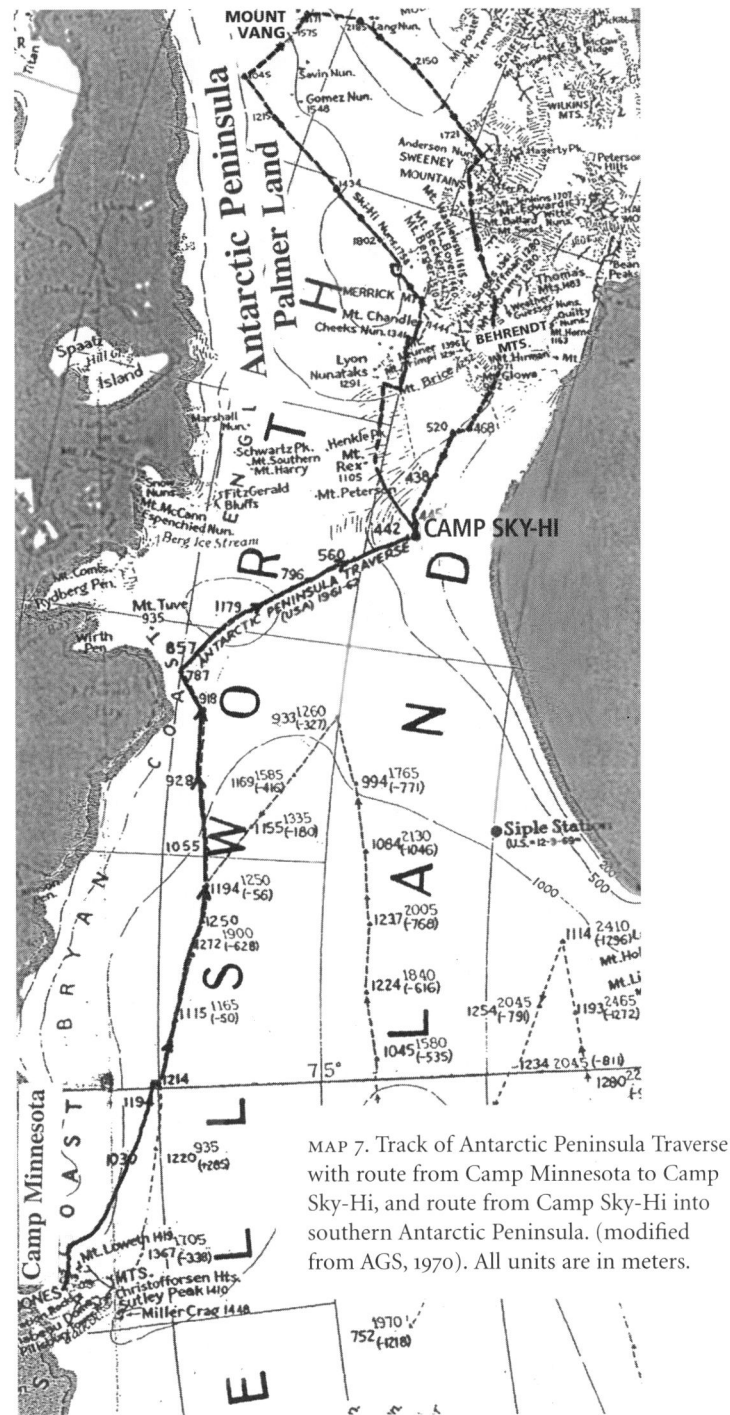

MAP 7. Track of Antarctic Peninsula Traverse with route from Camp Minnesota to Camp Sky-Hi, and route from Camp Sky-Hi into southern Antarctic Peninsula. (modified from AGS, 1970). All units are in meters.

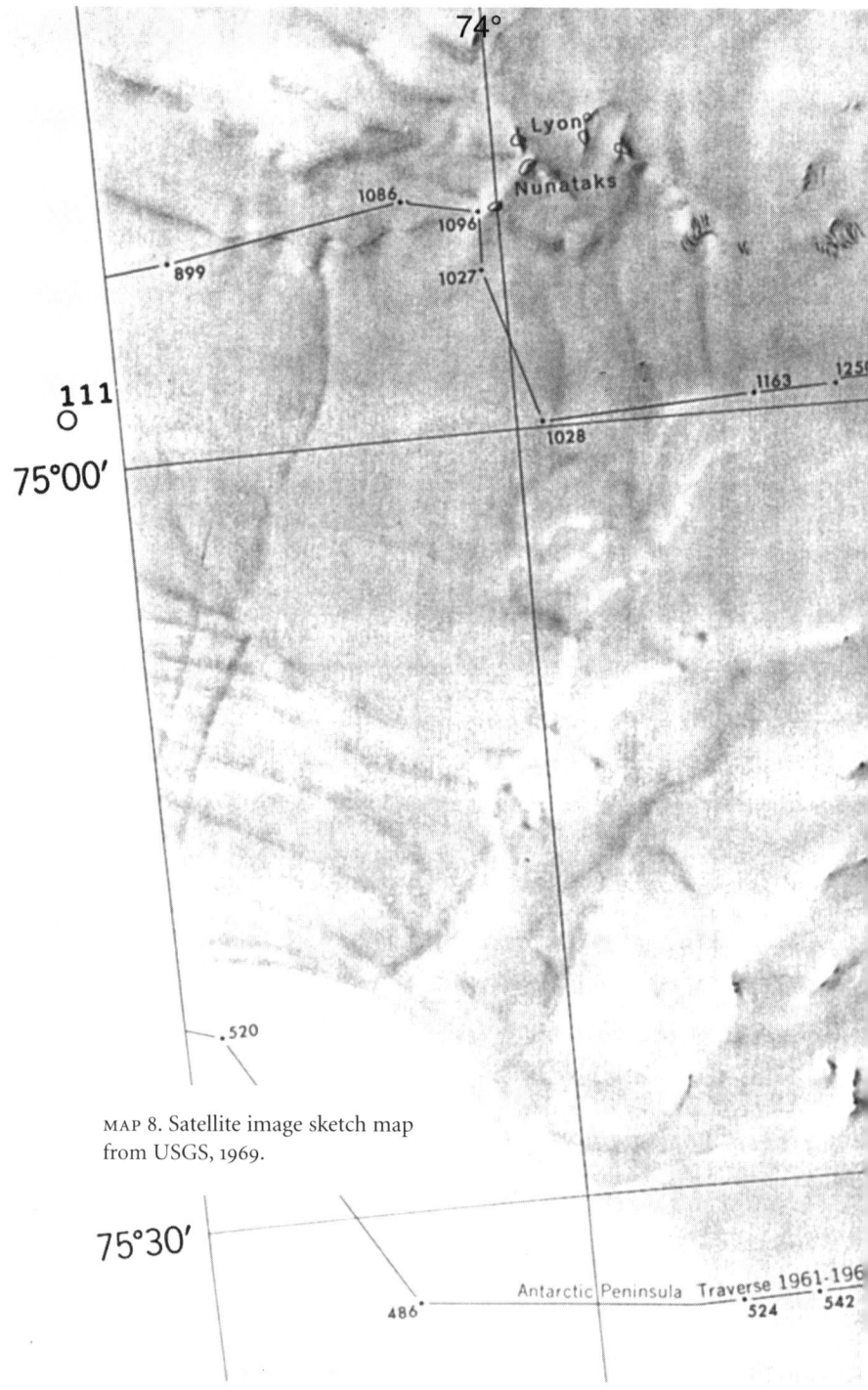

MAP 8. Satellite image sketch map from USGS, 1969.

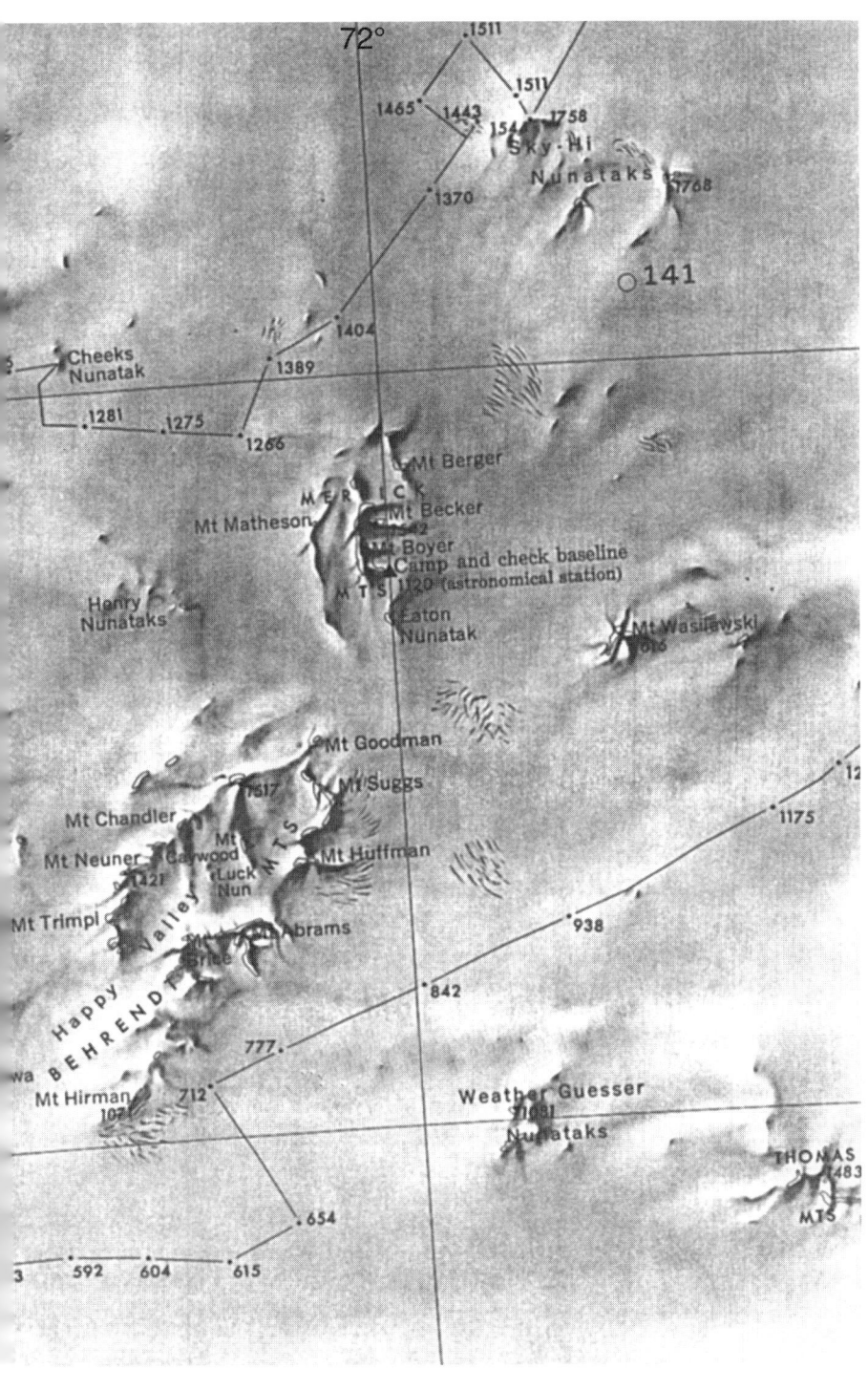

72°

.1511

.1511

1465 1443

1758

1465 1544

1370

Sky-Hi
Nunataks 1768

○ 141

1404

Cheeks
Nunatak 1389

.1281 .1275

1266

Mt Berger

MERICK

Mt Becker

Mt Matheson 1242

Mt Boyer

Camp and check baseline

MTS 1120 (astronomical station)

Henry
Nunataks

Eaton
Nunatak

Mt Wasilewski

Mt Goodman

1517 Mt Suggs

1175

Mt Chandler

Mt Neuner Gaywood

Mt Huffman

Mt
1421 Luck
Nun

938

Mt Trimpi

Abrams

Valley

842

Happy

Mt
Brice

BEHRENDT

777.

wa

712

654

Mt Hirman
1071

Weather Guesser
1061
Nunataks

THOMAS
483

MTS

3 592 604 615

# Notes

## Chapter 1

1. Aircraft distances and speeds were, and are, here reported in nautical miles. Elevations were always reported in feet. I have used metric where appropriate but mostly English units for clarity for American readers. All of the scientific measurements were made in metric units.

2. Jet-assisted takeoff. In the early 1960s "JATO" was used as a jargon term as a plural noun, e.g., "16 JATO were needed." "JATO" was also used as an adjective, e.g., "JATO takeoff" or "JATO bottles."

3. Local Byrd station time. Military (Z) or Universal time (UT) notation is used by the Navy or Air Force in flying in Antarctica. I have converted this to local Byrd time here.

4. Art Ford, John Aaron, and Pete Bermel, USGS; Capt. Joseph Walker, aircraft commander, Sergeants Andrew N. Holzener, F. W. Clark, Frederick W. Streitenberger (U.S. Marine Corps), Lt. Cdr. Lou Smith (not his real surname), copilot, PH2 L. Sayer (photographer), U.S. Navy, Richard Wold, Thomas Laudon, and I (University of Wisconsin) were on the plane (R4D-8 BuNo 11219).

5. Someone, a few years later (probably Lou), wrote an "*Anonymous*," (a non-attributed description of this incident in a Navy air safety magazine). An account of an incident such as ours was encouraged by the Navy and referred to as a "Minnie Mouse." The brief report described the occurrence as happening in a remote part of the world. Most significantly, the author did not include that the radar man had reported "targets 13 miles ahead."

6. There is an old Navy cliché I first heard at this time, which I paraphrased: "Aeromagnetic surveying consists of hours and hours of sheer boredom interspersed with occasional moments of stark terror!"

## Chapter 2

1. The U.S. IGY traverses were: (1) the Ross Ice Shelf (1957–58) and Victoria Land (1958–59), headquartered at Little America Station on the Ross Ice Shelf under Bert Crary; (2) the Little America-Byrd (1957) and Sentinel Mountain (1957–58) under Charles (Charlie) R. Bentley (geophysicist) and Verne Anderson (glaciologist) and Horlick Mountains (1958–59) under Bentley, operating out of Byrd Station on the West Antarctic Ice Sheet; (3) the Filchner Ice Shelf Traverse (1957–58), led by Ed Thiel and Hugo Neuberg (glaciologist) and the Ellsworth-Byrd traverse, led by John Pirrit (glaciologist), both out of Ellsworth Station on the Filchner Ice Shelf.

2. An incomplete list includes: Charles Swithinbank and John Hollin, glaciologists; Colin Bull, geophysicist (UK); Mario Giovinetto, glaciologist (Argentina); John Pirrit, glaciologist (Scotland); Feng Keng Chaing, geophysicist (Taiwan); George Doumani, geologist-glaciologist (Lebanon); Manfred Hochstein, geophysicist, and Peter Schoek,

glaciologist-aurora observer (Germany); Franz van der Hoeven, geophysicist (Netherlands); and Sven Evteev, glaciologist (USSR).

3. In 1959 Thiel was thirty-one, Bentley twenty-nine, Ned Ostenso twenty-nine, Hugh Bennett twenty-nine, Edwin Robinson twenty-four and I was twenty-seven. Mario Giovinetto, who would join us from Ohio State University, was twenty-six. All of us were single.

4. A two-week trip in January-February, with a gravity meter, had me tieing in base stations from Madison to San Francisco, Honolulu, Canton Island, Fiji, Christchurch, Sydney, Brisbane, Darwin, Bangkok, Calcutta, Karachi, Bahrain, Cairo, Rome, Paris, Dakar, Rio de Janeiro, Buenos Aires, Asuncion, Bogotá, New York, and to Madison. I stayed nights only in New Zealand, Australia, Italy, and Argentina. I continued studying throughout this grueling trip.

5. Rear Admiral David M. Tyree was Commander of Task Force 43 (TF 43) and Commander of Naval Support Force Antarctica during the 1960–62 period described in this book. In April 1959, he had replaced Rear Admiral George Dufek (CTF 43) in charge during the IGY years (Deep Freeze I–IV). The U.S. Navy had a large operation in Christchurch, New Zealand at the airport, which was the main staging area for United States operations into Antarctica from the beginning of Deep Freeze I in 1955.

By the 1970s the National Science Foundation (NSF) was budgeted for the entire program, and the Navy reduced its presence and downgraded its top position, Commander Naval Support Forces Antarctica, to the rank of captain. Dufek and Tyree were two star admirals. In 1960 TF 43 comprised nine ships including one Coast Guard and three Navy icebreakers, down from 12 ships during the IGY.

There were 2600 military personnel and 8 NSF staff supporting 142 scientific workers. Or perhaps the scientists, mostly graduate students and technicians, there "to do the science" (as it was referred to by the Navy) were a cover for the Navy expedition? Opinions still vary.

### Chapter 3

1. Named for a Seabee who drowned there in 1956, when his D-8 Caterpillar tractor broke through thin ice and sank.

2. Swithinbank, 1998.

3. By 1960 this had been changed to Naval Air Facility McMurdo (NAF McMurdo).

4. Charles Swithinbank, a British glaciologist, first went to Antarctica with the Norwegian-British-Swedish Expedition in 1949–52. He retired from the British Antarctic Survey (BAS) in 1986, and has since pioneered the use of wheeled aircraft landing on "blue-ice" areas throughout the continent. Swithinbank has continued lecturing on tourist cruise ships as recently as 2003. This made him, at the tender age of 74 (in 2000) the only person who has been in Antarctica in each of seven successive decades.

5. John "Jack" Tuck was a twenty-four-year-old Seabee Lt. j.g.[junior grade] when he was the Navy officer-in-charge at the South Pole Station during the first winter there in 1957 (but was a civilian in 1960). Paul Siple, a well-known geographer, was station scientific leader, and at forty-eight, was much senior, with many years of scientific and Antarctic experience. Although Siple was originally concerned about the dual command,

there were no problems because he was really in charge. I knew Tuck fairly well and Siple only slightly but was impressed by both.

6. By 1960 the University of Wisconsin Geophysical and Polar Research Center not only supplied most of the scientific personnel and equipment for the oversnow traverse program, but also the support people such as mechanics in Antarctica, and personnel, purchasing, shipping, and other staff in Madison. The Ohio State University supplied glaciologists; USGS, topographic engineers, and the USC&GS, geophysicists to make magnetic observations at stations on the traverses.

7. Twenty-five feet long, 10.5 feet high, and 9 feet wide.

8. Behrendt, 1998.

9. The Weasel was a World War II tracked amphibious vehicle that could theoretically float on water as well as operate on snow. It was about 12 feet long and, for Antarctic use, had an insulated cab. Weasels were fun to drive and could reach speeds of 20–30 mph on smooth snow. However, they were not very durable mechanically and broke through snow bridges over hidden crevasses more easily than the Sno-Cats. Therefore they were definitely not as safe as Sno-Cats.

A Weasel had the throttle and gear-shift controls in the usual places, and was steered by braking the right or left track with levers between the driver's knees. The engine was inside, to the right of the driver, and three passengers could squeeze uncomfortably in the back seat. By 1960 weasels were being phased out of the U.S. Antarctic Program. The only ones at the bases were leftovers from the IGY.

10. Hahn, 1961. The Operation Deep Freeze cruise books are similar to a high school yearbook with many photographs and names of everyone in the ships' crews and those who wintered over in the U.S. IGY program. All of the vital statistics for the names and locations of stations, ships, their itineraries, etc. are included. The cruise books were primarily paid for by the Navy ships' crews and station personnel (and also by the scientific personnel). These unpretentious but useful cruise books are essentially unavailable, except in personal libraries.

11. Filson, 1975.

12. A Navy project to measure the earth's magnetic field over all of the oceans of the world. Although this project made several flights to and over Antarctica, this was not their main area of operation. Consequently the pilots were not particularly experienced in Antarctic flying.

13. Although Carl Ecklund, a noted Antarctic ornithologist, had been the Station Scientific Leader at Wilkes Station during the 1957 winter of IGY, biology was not one of the scientific disciplines at that time.

14. The four turboprop engines in the Hercules C-130 used a kerosene type fuel called JP-4 (in 1960), which is less flammable than avgas, which meant that Navy had to keep separate supplies of both types of aircraft fuel, as well as automotive gasoline (called mogas) and diesel fuel.

15. The Polar 3 was a Dornier 228 ski-wheel plane in which I flew with the USGS-German GANOVEX 4 aeromagnetic survey in 1984–85. We mapped this very prominent, high-amplitude anomaly, which trends east-west for about 100 kilometers over the Ross Sea south of Hallett Station. On the return trip to Germany from Antarctica this plane

was shot down by Polisario guerrillas over Morocco and the three-man crew killed. I suggested the name "Polar Three" for this anomaly in remembrance.

## Chapter 4

1. Doumani, 1999.

2. Ibid.

3. David Bresnahan (NSF) explained to me at McMurdo in January 2003 how they had just successfully built a safe trail through a "shear zone" southwest of Ross Island by blasting open crevasses and filling them with snow as had been done for the Army-Navy trail from Little America to Byrd in the 1956–57 season. If successfully completed across the Ross Ice Shelf, up the Leverett Glacier (85°38'S, 147°35'W) and on to the Pole, this route will be about 1000 miles long compared to about 800 miles by air. They plan on carrying a cargo load up and back in 2004–05 using Challenger 95 tractors. Although a 30-day round trip is planned instead of 6 hours in a Hercules aircraft (LC-130), mostly fuel would be taken at a cost of $0.63–$0.84 per pound compared with more than $13 per pound by LC-130 (CRREL estimates, according to George Blaisdell).

4. The names of these features have only become more confusing in the past four decades. The formal definition of Marie Byrd Land is the part of the West Antarctic Ice Sheet centered about 80°S, 120°W where the ice is about 3000 meters thick. Early geologic and geophysical papers use this definition. However, geologists in the 1970s began to use "Marie Byrd Land" to refer to the coastal area bordering the Amundsen Sea where many nunataks are exposed; this coastal area is also known by various names for different sub areas. To further confuse things, small scale maps of Antarctica show Marie Byrd Land more or less correctly as the area of the West Antarctic Ice Sheet surrounding Byrd Station.

In like manner, the Byrd Subglacial Basin was originally defined in 1961 (U.S. Advisory Committee for Antarctic Names), "for its locus relative to Marie Byrd land and Byrd Station," as the vast subsea-level area (at about 1500 meters depth) underlying the 1500-meters-high ice of Marie Byrd Land. Because of an error in drafting on the Drewry, 1983, Scott Polar Research Institute Atlas, the words "Byrd Subglacial Basin" were printed over a smaller deep area to the north of the bedrock Sinuous Ridge beneath the divide of the West Antarctic Ice Sheet. The Byrd Subglacial Basin has since been redefined by the U.S. Advisory Committee on Geographic Names (*U.S. Geographic Names of Antarctica,* 1995) as this smaller deep area because it so designated in the Drewry atlas, although the original definition was used in scientific papers for more than 30 years. As of 2003 the vast subglacial area beneath Byrd Station and the West Antarctic Ice Sheet inland from Ice Streams A–E has no official name.

5. Dufek, 1957.

6. A replacement station called "New Byrd" was under construction six miles east of "Old Byrd" during the two summers covered by this book.

7. Ellsworth, 1937.

8. Ronne, 1948.

9. FM BYRD STA
    TO COMNAVSUPFOR ANTARCTICA
    INFO REP COMNAVSUPFOR ANT WASH DC

BUMED

USARP WASHDC

COMNAVANTSUPPACTY

191830 Z

1. Behrendt, John Charles— 3. Male 4. Cauc 5. 18 May, 1932.— 7. Civ USARP.— 9. Byrd Station Antarctica.— 11. E. F. Bartlett, Lt. MC USN. 13. A [admitted] 13 Nov. 60, DG-1 Appendicitis Acute——— D [discharged] 19 Nov, 60.

10. Naslund, 1999.

## Chapter 5

1. Behrendt, 1998.

2. The takahae is a flightless bird native to New Zealand. In the 1956 period at the beginning of the U.S. Antarctic program, there was a pub at the outskirts of Christchurch called "The Sign of the Takahae" (the building still exists with the same name but it is no longer a bar). VX6 pilots frequented the pub and later named an R4D *Takahae* after it. The aircraft *Takahae* resupplied Charlie Bentley's Sentinel Mountains Traverse in 1957–58. This traverse discovered the 20-mile-wide, 11,000-foot-high volcano and the field party named it after the resupply plane.

3. Pirrit, 1967.

4. They had a small grey kitten, which at the last minute was left behind when the major thought the smell was already bad enough in the wanigans.

Tom's mother sent him a narcissus bulb, which he has kept in a grapefruit juice can. [February] It sprouted and blossomed and is now hanging in the mess hall.

Neither cats, nor dogs, nor any other non-native species of plant or animal, are now permitted in Antarctica under the environmental protocol to the Antarctic Treaty, which entered into force in 1998.

5. The ice thickness at Station A was 3160 meters. As the elevation was about 1700 meters, this means rock is about 1500 meters below sea level. Allowing for isostatic rebound if the ice were removed, the rock would be about 200 meters below sea level, which is quite shallow. The ice sheet pushes the underlying rock down about a third of the ice thickness because of its weight.

6. The ice thickness was 3240 meters at [Station B] and 2710 meters at Station C. As the elevation at station [B] was about 1780 meters, the bedrock is 1460 meters below sea level. The rock surface would rebound to about −400 meters after ice removal. Station [C] is 2710 meters thick at about 1830 meters elevation, leaving the rock at −880 meters. If the ice were removed the rock surface would rebound to about sea level at this station.

7. I (with co-authors; Behrendt et al., 1998) reported a volcanic caldera complex in this area interpreted from the 1996 magnetic data. Our 1960–61 ice thickness measurements only hinted at the complex topography beneath the ice sheet, but these results and Bentley's ice soundings on the Ellsworth Highland Traverse were the first suggestions of the rugged landscape beneath the featureless surface of the West Antarctic Ice Sheet. The airborne and oversnow traverse seismic measurements of the 1950s and 1960s were too widely spaced for the necessary resolution. It was only when five-kilometer-spaced aerogeophysical surveys (including radar ice sounding) became possible in the 1990s that the

complex bedrock topography beneath the grounded Antarctic ice sheet could be successfully defined.

8. Behrendt, 1998.

9. Sponholz, 2003.

## Chapter 6

1. At 87°32'S, 78°W.

2. The bulk of the magazine comprised USARP supplies. There were 6200 pounds of Petrogel, with the remainder consisting of Nitromon, which we used for reflection shooting, Pelletol, and Dupont seismograph 60 percent gelatin dynamite. The Navy had only 1,200 pounds of M5A1 demolition blocks.

3. Henry Rosenthal [Brecher] told me of his experiences as a Jew in Europe during World War II. After the *Anschluss* his family, like all Jews, was persecuted by the Nazis in Austria. As he is just my age (I was born in 1932), and as he was only about five or six at the time he doesn't recall too much. But he did remember the German S.S. or S.A. sentries guarding his family's textile store after it was confiscated. His parents sent him to relatives in Zagreb, Yugoslavia, but remained behind themselves [to take care of their parents] and disappeared like so many millions of others. When the Germans invaded Yugoslavia in 1941, he was not immediately arrested like other Jews because he was technically a German citizen. He was sent by his relatives to live in Split on the Adriatic coast with friends of his parents, the Rosenthal family (who informally adopted him, hence the change of last name). This part of the country was occupied by the Italians, who did not persecute the Jews as much as the Germans. He did have to leave school (3rd grade), however.

When Italy surrendered, the Germans occupied the rest of Yugoslavia. They rounded up all the Jews in Split in big warehouses for shipment out. Apparently concurrent reverses in the war caused them to withdraw their occupying troops and turn the detainees over to the local authorities and he and his family were released. With the help of bribes and Tito's partisans, the family made its way on foot in several weeks to a place up the coast from where they were transferred by ship to the Italian city of Bari, which the British were occupying at the time. After being given clothing and medical treatment at a refugee camp, they were moved into a government-administered house in the countryside between Bari and Naples.

In the summer of 1944 President Roosevelt offered asylum in the U.S. to 1000 refugees for the duration of the war and he and his family were fortunate in being among the group. After being housed in a camp at Fort Ontario, Oswego, New York, until February 1946 they were allowed to immigrate formally by crossing over into Canada and immediately back into the U.S.

In 2001 CBS televised a miniseries on this forgotten episode, known as "Token Shipment." Henry changed his last name back to the original Brecher after his return from Antarctica. He was still at Byrd Polar Research Center at Ohio State University at the turn of the century.

4. The seismic wave reflected off the bottom of the ice, back to the surface of the snow, then back to the bottom and back again to the surface. This is possible under good conditions because the snow-air interface has a very high velocity and density contrast, which

makes it an excellent reflector. We tried to record "multiples" to insure that the first reflection was, in fact, the primary one.

5. What new skis? My journal makes no mentions of any, but apparently they were a significant help to us this day.

6. Fred Thwaites was an interesting fellow, who never received a Ph.D. because he refused to take the German exam during World War I. Consequently, he never was promoted above assistant professor despite being a world-renowned glacial geologist and geomorphologist. I had the privilege of taking geomorphology and glacial geology from him during the year before his retirement in 1955.

7. [Station 1] is 920 meters elevation, with 1930 meters ice thickness resulting in bedrock −1010 meters (below sea level). In the same order, the [Station 2] is 875 meters, 1580 meters thick, and −710 meters depth; [Station 3] is 580 meters, 840 meters thick, −260 meters depth; [Station 4] is 860 meters, 1590 meters thick, and 730 meters depth; [Station 5] is 930 meters, 1930 meters thick, and −1000 meters depth.

8. Behrendt, Laudon, and Wold, 1962.

9. Shepherd et al., 2002.

10. The aeromagnetic method was "invented" for studying geology, by James Balsley of the USGS about 1946 using a World War II Navy submarine detector sensor towed from an airplane. Balsley also made the first aeromagnetic measurements in Antarctica during U.S. Navy Operation Highjump in 1947.

11. Ferrigno et al., 1996.

12. Rignot and Jacobs, 2002.

13. Taylor, 1916.

## Chapter 7

1. Wright and Priestley, 1922. This is a famous book in glaciology circles.

2. Behrendt, 1967.

## Chapter 8

1. Behrendt, 1961.

2. Behrendt, 1998.

## Chapter 9

1. Our loads broke down thus:

| | |
|---|---|
| 3 Sno-Cats | 37,500 pounds |
| oil, antifreeze, etc. | 2,170 |
| diesel fuel, 2400 gallons | 21,700 |
| explosives | 4,000 |
| food | 6,100 |
| scientific gear and misc. | 2,050 |
| 7 men and personal gear | 2,450 |
| refrigerator for ice cores | 1,500 |

2. Hiro and I talked about World War II. He wanted to be a fighter pilot, but there weren't enough planes. He was a naval cadet at age 18 in 1945. He volunteered to be a kamikaze pilot

because he figured he wouldn't live long anyway and this was one way to get to fly.

Hiro's training was interrupted by the atomic bomb at Hiroshima, about 40 miles away. There was a blue flash, which at first they thought was the result of an electrical transformer exploding. The blast broke windows in their classroom. Years later, he told me that the mushroom cloud hung in the clear blue sky all day. Several days later, he and his fellow cadets were marched into the Hiroshima railroad station for evacuation and demobilization. New tracks had been laid amidst the devastation.

3. Burch, 1996, quoted with permission of the editor of *Aurora*.

4. There were only these four C-130s in the Antarctic program in the early 1960s.

5. All of the R4D-8 takeoffs this season were made using JATO, which I normally failed to mention in my journal. Obviously there was no shortage of JATO at Byrd as we experienced the previous season.

## Chapter 10

1. Behrendt, 1998.

2. Ibid.

3. Ibid.

## Chapter 11

1. The USGS had sent Merrick and other topographic engineers on the oversnow traverses to measure accurate positions of mountains and nunataks as controls for compilation of 1:250,000 scale topographic maps. Many of these maps were compiled and published using trimetrigon photographs. However, no such maps were made in the area of the Antarctic Peninsula Traverse. The USGS no longer has the equipment and expertise to compile maps using the oblique trimetrigon photographs. Vertical photography is not planned for this area due to lack of funds (and interest; they are essentially the same). As of 2002, the best available maps of the area we covered are two maps compiled from satellite images: Antarctica Sketch Map, Bryan Coast–Ellsworth Land, 1968 and Antarctica Sketch Map, Ellsworth Land (East Part)–Palmer Land (South Part), 1969, 1:500,000 scale, both U.S. Geological Survey.

2. These "miles" were approximately statute miles, but of course there was probably variable track slippage. Because we needed accurate positions, the recorded miles were adjusted to correct positions based on the very accurate control points Merrick determined at the overnight stops.

3. ±5 nT, nannoTesla.

4. Behrendt, J. C., 1998. op. cit.

5. Ronne, 1948.

6. The position they gave me is 75°14.6'S, 77°10'. Merrick's final position is 75°15'S, 77°06'W—quite close, which is several miles from the position sent in by Byrd.

7. The magnetic sources were probably Jurassic (about 180 million years old) rocks crystallized from magma intruded into the basement or sedimentary rock cover below the ice. We were over 500 kilometers from the nearest exposures of rift-related, late Cenozoic volcanic rock in the Jones Mountains and separated by a non-magnetic area associated with the several-hundred-year-old metasedimentary rocks of the Sentinel Mountains.

8. Mt. Rex as located by Ronne (1948) is only about 20 miles from its correct position. This is inconsistent with the much greater error for Mt. Peterson, Mt. Tuve, and other peaks named but mislocated by Ronne from the same flight in 1947. Possibly the peak he identified as Mt. Rex is a different peak. Ronne reported an elevation of Mt. Rex of 10,500 feet (3200 meters). The correct elevation is 1105 meters.

## Chapter 12

1. Ronne, 1948.

2. Neil Brice later became a highly regarded expert in his field, but was killed in a Pan American Airlines crash in Pago Pago in the early 1970s.

3. We had observed a strong reflection from the bedrock and a weak reflection from a horizon within the ice about 0.2 seconds earlier than the bottom reflection (corresponding to about 400 meters shallower within the ice). We planned to measure the velocity of this lower layer.

4. We tried various charge sizes, filter settings, and linear amplifier gains. A preset amplification rather than automatic gain control was always used to be able to compare reflection amplitudes. We shot and recorded numerous paper seismograms, the standard method at the time.

5. It was a dark gray igneous rock (dacite), somewhat pegmatitic with phenocrysts of feldspar and quartz. All rock identifications in this book are as reported by Laudon et al., 1964.

6. "1400 L (+5) 7 Jan., 1962. These nunataks were seen on 28 Dec., 1961 on a recon flight made by this party and were visited on 7 Jan., 1962 by us, the Antarctic Peninsula Traverse, which is part of the U.S. Antarctic Research Program.

"We are naming these nunataks the Johnson Nunataks after William F. Johnson, scientific leader of Sky-Hi Station. Rock specimens, soil, and lichen specimens were collected here. Angles and bearings were taken to the other outcrops and a gravity station was put in here, the value of which can be obtained from the University of Wisconsin.

"The traverse party is made up of: John Behrendt, Lee Kreiling, Conrad Merrick, John Molholm, Perry Parks, Hiromu Shimizu, and Peter Wasilewski."

7. The igneous rocks were dacite and andesite.

8. Quartz monzonite, hornfels, argillite, and andesite.

9. Behrendt, 1998.

10. I recorded several seismic arrivals, including a refracted wave through rock with an apparent velocity of about 6.2 km/sec (typical of granitic basement).

11. Geographic features were officially named after each of the Antarctic Peninsula Traverse party men: Behrendt Mountains, 75°20'S, 72°30'W; Kreiling Mesa, 83°13'S, 157°54'E; Merrick Mountains, 75°06'S, 72°04'W; Molholm Island, 66°16'S, 110°33'E; Parks Glacier, 77°07'S, 125°55'W; Shimizu Ice Stream, 85°11'S, 124°00'W; Mt. Wasilewski, 75°11'S, 71°24'W.

12. Ronne, 1948.

13. This is the closest I came to actually setting foot on what is now named the Behrendt Mountains. In 1977 Patrick Quilty (Quilty, 1977) published a paper on a new bivalve species he identified from his field work in the Behrendt Mountains, which he named *Astarte behrendtensis*.

14. The field safety technique taught at McMurdo in the 1990s involves clipping a rope into a harness with carabiners. This method works fine if you are preparing to enter a

known crevassed area on foot or start up a cliff. But it doesn't seem adequate for sudden emergencies such as this, and on at least two other occasions I have encountered in Antarctica and elsewhere I had to throw or lower the end of a climbing rope to someone, who needed rescue.

15. Data were carefully packaged and sent out of Antarctica by ship in those days—less risk than air shipment.

## Chapter 13

1. Behrendt, 1964a.
2. Auburn, 1982.
3. Behrendt, 1991

## Epilogue

1. According to information provided to me by NSF in 2002.
2. Basinger, 2001.

# Glossary

|              |                                                                                         |
| ------------ | --------------------------------------------------------------------------------------- |
| abort:       | Flight canceled after takeoff, i.e., abortion                                            |
| ACAN:        | Advisory Committee on Antarctic Names, United States Board on Geographic Names           |
| akio:        | Fiberglass banana sled                                                                   |
| airdale:     | slang for Naval Air Force man                                                            |
| annual ice:  | pack ice one year or less old (around six feet thick); contains saltwater                |
| APT:         | Antarctic Peninsula Traverse                                                             |
| aréte:       | a narrow snow or rock ridge                                                              |
| avgas:       | aviation gasoline                                                                        |
| balaclava:   | woolen knit hooded cap that pulls down to cover neck and expose face only                |
| *bergschrund*: | a large crevasse located at the head of a mountain glacier                             |
| blue ice:    | surface formed when wind and sublimation remove the snow leaving a polished ice surface  |
| C-124:       | Globemaster four-engine USAF aircraft used to air drop supplies from McMurdo to interior Antarctica, wheels only |
| C-130:       | Hercules four-engine aircraft (in ski-wheel combination in Antarctica); LC-130 is present designation for ski-wheel version of aircraft |
| cairn:       | conical pile of rocks left to mark a peak or trail                                       |
| casrep:      | casualty report                                                                         |
| Clement huts: | permanent base huts built at U.S. Antarctic stations in IGY                             |
| CO:          | commanding officer                                                                       |
| CPO:         | chief petty officer                                                                      |
| crevasse:    | a tension or shear crack in a moving glacier or ice sheet                                |
| CTF 43:      | commander task force 43 (Admiral Tyree)                                                  |
| EHT:         | Ellsworth Highland Traverse                                                              |
| fast ice:    | several-year-old sea ice attached to land or an ice shelf                                |
| firn:        | compacted snow in the process of changing to ice                                         |
| GPS:         | global positioning satellite                                                             |
| gravity meter: | also gravimeter, a small delicate instrument used to measure slight variations in gravity |
| Kiwi:        | slang for New Zealander                                                                  |
| magnetometer: | an airborne or surface-operated instrument used to measures slight variations in the earth's magnetic field |
| mogas:       | automotive gasoline                                                                      |
| motor toboggan: | snowmobile                                                                            |

| | |
|---|---|
| multiyear ice: | several-year-old sea ice less salty than annual ice |
| multiple: | multiple reflection, i.e., the reflection from the shot to the glacier bed, to the surface, back to the glacier bed and then to the geophones at the surface |
| NSF: | National Science Foundation |
| Nitromon: | ammonium nitrate explosive, trade name |
| nunatak: | a rock hill or mountain surrounded by glacial ice |
| OIC: | officer in charge |
| P2V: | Navy Neptune aircraft, ski-wheel |
| pack ice: | frozen seawater covering the sea around Antarctica (up to 25 feet thick) |
| Petrogel: | 60 percent nitroglycerine dynamite, trade name |
| R4D: | Navy designation for twin-engine Douglas DC-3 aircraft, ski-wheel |
| R7V: | Navy designation for four-engine Super Constellation aircraft, wheels only |
| RARE: | Ronne Antarctic Research Expedition, 1946–48 |
| SAR: | search and rescue |
| sastrugi: | windblown linear ridges on the snow surface |
| Seabee: | from Construction Battalion, CB, Navy men who built and maintained stations |
| seismic: | refers to sound waves traveling through ice, sea, and rock |
| SIPRE auger: | U.S. Army Snow Ice and Permafrost Research Establishment coring auger used to hand drill shot holes and obtain ice and firn cores |
| sitrep: | situation report |
| sun dogs: | pale rainbows to right and left of sun caused by ice crystals in air |
| UC1: | single-engine Otter aircraft |
| USAP: | United States Antarctic Program |
| USARP: | United States Antarctic Research Program |
| USAF: | United States Air Force |
| USC&GS: | United States Coast and Geodetic Survey |
| USGS: | United States Geological Survey |
| USMC: | United States Marine Corps |
| USN: | United States Navy |
| UW: | University of Wisconsin at Madison |
| VX6: | Air Development Squadron 6, the Naval Air Force unit operating in Antarctica |

# Bibliography

Alberts, F. G., editor. *Geographic Names of the Antarctic.* Second Edition. Arlington, Va.: U.S. Board on Geographic Names, 1995.

AGS, (American Geographical Society). *Antarctica.* Capitol Heights, Md.: Williams & Heintz Map Corporation, 1970. Map 1:5,000,000.

Auburn, F. M. *Antarctic Law and Politics.* London: C. Hurst, 1982.

BAS, British Antarctic Survey, 2000, Antarctic Peninsula and Weddell Sea, BAS Misc. Sheet

Basinger, J. "Research at what cost?" *The Chronicle of Higher Education,* v. XLVII (2001): 46.

Behrendt, J. C. *Geophysical studies in the Filchner Ice Shelf Area of Antarctica.* Ph.D. diss., University of Wisconsin, 1961.

———. "A statistical comparison of five geodetic gravity meters." *Geophysics,* v. 27, no. 6 (1962): 887–91.

———. "Seismic measurements on the ice sheet of the Antarctic Peninsula." *Journal of Geophysical Research,* v. 66, no. 21 (1963): 5973–90.

———. "Distribution of narrow-width magnetic anomalies, in Antarctica." *Science,* v. 144, 3641 (1964a): 995–99.

———. "Crustal geology of Ellsworth Land and the southern Antarctic Peninsula from gravity and magnetic anomalies." *Journal of Geophysical Research,* v. 69 (1964b): 2047–63.

———. *Antarctic Peninsula traverse geophysical results relating to glaciological and geological studies.* Univ. Wisconsin Geophys. and Polar Research Center Research Rept. No. 64–1 (1964c) 1–112.

———. "Gravity increase at the South Pole from 1957–1966." *Science,* v. 155, 3765 (1967): 1015–17.

———. "Scientific studies relevant to the question of Antarctica's petroleum resource potential." In Tingey, R. J., ed., *Geology of Antarctica.* Oxford: Oxford Univ. Press (1991) 588–616.

———. *Innocents on the Ice: a Memoir of Antarctic Exploration, 1957.* Boulder: Univ. Press of Colorado, 1998.

Behrendt, J. C., Laudon, T. S., and Wold, R. J. "Results of a geophysical traverse from Mt. Murphy to the Hudson Mountains, Antarctica." *Journal of Geophysical Research,* v. 67, no. 10 (1962): 3973–80.

Behrendt, J. C., and Parks, P. E. "Antarctic Peninsula Traverse." *Science,* v. 137 (1962): 601–3.

Behrendt, J. C., and Thiel, E. "Discussion of a gravity and magnetic survey of the Uinta Mountains." *Journal of Geophysical Research,* v. 68, no. 3 (1963) 857–68.

Behrendt, J. C., and Wold, R. J. "Depth to magnetic 'Basement' in West Antarctica." *Journal of Geophysical Research,* v. 66, no. 4 (1963): 1145–53.

Behrendt, J. C., Wold, R. J., and Dowling, F. L. "Ice surface elevation of Central Marie Byrd Land." *Journal of Glaciology*, v. 4, no. 31 (1962): 121–23.

Behrendt, J. C., Wold, R. J., and Laudon, T. W. "Gravity base stations in Antarctica." *Geophysical Journal*, v. 6, no. 3 (1962): 400–405.

———. *Aeromagnetic survey in West Antarctica*: Univ. Wisconsin Geophys. and Polar Research Center, Rept. No. 63–1 (1963) 1–29.

———. "Aeromagnetic studies in West Antarctica." *IGY Bulletin*, 73, Am. Geophys. Union Trans. (1963): 793–98.

Burch, Bill, *Aurora*, 1996, p. 7–8.

Dewart, Gilbert. *Antarctic Comrades; An American with the Russians in Antarctica*. Columbus: Ohio State University Press, 1989.

Doumani, G. A. *The Frigid Mistress; Life and Exploration in Antarctica*. Baltimore: Noble House, 1999.

Drewry, D. J. *Antarctica: Glaciological and Geophysical Folio*. Cambridge, England: Scott Polar Research Institute, Cambridge University, 1983.

Dufek, George J. *Operation Deep Freeze*. New York: Harcourt, Brace and Company, 1957.

———. *Through the Frozen Frontier*. New York: Harcourt, Brace and Company, 1959.

Ellsworth, Lincoln. *Beyond Horizons*. Garden City, New York: Doubleday, Doran & Company, 1937.

Ferrigno, J. G., J. L. Mullins, J. A. Stapleton, P. S. Chavez, Jr., M. G. Velasco, R. S. Williams, Jr., G. F. Delinski, Jr., and D. Lear. *Satellite Image Map of Antarctica*, USGS Map I-2560, Reston, Va.: The Survey, 1996.

Filson, J. V. *Antarctic Journal of the United States*, 1975: 195.

Hahn, J. S. Ed., *Operation Deep Freeze 61*. Boston: Burdette & Company, 1961.

Joerg, W. L. G. "The Topographic results of Ellsworth's Transantarctic Flight of 1935." *The Geographical Review*, v. 26 (1936): 454–63.

Laudon, T. S., Behrendt, J. C., and Christensen, N.J. "Petrography of rocks collected on the Antarctic Peninsula Traverse." *Journal of Sedimentary Petrology*, v. 34 (1964): 361–64.

Lythe, M.B., Vaughan, D.G., and the BEDMAP Consortium, BEDMAP–bed topography of the Antarctic, 1:10,000,000 scale map. BAS (Misc) 9, 2000, Cambridge, British Antarctic Survey.

Naslund, S. J. *Ahab's Wife*. New York: Harper/Collins, 1999.

Nielsen J. and Vollers, M. *Ice Bound*. New York: Talk Miramax/ Hyperion, 2001.

Pirrit, J. *Across West Antarctica*. Glasgow: John Smith and Son, 1967.

Quilty, P. G. "Late jurassic bivalves from Ellsworth Land, Antarctica: Their systematics and paleogeographic implications." *New Zealand Journal of Geology and Geophysics*, 20 (1977): 1033–80.

Rignot, E., and Jacobs, S. *Science*, v. 296, (2002): 2020–23.

Ronne, F. "Ronne Antarctic Research Expedition, 1946–1948." *Geographical Review*, v. 38 (1948): 355–91.

———. *Antarctic Conquest*. New York: G. P. Putnam's Sons, 1949.

———. *Antarctic Command*. New York: Bobbs-Merrill, 1961.

———. *Antarctica My Destiny; A Personal History by the Last of the Great Polar Explorers*. New York: Hastings House, 1979.

Shepherd, A., Wingham, D. J., and Mansley, J. A. D. "Inland thinning of the Amundsen Sea sector, West Antarctica." *Geophysical Research Letters*, 10.1029/2001GL014183, 2002.

Sponholz, Marty. "Among the Magi: Research Tracks in the Desert." Available at *http//:205.174.118.254/nspt/home.htm.*, 2003.

Siple, P. *90° South*. New York: G. P. Putnam's Sons, 1959.

Sullivan, W. *Quest for a Continent*. London: Secker and Warburg, 1957.

Swithinbank, C. *Alien in Antarctica*. Granville, Ohio: McDonald and Woodward Pub. Co., 1996.

Swithinbank, C. *Forty Years on Ice; A Lifetime of Exploration and Research in the Polar Regions*. Sussex, Eng: The Book Guild Ltd., 1998.

Swithinbank, C. *Foothold on Antarctica; The First International Expedition (1949–1952) Through the Eyes of its Youngest Member*. Sussex, Eng.: The Book Guild Ltd., 1999.

Taylor, Griffith. *With Scott: The Silver Lining*. London: Smith, Elder and Co., 1916.

USGS *Antarctica Sketch Map, Bryan Coast-Ellsworth Land, Antarctica Sketch Map, Ellsworth Land (East Part)–Palmer Land (South Part), 1969.*

Wright and Priestly, 1922

Wright, C. S. Glaciology. London: Harrison adn Sons, Ltd., 1922

# Index